Everest and the Rest of Us

Four Journeys in Search of Adventure
Cycling, Rowing, Trekking and the Quest for Meaning

James Nehring

Black Rose Writing | Texas

©2025 by James Nehring
All rights reserved. No part of this book may be reproduced, stored in a retrieval system or transmitted in any form or by any means without the prior written permission of the publishers, except by a reviewer who may quote brief passages in a review to be printed in a newspaper, magazine or journal.

The author grants the final approval for this literary material.

First printing

Some names and identifying details may have been changed to protect the privacy of individuals.

ISBN: 978-1-68513-702-1
LIBRARY OF CONGRESS CONTROL NUMBER: 2025944176
PUBLISHED BY BLACK ROSE WRITING
www.blackrosewriting.com

Printed in the United States of America
Suggested Retail Price (SRP) $22.95

Everest and the Rest of Us is printed in Book Antiqua

*As a planet-friendly publisher, Black Rose Writing does its best to eliminate unnecessary waste to reduce paper usage and energy costs, while never compromising the reading experience. As a result, the final word count vs. page count may not meet common expectations.

For Chuck, my first and best adventure buddy

Praise for
Everest and the Rest of Us

"With its beautiful prose, *Everest and the Rest of Us* is a meditation on meaning, action, and discovering who we are through challenges and overcoming – no matter how large or small the scale."
–James Hibbard, author of *The Art of Cycling: Philosophy, Meaning and a Life on Two Wheels*

"Absorbing and thought provoking, *Everest and the Rest of Us* takes us on a deep dive into the meaning of adventure. It affirms what I've always felt, that my own journey into motherhood was just as life changing/transforming as sailing around the world.
–Tania Aebi, first American woman to sail solo around the world and *New York Times* best selling author with Bernadette Brennan of *Maiden Voyage*

"Getting away has never been so tempting. Nehring, with candor and eloquence, explains why a brief respite from the grind of life is so essential (and often so hard to manage). Thoreauvian in spirit, humble yet ambitious, this is a book for ordinary readers, who long to take extraordinary adventures."
–John Kaag, author of *Hiking with Nietzsche: On Becoming Who You Are*, Editor's Choice *New York Times* and NPR Best Book

"This is adventure panorama at its best, serving up greater meaning within by turning one's ears, eyes and heart to the open road and all its wild secrets."
–Scott V. Edwards, Harvard University Professor and solo cyclist who carried a *Black Lives Matter* sign across the United States

"*Everest and the Rest of Us* is a compelling blend of well-crafted adventure tales and critical self-examination."
-Tori Murden McClure, first woman and first American to row solo across the Atlantic Ocean and author of *A Pearl in the Storm: How I Found My Heart in the Middle of the Ocean*

"I loved delving into the deeper meanings of our search for new, challenging experiences. It's a unique and fascinating adventure tale. 5 stars!"
–Joan Griffin, author of *Force of Nature: Three Women Tackle the John Muir Trail*

"[Nehring] extends an invitation for readers to tag along, but the invitation does not end with the physical journey. We are invited also to consider what adventure is, how it is experienced and why we seek it... A joyful read!"
–Karen J Fluet Roy, Camino Companions Support, Pilgrim Office, Camino de Santiago

Praise for James Nehring's previous books
"...colorful and soberingly realistic."
– *Publisher's Weekly*, **starred review**

"The evocative scenes...are so true you can nearly smell them."
– *Library Journal*

"... a real good story–an ethical and intellectual adventure."
– *Jonathan Kozol, National Book Award Winner*

"...wonderfully written, it was hard to put down."
– *Deborah Meier, MacArthur "Genius" Award Winner*

"... a page turner"
– *Alfie Kohn, author of* The Brighter Side of Human Nature

Twenty-five percent of author royalties from this book go to the Mary, Joan, and Nancy Scholarship for Courage and Compassion at the University of Massachusetts Lowell and the Michael J. Fox Foundation for Parkinson's Research

Everest and the Rest of Us

Prologue
Four Journeys

Prologue

Do you remember your childhood adventures? When we were ten, Chuck and I crawled through the storm sewer near his house. I don't remember how we found our way in, but, on that dry autumn afternoon, it was free of muck and debris, and, because it was for storm run-off only, and not an actual sewer, it was, well, not disgusting. After crawling through the dark, inside a two-foot high, underground, concrete pipe, for what felt like an hour, but was probably more like ten minutes, we came to a place where light surrounded us. We could stand up and looked through a window right at eye level. It was actually a street drain cut into the curb, and we had a good view at shoe level of people crossing the road. We hollered to a pair of passing business shoes, like my Dad wore to work - black, shiny leather with skinny black laces.

"Where are we?" we shouted. The shoes stopped. Then they turned, and a moment later, a man's face, sideways, came into view.

"What the--" said the man. Then he paused, taking us in. His tie flopped out of his suit, and the tip brushed the street. He tucked it back in and said, "You're in New Rochelle." Then his face vanished, and his shoes turned and continued across the street. My friend and I looked at each other unable to contain our excitement.

"Cool!" we exclaimed together, for we had crawled from our town to the next.

Growing up, I loved adventure books, like *The Hardy Boys*. Their blue bindings were lined up on my shelf. Each book had a suspenseful picture on the cover—brothers Frank and Joe, staring with a look of deep concern into a hole on a wooded path. A lone glove lies on the ground right next to it. Another favorite, early on, was *My Side of the Mountain*, in which young Sam Gribley runs away from his parents' New York City apartment to a woodland in the Catskill Mountains and proceeds to live a full year in a hollowed-out tree. *The Box Car Children* captivated me. I dreamed of finding something like an abandoned train car in the woods and setting up house in it. In high school, when the only kinds of books teachers assigned were famous novels, I generally only read the first few pages before I got bored out of my mind. Meanwhile, I devoured true-life adventure stories, like Robin Lee Graham's *Dove*, about his solo round-the-world sail, at age sixteen and Peter Jenkins' *Walk Across America*, serialized in *National Geographic* and, later, a book.

In my twenties, Laurie and I took up backpacking. We hiked the Gallatin Mountains in Montana, the upper reaches of Yosemite, the Adirondacks, the Catskills. Then we got married and kept hiking. In my thirties, I bought a sailboat and traveled for eight days, 150 miles, down the Hudson River from our home in Albany past rolling farmlands and forested highlands to New York Harbor. It almost ended badly when my sixteen-foot vessel just missed getting run down by the Staten Island Ferry, but the scary encounter made for a better story. I continued reading adventure tales. I loved survival stories like *Adrift* about Steven Callahan who survived for 76 days in a life raft after he lost his boat in the middle of an Atlantic crossing. I loved Tania Aebi's *Maiden Voyage*. Offered the choice, by her father, of a college education or a sailboat, as long as she sailed it around the world, she went for the boat and then wrote a fantastic book about her three years at sea.

When I was forty-six, I wrecked my right knee training for a marathon. The doctor said I was done as a runner—worn out cartilage, torn meniscus. So, I took up cycling, which was like running, only a whole lot easier on my joints. I wasn't interested in racing. I just wanted to ride, and, as I discovered that, unlike running you could actually *get somewhere* after an hour, I was smitten. I'd go for a ride on a Saturday morning and then call home.

"Guess where I am, Laurie?" I'd say.

"I don't know Jim, where?"

"I'm in Pepperell!" I'd exclaim with excitement to match my storm drain experience. Pepperell was just two towns up.

"Wow!" Laurie would cheer with playful enthusiasm.

The farther I rode on my bike, the farther I wanted to go. Eventually, I rode it across North America, from sea to shining sea. It was a grand adventure, and before long I was asking, what's next? Then, one day at work while I was sitting in my office, which overlooks the Merrimack River in Lowell, MA, I noticed people rowing. It looked like a lot of fun. So, I signed up for lessons on "how to scull", or row skinny boats with a sliding seat like college crew teams. I liked it, and just like cycling, I wasn't interested in racing. Instead, I wanted to explore bays and rivers with hidden tributaries, carry gear with me, and camp out on the shoreline. However, I couldn't do that with a racing shell. So, I bought a kit for an expedition rowboat, built it in my garage, and then rowed it from New York City to Cape Hatteras. Another exciting adventure!

One day while rowing hard into a gusty headwind on a long passage that followed North Carolina's Outer Banks, I noticed people walking a road on the other side of the beach in a happy, care-free way while I was huffing and puffing with every stroke. They were going faster than me! I decided then and there that once I tagged Hatteras, I'd say good-bye to rowing and do a big walk. Shortly after that, the idea of the Camino came into view. The Camino de Santiago is a medieval pilgrimage route that crosses Northern Spain. It starts in the French Pyrenees and, 500 miles later, winds up at the cathedral in the city of Santiago de Compostela where the bones of St. James are said to be interred, minus his skull because he was beheaded. That, too, was a great adventure, but very different from the other two, which I'll explain later.

I've wondered, at times, what draws me to adventure. The thrill? The challenge that goes into planning a big trip? The feeling of accomplishment once it's done? The bragging rights? Is it the pleasure of solitude I experience on a stretch of empty highway? The wonder that accompanies summiting a mountain? Is there a spiritual element to the adventure experience that can be found between the hardships and the pleasures? Is it the excitement of seeing someplace new, entering, exploring, eating the food, enjoying the sights, and then leaving without any lingering obligation? Is it that, by burning 4000 calories a day, I get to eat anything I want—cheese laden pizza, cold beer, more cold beer, chocolate-peanut butter ice cream, fudge brownies, an enormous breakfast of scrambled eggs and blueberry pancakes swimming in maple syrup and butter—and not get fat? Is it the simplicity found in the fact that all I have to do in a given day of adventuring is get myself from point A to point B — so different from my everyday life, crowded as it is with hundreds of tasks and all the required interactions with people, each of whom comes, annoyingly, with a personality.

I didn't plan to write a book about adventure, but it was inevitable from the start. I should have realized. I've compulsively kept journals for all my trips *just because*, and even though I told people these trips represented a break from the writing I regularly do about schools and teaching, lurking at the back of my mind was... something. I didn't know what, but, when the time came, I'd have notebooks filled with messy entries for each day of every adventure.

Adventure books are a dime a dozen, and, as book-worthy adventures go, my trips are not exactly world-class. A cross country bike ride? Thousands of people have done it. Rowing a small boat on a coastal adventure for a few weeks? No big deal. And the Camino has become so popular, you have to reserve your accommodations months in advance. No, this book would have to be about more than just my average-guy adventuring. Then again, maybe not.

Everyone likes a good adventure, but most of us will never climb Mt. Everest. The good news is you don't need to. That's because adventure is a *relationship* between you and whatever experience you find challenging. If it challenges *you*, then it can be your adventure and you can derive the kind of satisfaction akin to what Tenzing Norgay and Edmund Hillary experienced when they were the first to summit Mt. Everest in 1953 — as long as for *you*, the experience is new, challenging, maybe a bit risky, and chosen *by you* for all those reasons. Elite women adventurers, interviewed in one study, claimed the greatest adventure they had experienced was raising children. These are people who are accomplished rock climbers, kayakers, surfers, etc.. Society's understanding of adventure, as defined by most of the books that make it to the Travel and Adventure section of the bookstore, is way too narrow.

This is a book for the rest of us — people who will never sail alone across the Atlantic, climb the tallest peaks on six continents, or surf a 50-foot monster wave on a beach in Hawaii. But people who nonetheless *love* adventure and are not satisfied with just reading about it. This book is an affirmation of *your* adventuring. And it is more.

After I'd completed all three adventures chronicled in this book, I had the opportunity to take a sabbatical leave. I spent the better part of a year reading about adventure. I had some questions, in addition to the ones I mentioned, like, what are the elements of a great adventure? Are they the same for everyone? I like solo journeys that require endurance and long-term planning and training. I don't like risk, heights, and going fast downhill. Some people I know thrive on risk and speed and daring heights but have no interest in slogging through a 4000-mile bike ride. I had other questions too; for instance, are the impulses that drive adventure benign? I am well aware that *adventure* in some contexts is deeply problematic. For centuries, White Europeans adventured into Asia, Africa, and the Americas, subjugating people who live there. I wondered about that and its connections to contemporary adventuring. What is the impact of my adventure on the people in whose space I'm adventuring? Do they benefit from my adventure? Do they get to have adventures too? I also wondered about the psychology of adventure. Flying downhill on a highway in North Dakota toward a two-lane bridge just as two big rigs were passing, I saw, briefly, a look of terror on the face of the driver coming my way. It said, there's no room on this bridge for two trucks and a bicycle and I know who's going to lose. But I saw a perfectly serviceable shoulder, a little narrow, but enough room for a bicycle to ride without even the widest vehicle having to swerve. In hindsight, I've sometimes wondered, was I too casual in that moment? Over-confident? Was I toying with life and death? Had a thousand accident-free miles lulled me into a false sense of security? What sort of person free climbs the sheer face of El Capitan in Yosemite Valley, as Alex Honnold has done?[1] What's behind the thrill? I have other questions. Riding my bike along rural roads frequented by pickups with gun racks and the occasional confederate flag fluttering somewhere nearby, I've been aware that I can be out here all by myself traveling in relative safety mainly because I'm a man and my skin is White. A person of color, or a woman, riding way out here, alone? I wouldn't be the first to call it crazy. How do race and gender play out in outdoor recreational spaces? Why is it that, as I adventure on my bike along America's highways, and its mountain footpaths with a backpack, I see so few people of color? I've also noticed that sometimes I'll be daydreaming about some kind of adventure, and it starts to look like a Nike ad, or a Subaru commercial. I've bought a bunch of stuff over the years because I just had to have it. But it sits in my basement rusting or gathering dust. How do the big brands and all their advertising money shape what I think about adventure? Has adventure been turned into just a thing that people like me are lured into buying? When does the stuff become more important than the experience? Finally, and maybe the most magnetic question for me, as an educator, is how can the benefits of adventuring be put to good purpose in the growth and development of people young and old? Recent decades have seen the emergence of *outdoor education* and adventure tourism. Outward Bound, the most well-known adventure-based educational program, has centers all over the world. What do participants gain from the experience? Does it last? How can we make greater use of adventure as a resource for learning? How can adventurous travel build understanding across cultures? And what have I learned? How has all this adventuring changed *me*?

This book combines three true-life adventure stories over a span of fifteen years and explores a host of questions about the nature of adventure. I hope to entertain you with adventure tales, make you laugh, put you at the edge of your seat, hold you in suspense from chapter to chapter, as a good adventure story should. Along the way, I hope to demonstrate the sorts of adventures *the rest of us* enjoy are just as exciting in their own way as the ones that set fantastic world records. And I hope also to take you on a parallel journey as we explore the nature of adventure, examine its darker sides, its deeper meanings, and benefits that enrich our own adventure experiences. This latter exploration constitutes the fourth journey of the book's title because, like any good adventure, it includes hazards, risks, an uncertain outcome, and, I hope, reward. But, first, there's the question of what really happened on the five thousand foot descent, by bicycle, down the western slope of the Northern Cascades Mountain Range.

Part I:
Bike to Anacortes

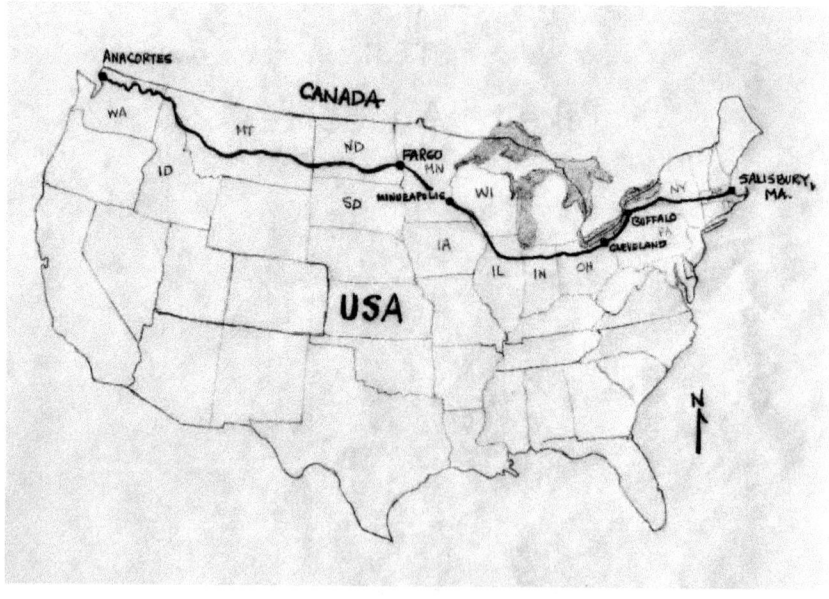

Chapter 1
Downward to Darkness

There are any number of dangers I might face riding a bicycle across North America. Taken singly, they are, by and large, manageable. But on a clear blue-sky day in August, descending from the 5477-foot Washington Pass in the Northern Cascades, on my way to Puget Sound, at what was meant to be the tail end of a 4000-mile journey, spread across four summers, they all came screaming at me as one big package deal. Would my epic trip come to an untimely and, possibly, painful end, just three days short of the finish?

The morning started with promise. I'd slept well in *The Bicycle Barn* outside of Winthrop, Washington, just off Route 20, my main bike route through that region. Recently constructed, the post and beam barn was sheathed with cheerful yellow pine boards and topped with a brown metal roof. It was nestled into a hillside meadow and maintained by a retired couple whose house was on the same property. Inside were rows of bunks against walls that smelled like fresh cut lumber. Outside there was a solar heated shower and a nicely maintained outhouse. I slept like a rock. Fresh and ready to hit the road the following morning at 6:30 a.m., I was straddling my bike, grooving to the crisp mountain air when Jeff, the owner, approached me from up the driveway. Pebbles crunched under his big boots, and he had a serious look on his face. The night before, he and his wife, Jan, had me up to their patio for ice cream. He was just retired from the forest service, and, avid outdoors people—skiing, hiking, cycling-- they'd bought this property and built the barn to serve the steady stream of cross-country cyclists riding past their front door. Jeff came right up to me and stopped a little out of breath. He must have seen me from the kitchen window and knew he needed to catch me before I took off.

"A cyclist was struck and killed on the road up to Washington Pass last night," he said, before I had a chance to say hi. We both paused for a beat and regarded each other. I nodded, trying to think of what to say. Then he said, "Police report said the cyclist was weaving in the road. Likely what the driver claimed." He paused again then said, "Well, I just thought it's something you should know. It happens, and you should be aware."

"I'm aware. And I'm careful," I said. "Thank you for letting me know." I clipped into my pedals.

"Ride safely," Jeff said.

"I will," I said and pushed off.

Shortly, I found myself on a steady climb. The two-lane highway was quiet, a morning mist shrouded the surrounding hillsides. I knew, from the previous day, that once that mist lifted, I'd be staring at a towering landscape, surrounded by craggy, snow-covered mountains. To my west were Gardner and North Gardner Mountains, both just under 9,000 feet. To my north, Fawn Peak which is 6600 feet. Ahead of me, The Needles, 8100 feet, and Tower Mountain, 8400 feet. Thirty miles uphill, I'd cross Washington Pass, cutting through the gap between Cutthroat Peak and Kangaroo Ridge. There would likely be snow by the road.

I was checking the shoulder as I pedaled in a low gear at about six miles an hour. *Weaving*, I thought. Sure, if you're weaving into the traffic lane, and you're not paying attention to the cars and trucks behind you, you are likely to get hit. Just then, I heard a familiar rushing sound behind me, checked my mirror. A logging truck was roaring up the hill. I looked down and sized up the shoulder, made a note of my escape path, looked in the mirror again. The truck was on me, but he saw me and was giving me a berth. I pedaled through the noise and shortly he was past me, powering up the rest of the hill with a full load of logs in a stack that got wider the higher it went.

I, on the other hand, did not weave. I rode the shoulder whenever it was good enough to ride, and I checked my rearview mirror regularly while always listening for road noise coming from behind. I also mentally registered my bailout plan every time road conditions changed — what I'd do to get off the road fast if I had to. I comforted myself that such precautions would keep me safe.

Three hours later, I was approaching Washington Pass. The mist had burned off, revealing a landscape of brown, grassy meadows, alternating with pine forests. Those tall mountain tops were right above me now. The air was alpine cool, thankfully, as the climb got steeper. If I kept my bike in the three lowest gears, it was sustainable. Slow and steady. I could keep this up for hours, I told myself. Good thing because that's exactly what I had to do. Plugging along, I recalled how back in February, I was studying the bicycle map for this section of my cross-country route. It was Map 1 because the route is designed for west to east travel in the series of 11 maps produced by the Adventure Cycling Association. Map 1 goes from Anacortes, Washington to Sandpoint, Idaho, 462 miles. For me, it was not the first map. It was the last. And in February, I felt great anticipation that in a few short months, I would be riding those roads. I also felt great apprehension because the map included an insert showing the elevation profile of the ride. It looked like an EKG reading of a healthy heart, with four big spikes for the major passes I would cross: Sherman Pass, Wauconda Pass,

Loup Loup Pass, and Washington Pass. Back in February, I would lie in bed at night, trying to fall asleep and my mind's eye would follow a spike up, and, as it neared the top, it was so steep, it seemed to bend slightly backwards before cresting and falling away on the other side, like a mad roller coaster that goes beyond vertical just before it hits the top of the ride and then sends you screaming nearly straight down.

This isn't so bad, I thought, now that I was actually on the road pictured in the map that had so terrified me a few months earlier. The roadside began to open up as I approached Washington Pass. I was no longer in the narrow valley where the Methow River flows. I'd left the river some miles back. It had been my occasional companion as Route 20 meandered back and forth across its sparkling surface, in places just a few feet deep and so clear, I could make out individual rocks at the bottom. I was approaching what would be for me, the summit, but in terms of mountains is actually a kind of low point. A pass is the notch in the otherwise relentless ridgeline of imposing rock and ice and snow. Like a free pass, a get out of jail free card, it lets you through without forcing you to climb up into a region completely unfriendly to hikers and cyclists and motorists, a place where you need climbing ropes and ice ax. I felt gratitude that people before me had found this pass and developed it over many years into a paved road that could carry me without too much difficulty up and over, then down the other side.

I was starting to crest the pass. I picked a spot, without any clear indicator, that felt like the top. I stopped, got off my bike and laid it down in the grass. I stood up straight and stretched, my back stiff from the constant crouch of a 30-mile climb. I took a look around. To my left and right were broad sheets of land sloping gently away at different angles. It was as if I had crested an ocean swell in a tiny, tiny boat. I was no longer in the trough; I was now on top and the view was majestic. I was no longer looking *up* at the mountain tops. I was among them, looking with them at the land below. The sky, blue and clear, and the land, brown and green, were both enormous. In the moment, I understood the motto I'd seen miles back on so many Montana license plates, which speaks for this entire part of the country. "Big Sky". A patch of snow was a hundred feet up slope. I walked over, and with my bike shoes, crunched into its white surface, blinding bright in the mid-day sun. I bent down, took off my gloves and stuffed them in the pocket at the back of my jersey. I reached down and ran my fingers into the snow, cold and crystally, old snow, not fresh. I formed a snowball, packed it, stood up, and gave it a hurl, as if I might throw it far enough to ride across the giant ocean swell and follow a broad, gentle arc down toward the distant flat land at the bottom. My snowball went plunk in the middle of the snow patch fifty feet away.

It was time to begin my descent. By now, having crossed an entire continent, and, in particular, three previous passes in this mountain range, I knew what to expect. Or I thought I did. I could expect I would not have to exert myself pedaling, which is a way of saying that, even though I'd be going downhill, I might still do *some* pedaling. Strange as that may sound, pedaling downhill sometimes makes sense. On a long descent, like the backside of the three passes I'd just crossed (i.e., sixteen miles at Sherman Pass, twenty-six miles at Wauconda Pass, twelve miles at Loup Loup Pass), it feels odd, after a mile or two, to not pedal. Then another mile or two on, I start to feel wobbly, like I'm losing my balance, like the rhythm and the subtle, metronome-like weight-shift that goes along with pedaling is a stabilizing force, and without it, I might just flop over, in the same way you flop over on a bicycle if you're not moving forward. For that reason, I sometimes pedal for parts of a long descent. The really strange part is I'll pedal with the brakes on to get some resistance. If I'm pedaling slower than the bike is traveling and there's no resistance, it doesn't work, that metronome balancing effect doesn't kick in. But if I apply the brakes, and I slow the bike down enough to get even a little resistance in a top gear, then my balance is restored. I may be the only long-distance cyclist in the history of the modern bicycle who does not like going fast downhill. I don't like feeling out of control and flying down a road with no end in sight. Just freaks me out. And I don't like going faster than my brakes will work on a continuous descent. If I'm descending a continuous, steep twelve miles, my velocity will just keep increasing, and as it increases the amount of time it would take me to stop the bike using my front and rear brakes also increases, and I don't like the feeling that I wouldn't be able to stop my bike quick enough were there a sudden need, like maybe a branch in the road, or a bunch of fallen rocks scattered across the lane, or a car appearing out of nowhere from a side road and suddenly blocking my way, or any number of hazards around a blind turn. I don't like riding faster than I'm willing to fall. That means, unless I can see a clear, unobstructed path to the bottom of whatever hill I'm on, with a clear view beyond for deceleration, I don't like going much over thirty miles an hour. In the world of cycling, that makes me a super-chicken. I know people who descend at fifty miles an hour, and faster.

The descent from Washington Pass to Newhalem, my destination for the afternoon measured 5000 feet over a distance of forty-two miles. This promised to be the mother of all downhill rides. Ten days before, I'd crossed the Continental Divide at Marias Pass in Montana, and from there to West Glacier, Montana, my stopping point for that day, was a descent of just 2000 feet over roughly the same distance. Piece of cake. This was more than double the steepness. At a steady rate of descent, the distance-to-drop ratio is not extreme, but the rate of descent from most mountain passes is not steady. There are often long flat-ish sections when the road is hugging a mountainside, and then, suddenly, a hair pin turn, and the road falls away. Unless you have a really good topo map and care enough to study it, you just don't know what's around the next bend.

At the top of the pass, I was anxious to get underway, blissfully unaware of the next hazard about to greet me. I picked up my bike, threw my leg over and clipped in my right foot. Then I thought maybe I should eat something and have a few swigs of water before I begin this epic descent. I tore open a meagre granola bar from my handlebar bag and consumed it as fast as I could, took a few swallows of water, made a quick check of my helmet, sunglasses, brakes, panniers--everything secure-- and pushed off. The first mile or two was a moderate descent. That went fine. I pumped the brakes now and then, did a short bit of pedaling to maintain my balance. The tree-lined roadside was whizzing comfortably past. Not bad. I can do this.

An orange sign came into view. "Road work ahead." Road work usually means either a disturbance of the road surface or lane-shifting that eliminates the shoulder, or both. For a cyclist, that's trouble. Another sign came into view. "Loose Stones". I'd seen that message numerous times on my cross-country journey and it always meant a chip seal operation. Chip sealing is a cheap way to fix a paved road that's deteriorating. A road crew pours hot tar on the road, next they dump gravel, spreading it out evenly over the hot tar. Then they might drive heavy rollers over the whole thing to smoosh the gravel into the tar and make a nice clean surface. More often, in my cycling experience, they skip the last step and let the traffic do the work. Depending on how busy the road is, the job gets done in a matter of days or, on some rural country roads I was riding in Indiana the previous summer, a whole season. Thing is, either way, the edges of the road stay pebbly much longer than the lanes because the traffic generally rides where it rides and it's rare for a car to veer toward the shoulder. For a bicycle, chip sealing is bad news—for two reasons. The first is obvious. The part of the road where a bicycle rides remains loose gravel often months after the chip seal operation, and riding on loose gravel when you're trying to make distance on a touring bike with panniers is miserable. It's like running on a beach through wet sand. Carrying a backpack filled with encyclopedias.

The second reason is less obvious and worse than the first. On a hot day, the tar goes soft, like hot fudge when you take it from the fridge and cook it in the microwave for a minute. The weight of your bike tire pushes through the loose layer of gravel to where it hits the soft tar. The rubber of the tire is very attractive to the tar and before long it acquires a layer of sticky tar all the way around. The pebbles in the road are meant to stick to tar and they don't care if it's on the road or on your tire. Pretty soon your bike tire resembles a frosted donut with sprinkles. That's bad enough, but it gets worse. The pebble that catches a ride on your tire as it smooshes into the pavement, continues to ride along as the tire rotates. At the top of its ride, that pebble comes up against your brake caliper. If it's a flat pebble it might ride right under the caliper, but if it sticks up a little, it hits the caliper with a loud ping and flies off in whatever random direction its shape and angle of impact dictate. Of course, if it's just the wrong size, it might get stuck under the caliper, and then other pebbles pile up, causing the tire to jam, sending the rider head over heels. That's never happened to me, but it's what I think about continuously when I'm navigating a chip seal mess and pebbles are making a racket like an old-fashioned arcade machine. Fortunately, the day was still cool, and the tar appeared to be hard. The downside was that because the tar was hard, more pebbles were loose. I started grinding through the gravel, manhandling the handlebars to keep my front wheel aiming straight ahead. Traffic was light so I could occasionally drift into the lane where the surface had been worn smooth by traffic. But I had to keep a sharp eye and ear behind me. I thought about the fatality the day before. *Weaving.* This kept up for several miles. I'd occasionally sneak out into the lane when there was a clear stretch of no-traffic behind me and a good straightaway up ahead. Then a car would appear in the distance behind, and I'd wrangle the bike over toward the shoulder and loose pebbles. The car would whizz past at fifty miles an hour with no appreciation for my effort getting out of their way.

The downhill ride started to get steeper. The loose chip seal surface was unrelenting, and traffic was starting to pick up. So was the wind. I was now on the westernmost slope of this part of North America. West of here was 100 miles descending to sea level. Beyond that, Puget Sound, a little piece of Vancouver Island and then the Pacific Ocean, 4300 miles to Hokkaido, northernmost of the four main islands of Japan. Because the prevailing winds on planet Earth travel from west to east, and, a blowing wind will tend to pick up speed when there's nothing in its way, the breeze exhaled by Asia starts to gather force and speed as it leaves Japan and continues to do so as it rolls across the 4000-plus miles of Pacific Ocean. Add to this the fact that wind tends to travel faster the higher you go and you get what was now hitting me at elevation, full in the face. Riding west downhill, I was literally the first hard object, at this elevation, to make contact with a force that last encountered resistance in Asia. I'm sure weather science is more complicated than that, but it's how I imagined it in the moment. My handlebars' unruliness was due to more than just pebbles. The wind was becoming a factor. Mild for now, but experience suggests, if I have a stiff breeze in the morning, and I'm riding the same direction all day, more often than not, the wind will grow continuously all day from the same direction. Today's ride forecast: loose gravel with increasing headwinds and irregular descent. But it turned out still more hazards lay ahead.

An hour later, the wind was picking up, but the chip seal operation had ended. Thank goodness! Traffic was picking up, too. Because it was August, and because the Northern Cascade

Mountain range is a big outdoor recreation destination, a lot of the traffic was RVs. When I was a kid, family camping meant a canvas tent that you rolled into a duffel bag and stashed in the back of the station wagon. A few families, not mine, had a pop-up camper that they towed. I got to step inside one once and couldn't believe my eyes. It had a sink and beds and a table where people ate breakfast and played cards on a rainy day. It was like a hotel. There were also, back in the day, very occasionally, little trailers. Teardrops they were called because of their shape. No one had anything bigger than that, at least not in my circle of experience. But times change. These days, it's not uncommon for a family to ride a forty-foot motorhome with two bathrooms and a big screen TV into the wilderness for a week of roughing it. Because they're expensive and because most families will use a giant motorhome just one or two weeks a year, the RV rental industry flourishes. With just a regular driver's license, you can operate an RV up to 40 feet in length, weighing up to 26,000 pounds, in most states.

 I've often contemplated these facts, especially the last one, while riding my bicycle on highways in vacation areas. It occurred to me afresh as traffic picked up, and I heard what sounded like a freight train behind me. I checked my mirror to see the front end of a Cruise America rental monster headed my way. I've come to recognize the brand because their RVs have a mural of a scenic location-- Grand Canyon, Yosemite Valley, etc.-- plastered like a billboard on the front of the overcab. The driver was showing no sign of giving me any room so I held out as long as I could, riding the white line marking the right edge of the traffic lane. When it was clear he (almost always he) was not making an accommodation for me, I angled onto the shoulder, which, good thing, was wide enough and paved. Vrooooom. The roaring beast went rushing past. I felt like I was a little boat inches from a container ship. Its mass was intimidating, and it lingered. It wasn't a quick whoosh and gone. It took a while for the full length of it to go by.

Thing is, there's a good chance the driver was new to large vehicles, accustomed, more likely, to steering a minivan. And this may well have been the first time ever he was in charge of a vehicle about which he had no clue where it ends. He weaved a bit as he went by as though he decided, after the fact, to give me some space. Too bad he was already a football field down the road. I kept watching. He drifted briefly into the opposing lane and then adjusted abruptly back to where he belonged. I pictured plates flying out of the cupboard. I sometimes imagine what goes on inside an RV as they roar by, based on brief glimpses through the windshield. Maybe the stereo is going full blast, maybe Dad (driver) is shouting at the kids and checking his map, which he insists on looking at because he doesn't trust the one on the screen embedded in the dashboard. Maybe Mom is trying to keep him calm since she realizes he could potentially crash. Maybe she pointed out he'd just passed a bicycle which is why he took supposed corrective action after the fact, then overcompensated, veering into the opposite lane. The inexperience of RV drivers is frightening, and this morning, they were all headed my way as they descended the winding highway after a week in the mountains, tired and cranky from a little too much family togetherness.

Winding highway indeed, and windy, too. For much of the descent so far, the highway had run along the bottom of a rift in the undulating terrain following the course of Granite Creek as it flowed west toward Puget Sound. At some point a ways back it joined East Creek and now, with a bigger volume of water flowing at the bottom of the rift, it appeared that the highway engineers chose to move the highway up above the level of potential flood waters. That meant, just beyond the highway shoulder, the land started to fall away, in places at least 10 feet, in other places, several hundred. The range of distances was growing as was the frequency of big fat RVs, and the wind, which was becoming a considerable headwind with that 4000-mile fetch behind it. Turns in the road were coming up faster and sharper, and with each turn, the wind would come at me from a slightly different angle. No apparent pattern was discernable. For example, I'd be riding due west, the road would bend left, and I'd get a fresh headwind over my right shoulder. Then half a mile later after a turn or two got me traveling due west again, I'd come around a similar bend to the left and the wind would hit me on the left, as though it had decided to come straight down the mountain instead of crossing the Pacific Ocean.

Two hours after Washington Pass, I approached Ross Lake and Diablo Lake. The wind was blowing hard and unpredictably. I'd already descended over 3,000 feet and that Pacific breeze, uninterrupted at the top of my ride, was now getting channeled through a crazy maze of mountainous terrain before reaching me. Peaks and valleys rippled like a sheet of aluminum foil that's been wadded up, then pulled open and laid not quite flat, which meant the wind could hit me from any angle. The road made more turns now, too, as it began to skirt the lakes and wind through the maze-like terrain. At Ross Lake, I came around a hairpin turn just as an RV went roaring past and I got hit by the turbulence of its wake on my left just as a fresh burst of headwind hit me from slightly off to the right. Managing the handlebars was getting tricky, and, mostly, there was no guardrail so I had to be especially mindful of the drop off on my right, several hundred feet to very chilly water. Of course, when there was a guardrail, it left me at the mercy of the vehicle mob to grant me enough room to ride. This precarious dance carried on for a good hour and then, gradually, the wind died, the ride started to level off, and the road got straighter. I was surrounded by a thick pine forest, as the road relaxed into a gentle descent.

Relief, at last, I thought.

But it was not meant to be. A sign appeared. It said, "Bridge Ahead". Bridges can be tricky business. Sometimes the shoulder disappears, forcing me into the traffic lane. Sometimes, expansion joints interrupt the pavement at sharp angles that can catch your front tire if you're not careful. And sometimes, the pavement abruptly ends and you're riding on steel grating. If it's the wrong kind of grating, the gaps can swallow your tire and you crash. Sure enough, another sign appeared on the approach, "Open Grate Bridge." I braced myself and readied to stop, but as I got closer, I could tell it was the kind of grating that will support a bicycle. Nonetheless, riding across a grated surface is usually a wobbly experience. I took a quick look behind and, amazingly, nothing was coming. So, I took the lane and scampered across, happy to be back on pavement on the other side.

I was getting closer to my destination for the day, and the road had settled into a straightaway that hugged the very long and skinny George Lake. Traffic remained heavy but in the absence of loose pebbles, unpredictable headwinds, and steep drop-offs, the ride was feeling relatively calm. The only remaining unknown was the tunnel I'd read about in my ride notes, but I wasn't too worried. I'd done plenty of tunnels in recent weeks, and sure enough it turned out to be no big deal. I could see daylight from the other side. I waited for a break in the traffic and scooted through. I was now approaching Newhalem and was fantasizing vividly about food—pizza, hot from the oven with stringy cheese, cold beer, an ice cream sundae. That's when a "Tunnel Ahead" sign appeared. A second tunnel. My day was about to get a whole lot worse. I approached. It looked dark inside. I slowed, pulled onto the shoulder, and stopped. A big RV roared by and dropped into the tunnel like a half-peg into a hole that just fit. At that moment, a truck came flying out from the other direction. Together, the two vehicles neatly filled the circumference of the tunnel entrance, leaving barely an inch on either side. I stood there straddling my bike as I watched cars and trucks fly in and out of the hole at alarming speed given the close tolerance. I tried again to notice any light from the other end, any sign that it didn't just go on forever. No way would I ride my bike into this cave of death. Besides the unrelenting traffic, darkness, and absence of any shoulder, there was the ever-present threat of debris in the road: an eight-foot two-by-four that bounced off a pick-up truck, loose rock crumbling from the tunnel wall, random car parts, like a broken bit of bumper, piece of a roof rack, or tail light assembly. That dark road surface was a potential minefield.

I looked around the entrance, wondering if maybe there was a dirt path that skirted it. No such luck. It was all rock. That's why they made a tunnel. Just ahead, I saw another sign. I got off my bike and walked it along the shoulder to the sign. It read, "Bicycle in tunnel", and had caution lights that apparently could be activated if I pressed a button attached to the signpost. I'd never seen such a thing, and felt some relief. Just then an eighteen-wheeler roared by, kicked up dust, and flew into the great mouth of the tunnel at sixty miles an hour, then disappeared. Oy. I was going to have to do this. I checked my gear, making sure everything was secure. I watched the traffic, waiting for a gap. I almost started a couple times, and then held off. Finally, a gap bigger than a few car lengths appeared. I hit the button on the sign and the caution lights started to blink, I jammed my feet on the pedals and took the lane, hoping my bright yellow neon jersey would be visible. I accelerated as fast as I could and flew into the tunnel. Instantly everything went black.

Chapter 2
The Hero's Journey

It turns out all adventures have roughly the same story line, whether it's climbing the North Face of the Eiger, backpacking the length of the Pacific Crest Trail, driving a dog sled across Greenland, kayaking around the whole of South America, or maybe riding a bicycle across the United States. It doesn't matter whether your quest is monumental: the first, the best, or the most extreme. It doesn't matter if it is completely inconsequential to the rest of the world: sneaking into a neighborhood after your mother said stay out, following the snowy tracks of a rabbit into the woods behind your house, or exploring a new beach destination for your family vacation. They're all the same. The adventure plot goes like this: you leave your normal life as the result of a calling. You enter a world that is different and mysterious, possibly dangerous. You face challenges, but, along the way, you get help from others. You either save people or learn something. Then you return, a changed person. Pick any adventure book off the shelf, read it, and you'll see.

Here's an example. In *Wild: From Lost to Found on the Pacific Crest Trail*, Cheryl Strayed tells the story of her 1,100-mile hike along the famous west coast hiking trail.[2] Having recently lost her mother to cancer, and, with her life unraveling from heroin use, divorce, and an abortion, she decides she will drive from

Minneapolis to Tijuana and set out on an epic walk, having never carried a full backpack. And she will do it alone. Under the burning sun of the Mojave desert, and the crushing weight of her backpack, which she nicknames Monster, she nearly gives up, but, with the encouragement and aid of fellow hikers, she somehow continues. Actually, she nearly gives up many times, from the blisters, the sore muscles, the loss of her hiking boots (she duct-tapes her sandals to get by), and the demons that torment her and with which she wrestles as she climbs rocky slopes and descends into lush green valleys. All along the way, people help her, and slowly, she heals. She calls out her mother's name in a dramatic moment of self-realization as she approaches her destination, the Bridge of the Gods.

Strayed's memoir is a moving account of personal transformation. Her art as a writer is powerful, and the book, published in 2013, was an enormous success. It remained at the top of the *New York Times* Best Seller list for weeks, was featured by Oprah, and got turned into a movie starring Reese Witherspoon. What's also true is her story perfectly follows the adventure formula. Consider this:

Adventure Formula	*Wild: From Lost to Found on the Pacific Crest Trail*
Person receives a calling	Strayed sees a map of the Pacific Crest Trail in a store and feels drawn to it.
Person enters a world that is different and possibly dangerous.	Strayed takes off on The Pacific Crest Trail, with over a thousand miles to cover, starting in a desert.
Person faces challenges.	Strayed endures extreme heat, deep snow, water shortage, losing a boot,

	threatening men, and more. She also faces the demons of her past.
Person gets help along the way.	About to give up, Strayed is encouraged by Paul, a fellow hiker. She meets many others who provide support and advice.
Person saves others or learns something.	Strayed gains confidence and the strength to overcome the pain and sorrow in her life.
Person returns, changed.	She crosses the Bridge of the Gods, concluding her hike. In the years after her trip, Strayed achieves a stable life with a loving partner and children. She is a stronger, more confident person.

Did Strayed plan her book to follow the adventure formula? Did she chart out her story like above? I haven't read anything to suggest she did, but, nonetheless, her story checks all the boxes, just like lots of other adventure stories. Think of Homer's *Odyssey* with the hero, Odysseus, facing monsters, swirling seas, and a witch on his way home from the Trojan War. Consider *The Adventures of Huckleberry Finn*, featuring two escapees facing trials and finding help as they raft down the Mississippi River. How about movies: Harry Potter, Indiana Jones, Star Wars? Or, consider a guy who rides his bicycle across the United States. They all fit. They all follow the same formula. Why? The answer requires a slight detour.

Joseph Campbell, an aspiring novelist, came from a wealthy family in New York. After college at Dartmouth, he traveled and read widely. He spent a year in Monterey, California, in the 1930s, where he became friendly with John Steinbeck and his wife, Carol, a little too friendly with Carol, as it turned out. After the affair, Campbell headed back east where he taught for a year at the Canterbury School, the prep school he had attended, and then accepted a job offer to teach literature at Sarah Lawrence College. Fascinated by mysticism and American Indian culture from a young age, Campbell became an expert in myth and folklore. He never finished his novel, but in 1949 published a book that would eventually change how millions of people think about myths. In *The Hero with a Thousand Faces*,[3] Campbell argues that every culture in the world has stories with heroes and that, in all those stories, the hero goes on a quest, following the template laid out above. The trappings differ across cultures, but the basic elements are the same. First there's a "calling". For instance, in a story beloved of the Arapaho of the North American Plains, a girl is drawn by a porcupine that climbs up a cottonwood tree. The girl follows and begins an adventure in a magical realm. Another example is the famous story of the buddha, Siddhartha Gautama, who led a princely life sheltered from anything unpleasant. One day he came upon an old man bent over a stick. The next day, he met a man who was diseased, then he saw a dead man. The prince was shocked by the pain and suffering. Finally, he met a monk who called him to renounce the world, and the prince followed. Campbell writes, "This first stage of the mythological journey — which we have designated the 'call to adventure' — signifies that destiny has summoned the hero and transferred his spiritual center of gravity from within the pale of his society to a zone unknown" (p. 48).

Once called, the hero enters a strange world, which, Campbell points out, often swallows the hero, literally. In an Eskimo tale, it's a whale, much like Jonah. In Zulu culture, it's an elephant. For Finn MacCool of Irish lore, it's a monster. But it doesn't have to be the belly of a beast, it can be an underworld, a forest, a heavenly kingdom, the depths of an ocean, or a mountaintop (think Moses). Or maybe a dark tunnel along a mountainous highway. Once there, the hero faces ordeals, for which helpers mysteriously appear. In Greek mythology, Psyche, in search of her lover, Cupid, is commanded by Cupid's jealous mother to sort a mountain of beans and grains before nightfall. An army of ants helps her. Then she has to gather wool from a flock of sheep with sharp horns and a poisonous bite. She learns from a reed (which talks, apparently) that she can just pull bits of wool from the grasses that snare it as the sheep pass.

Ultimately, the hero gains a prize, what Campbell calls "the boon". For Psyche, it's getting reunited with Cupid. For Siddhartha Gautama, it is enlightenment. For Moses, it's the Ten Commandments. But then comes the final step in the hero's journey. The hero must return to the world that they left, and that part can go well or poorly. In the end, Psyche is united with Cupid, and with the blessing of Zeus, the couple weds and lives happily ever after — truly ever, as Zeus grants them immortality. Moses, on the other hand, comes down the mountain to find the Hebrews breaking all of the freshly chiseled holy commandments. Drunk and fornicating around a giant bonfire with a golden statue for worshipping, they shortly realize they're in big trouble, and are forced, as punishment, to wander in the desert for 40 years eating dry crackers. Then Moses dies.

Campbell's book lays it all out. The examples above, except the bicycle-in-tunnel, are all taken from *The Hero with a Thousand Faces*, which describes, in great scholarly detail, hundreds more examples from around the world and across history. It's all pretty convincing. Every adventure is basically the same story with different details. Hence the title: *The Hero with a Thousand Faces*. Campbell's book was well received in the academic world and became a staple of college courses in literature and mythology. But something happened 40 years later that turned it into a cultural phenomenon. Bill Moyers, the peripatetic TV journalist, and former press secretary for Lyndon Johnson, had interviewed Campbell in the 1970s and was so struck by his presence on screen, he later wrote, "I vowed then that I would come after him again, this time for a more systematic and thorough exploration of his ideas."[4] Six years later, he did. Camping out at George Lucas' Skywalker Ranch an hour's drive north of San Francisco, Moyers and his crew taped 24 hours of the two men sitting across from each other in a library setting, chatting about mythology. It was edited down to six hours and ran nationally as a series of one-hour episodes on PBS in June of 1988. It's hard to imagine anything more boring for TV than a couple of talking heads in an academic discussion, but *The Power of Myth* was an instant hit. Between Moyer's perfectly pitched *everyman* questions and Campbell's artful commentary refined from 40 years as an extremely popular college teacher, the show's exploration of deep questions and our connection to them, drew people in. It helped that, sadly, between the taping and the broadcast, Campbell, by then in his mid-80s, succumbed to cancer and was already widely in the news with tributes to his life and work. Because of *The Power of Myth*, Campbell's ideas, already in the societal mainstream, exploded across American culture and beyond. Everyone started seeing Campbell's journey of the hero, what he called the *monomyth* (borrowed from James Joyce), everywhere. Authors and artists reacted viscerally, some with trepidation. British novelist Neil Gaimon was so freaked out by Campbell's analysis that he stopped reading the book. From an interview in 2007:

> Interviewer: Can you tell us if you've had particular influences from thought-leaders in this realm—particularly Joseph Campbell?
> Gaimon: I like Campbell—but, I sort of met him second. And the truth is, the stuff that I've always really enjoyed most of all is the primary influences. It's always

interesting to see what people say about things. But I tend to be more interested in the actual myth. I think I got about halfway through *The Hero with a Thousand Faces* and found myself thinking if this is true—I don't want to know. I really would rather not know this stuff. I'd rather do it because it's true and because I accidentally wind up creating something that falls into this pattern than be told what the pattern is.[5]

Some authors embraced Campbell, studied his work, and used it to punch up their adventure stories. Popular apps, like Scriptstudio.com, offer tutorials in the hero's journey for script writers. George Lucas, who hosted the taping sessions for the *Power of Myth* at his recording studio/ranch, is the most famous example of an artist who intentionally drew on Campbell's work – for the creation of Star Wars. Lucas was familiar with *Hero with a Thousand Faces* when he conceived Star Wars and acknowledged his debt to Campbell. When they finally met in person in 1984 at a talk that Campbell gave in San Francisco, they quickly became friends. Campbell had not seen any of the Star Wars movies, so Lucas invited Campbell and his wife to Skywalker Ranch for a one-day, three-movie marathon. When the third movie wrapped up, Campbell said, "You know, I thought real art had stopped with Picasso, Joyce, and Mann. Now I know it hasn't."[6]

So how does the hero's journey track on to Star Wars? Short answer: perfectly. Young Luke Skywalker responds to his calling from Obi-wan and the adventure takes off. A celebrated modern epic, the series of *Star Wars* movies comprises an elaborate and complex version of the hero's journey. No wonder Joseph Campbell instantly fell in love with it. But the hero's journey needs not the grand scale of the entire universe to play itself out. Small moments of everyday life can follow the same adventurous path with the same excitement and delight, but on a much smaller scale. Most mornings I go for a walk in the woods. One day recently, I got up at 5:30 a.m., and, stiff from sleep, hobbled down to the kitchen, made a pot of tea, and carried it up to my office. I settled into my recliner facing the east window with my laptop, my usual routine. For two hours I worked on the pages you just read. When I began, the window was dark, but as I worked, sipping tea from my favorite mug with swirly green and yellow Celtic designs, I occasionally looked up, and, after a while, I could faintly make out the branches of the oak tree that stands in the corner of our yard. A little later, the sky shifted to a lighter shade of gray. More tea and a paragraph later, there was a pink-orange glow. I felt a familiar calling. If I wrote for another half hour, it would be time to quit, and I could head outdoors to see what the day has to offer. Shortly, I finished off my tea pot and headed downstairs. It was January. I checked the thermometer: 23 degrees. I pulled on my boots and laced them up, grabbed my down coat, insulated gloves, hat, and muffler. As long as my neck and my back are warm, I love heading out into the cold. I walked to the end of the street and headed into the woods, assisted by a well-worn trail, and cheered on by a few bird tweets as the sun hit the tops of the trees. As I walked, I worked through problems. Our daughter in Brooklyn can't afford her daily commute to the Bronx. The paragraph I just wrote isn't right. How should I package the late Christmas gifts I need to mail? I stepped lively, frozen leaves crunching underfoot. Light coming up. I felt a surge of energy, the possibility of a new day with fresh ideas. Maybe Brooklyn daughter should get an EZ pass. The paragraph is missing a sentence. Is there an empty box in the attic for the Christmas gifts? I returned home refreshed, eager to plunge into the day.

My bike ride across North America is no different, just a bit more extended. I fell into cycling, found I loved it and felt an urge to go further and further, until nothing less than the whole span of our great continent would do. Along the way I had help from strangers—a farmer who gave me shelter during a massive thunderstorm, and the deputy sheriff who drove five miles ahead to see if the bridge was passable. In the end, well, we'll see how it turned out, but, meantime, it sure seems like Campbell's monomyth works. Whether it's a blockbuster movie series spanning the universe or my daily walk in the woods in Central Massachusetts—we're all really about the same business. There's just one problem: it's not that simple.

Chapter 3
"Hey, Buddy"

How did I end up in a pitch dark tunnel on the downside of the Northern Cascade Mountains at the far end of a 4000 mile cross-country bicycle journey? It started as a weekend jaunt from my house in Central Massachusetts, 55 miles east to the coast, Salisbury State Reservation, with its sweeping sugar-sand beach that extends for miles and the Atlantic Ocean that comes crashing ashore unobstructed by any capes or barrier islands. It was early May. My father was in hospice care. Thirty years of adult-onset type 1 diabetes had taken a toll on his body, despite the expert care provided daily by my Mom, a registered nurse. His body was worn out and his mind, the once subtle mind of a philosopher and theologian, was in a permanent fog. Until recently, he could still tell a joke, improvise a beautiful prayer woven with verses from the Book of Isaiah and the Gospels when the extended family met at mealtime, and sing a Lutheran hymn with his deep, well-regulated baritone. But all that was gone. He was in bed, mostly incoherent, with 24-hour care.

Strange how very different things happen at the same time. As my Dad was failing, I was getting interested in biking. After the doctor said I shouldn't plan on any more running, due to a torn meniscus and worn-out cartilage in my knee, I'd started experimenting with my old three-speed bike, up and down the rail trail that cuts through our neighborhood. I talked with my brother, an avid racing cyclist. He endorsed my taking up cycling. I started looking at new bikes. Laurie didn't like the price tags. I countered that taking up a new sport will keep me from getting moody and fat, or fatter. I'd been picking up pounds through my 30s and into my 40s because I was carrying on with chips and beer and Mac & Cheese like I was a teenager. When she still hesitated, I pointed out that what I made in a day of consulting would pay for the bike. That clicked, and the next weekend I bought a Specialized Sequoia, which Gene the bike store guy described as a "light touring bike." Crucially, it had two screw holes near the rear wheel hub, where you could attach the frame that supports a set of panniers, and in those panniers would go the gear needed for a multi-day trip.

At Salisbury Beach I scooped a tiny jam jar I'd brought with me into the retreating water of a spent wave. I was barefoot, and the cold, rushing water and gritty sand was a massage to my newly christened biker's feet. I held up the jar, and shiny specs of sand swirled like a snow globe, then settled at the bottom with water filling the rest of the way to the top. My own mini beach. I capped it and told myself, I'd carry it with me to the west coast to be tossed into the Pacific. I had no plan to ride my bike cross-country. It was a *just-in-case*.

I started riding my bike everywhere. I rode it west to Great Barrington, MA, for our daughter's start in college. Which meant I'd now ridden my bike the breadth of my home state. If I was going to launch some epic ride west the next summer, I could start at the Massachusetts-New York border and ride to … where? Buffalo?

In the fall, Mom called. "If you want to see your Dad one last time, I think you should come this weekend." I rode my bike to Connecticut. He was unconscious. His face looked relaxed and rosy-colored.

I was glad to see that because Mom had recently reported one of the last things he said was, "I'm suffering," a striking admission for a man who lived a life of guarded emotions. He died that weekend. We were all there, my brothers, my Mom, and me. Laurie drove down with our youngest daughter, Anna. When he drew his last breath, I was the only one in the room.

I said, "I love you, Dad." I think that's the only time I ever said that, maybe because it was the only time I could say it without making him or me feel embarrassed. He was already gone.

Fast forward.

"Hey, Buddy, where you goin'?" I turned around and saw four beefy guys in uniform, hands poised over the holster of their side arm.

I stuttered, "Uhm, Buf, Buffalo, I think?"

"Well, you're goin' the wrong way. That's a secure area."

"Oh. Sorry," I said, and turned my bike, which I was walking, to face the other way. I smiled weakly. "Thanks," I said. The lead guy gave a smug little smile that said, *Idiot, toad, 'Spooked him'*, all in one.

I'd started in Pittsfield, Mass, right up against the New York State border. It was mid-May. I'd done my Salisbury Beach ride the previous May. My Dad had passed in November. The spring semester had finished up. I submitted my grades and had no other work obligations. Laurie dropped me off on a stretch of road just before the *Welcome to New York* sign. After a short ascent, it was downhill, pretty much the whole way to Albany. The announced plan was to get as far as Buffalo, 383 miles. But I had a secret ambition to push through to Cleveland. At 600 miles, that would mean 75 miles a day for the eight riding days I'd budgeted to make it back in time for Commencement. I also had a secret-secret ambition to eventually ride much farther than Cleveland.

The morning of day five, I was approaching Buffalo. I couldn't believe it. I was doing close to 90 miles a day. My months of training were paying off. Map said best route would take me into Canada and included 25 miles on a lightly trafficked parkway. The "park" part of that got my attention. After experiencing Rochester rush hour, where I got very lucky to fall-in behind a slow-moving farm tractor while crazed commuters went flying past in the three other lanes, and, after getting beer cans thrown at me across upstate New York – me all skinny legs in neon, someone yelled, "faggot"-- I was all for a break from heavy road traffic. I paid my 50-cent toll at the Lewiston Bridge, and crossed into Canada, land of sensible people. My butt was sore. Never in my life had I ridden anything like 90 miles in a day, let alone every day. But riding along the Niagara River Parkway, where the cars were few and slow moving, there was a comfortable shoulder which sometimes split off to a separate bike path, and I could enjoy the view, my mind got free from its accustomed thinking. I realized I could shift my butt back on the seat about a half inch, and everything suddenly felt great.

I continued to feel good as I approached the Peace Bridge with the US on the other side. I noticed it went kind of high in the sky. I don't like heights, but I figured I'd be fine. It probably has a ten-foot high mesh fence between the shoulder of the road and the edge of the bridge, I thought. And it probably has a protected bike lane. I got there and, of course, neither was true. A faint white line separated the highway traffic from a shoulder littered with debris. The right edge of the shoulder was a jersey barrier, and then, a couple hundred feet down, the river. Thing about a jersey barrier is, you hit it with a bike and, because the barrier rides just below hip level, you kind of roll over the top and down the other side, which, in this case, was a long way down. I started cautiously up the bridge and was dismayed to encounter crosswinds that increased, the higher I got. White knuckling it all the way, I made it over, negotiated a maze of off ramps, and parked my bike. After peeling my fingers from the handlebars, I walked into the customs office, where I was directed, incorrectly as it turned out, down the little path where, after a few minutes, I was approached from behind by armed customs officers. *Hey, buddy* ... All in a day's ride.

The beer can thing was weird. It happened a total of seven times, all while riding through economically depressed places in New York and Pennsylvania. It was always teenage boys driving by in a beat-up sedan. It felt like the same gang was dogging me the whole way. Of course, it wasn't, but something about me was universally threatening to a particular demographic—young, White males with no money and maybe no future. Perhaps my neon jersey and my tight shorts said I was gay. Maybe my bike's skinny tires and sleek look said European (French, socialist, intellectual, softie). Maybe it's that only people with money and time on their hands ride fancy bikes with panniers. It all somehow made me the enemy. Besides having beer cans thrown at me, I got honked at, swerved at, and airhorned once. I nearly fell off my bike when I got airhorned. Side note: The following summer and thereafter, I rode with an American flag on a wood dowel sticking up from my left rear pannier. Flying in the breeze, that flag was the first thing anyone approaching from behind would see. No more beer cans after that. The flag was my talisman. The series of episodes got me thinking, what if I was Black? What if I was a woman, riding by myself along some lonely highway? I don't think I saw a solo Black touring cyclist my entire ride. The one solo woman I ran into, on a stretch of road where it was just us two, said her friend was a mile back and would catch up soon. I don't think there was a friend. She was being cautious.

It wasn't all butt sores, beer cans, and scary bridges going across New York State. There were moments of sublime beauty. Riding west of Palatine Bridge on Route 5S, almost no traffic was present on the series of rolling hills. I climbed and coasted, climbed and coasted. On either side were broad, sloping fields, some, a fuzzy green and gold with just-sprouting crops, others tawny with long, unmowed grass left over from last year. The air smelled like mud and hay. The Mohawk River meandered close by. Sometimes I looked down on the river from high on a hill. Then, a few minutes later, it would be rushing by me, going the other way, swollen with spring melt from the Adirondacks. I'd dig into a big gear with the push of the hill I just descended. With almost no effort, I was averaging 20 miles an hour. Through the almost-magic of happy brain chemicals induced by vigorous exercise and a landscape worthy of a Bierstadt, Cole, Durand, or Church, all Hudson River School painters from the two centuries past who rendered the drama of the surrounding landscapes, I experienced a magnificent high most of the daylong.

There were moments of sublime pleasure, too. Approaching the eastern shore of Oneida Lake later that same day, a storm threatened in the west. I pedaled hard to the state campground. The ranger, noting the storm and my bike, directed me to a covered pavilion right on the shoreline. She said I could spend the night there. The campground was just about empty. That night the rain poured, lightning flashed, and I was cozy indoors. The pavilion had walls and windows, too, with a big piece of plate glass between me and the lake. I hunkered down with a 12-inch sub I'd picked up on the way in. I read, wrote in my journal, and watched the sky over the water.

But I couldn't call my Dad with a report from the road. Bizarrely, Laurie's father, too, had died, within three weeks of my father's passing. In addition, a good friend, someone who had been my mentor and my boss, and about the same age as my Dad, was sick with cancer, the kind that is sure to kill you, and he was declining. Bald from chemo, surrendered, after a big fight, to a wheelchair, Ted, a fundamentally joyful person, was making the best of it. All three men had the good fortune of a *til-*

death-do-us partner who was lovingly tending to their spouse through the *or worse* after a life-time of mostly *better*. For all three men, the decline was years long, which meant that for all three women, the emotional and physical labor of caregiving was a monumental pull.

When I left Oneida Lake the following morning at 6:30 a.m., the temperature was 39 degrees. I hadn't brought full-finger gloves because I thought, wrongly as it turned out, that May was a relatively warm month. But the sun climbed into a cloudless sky and the day warmed. I was getting used to biking every day, all day. The road was starting to feel like my home, maybe in the way sailors feel the sea is theirs. When they come into port it feels temporary and foreign. They long to leave. Back on the water, feeling the wind and spray, they are once again in their element. Today's ride was to include a lunch meet-up with Laurie's Mom in nearby Weedsport. A widow of just a few months, we'd all been concerned about how she was getting along. Lunch cheered us both and she seemed to be doing remarkably well. Heading west out of Weedsport on New York State Route 31 offered some gentle up and down through farms with tracts of land spreading to the horizon. It made me feel like a knob on the top of the planet, with Earth curving away on all sides. Mid-afternoon, I began a descent into the vast, flat Montezuma National Wildlife Refuge, a 10,000-acre swamp and a big stop-off point for migratory birds along the Atlantic Flyway. Would I get dive-bombed by flocks of sharp beaks and rasping talons? *My helmet would protect me!* Route 31 shot straight across. A headwind made me earn my transit, but there were no angry birds, only an enormous expanse of marsh. On both sides of the road cat tails, long grasses, patches of open water, and natural canals here and there. The road was maybe five feet above the water table, and I was glad it wasn't flooded because there was no other passage in view to the north or south. Several miles of swamp ended abruptly in a hill that quickly returned to the familiar roadside scenery: farmhouses, trees, rolling meadows, and cultivated fields. The abrupt change marked off Montezuma as a singular feature of the land. No wonder it had become embedded in the annual migrating patterns of so many species of bird.

Seeing Laurie's Mom in good spirits and enjoying a sit-down meal at midday had given me a burst of energy. I ended up covering more miles than planned. Which meant, the very accessible campground I'd been planning to stop at for the night would be well behind me and the only option where I'd likely be ending the day's ride was a campground four miles off route. Too far because it would add a total of 8 useless miles. I decided I would stealth camp, meaning, in the absence of a developed campground, I would wait for a stretch of open country along my route, then pick a spot by the side of the road, walk in far enough so my bike and my tent would be hidden from traffic, and set up camp. I'd arrive at twilight and leave near dawn to further hide my clandestine activity. I'd only read about stealth camping. I'd never done it.

The late afternoon remained warm and sunny. I began noticing side-of-the-road spots that would be good for the night. A grove of pine trees with no houses around, an old barn, apparently abandoned, with no other structure nearby. It got to be 6 o'clock. I decided I should have a good dinner. A diner presented itself. Leaving 45 minutes later, the sun was getting low, and the temperature was falling. Stealth camping suddenly seemed less attractive. I continued along Route 31. Between the Taco Bell, the Walmart Super Center, the closed-up storefronts and the occasional industrial parking lot, nothing looked good for a night of camping. Shortly, I was six miles out of downtown Macedon stuck in a relentless industrial, strip-mall wasteland. There were no secret camping spots. At least none that felt marginally safe. It would be dark soon and all maps indicated no motels. Just then, lo and behold, a motel came into view on the left. I got closer. It was an old-style, one-story with doors opening onto the parking lot out front. Probably why it wasn't listed anywhere. I pedaled eagerly. It looked a little gloomy. That's okay as long as there was a room with a bed, a toilet, and a shower. I got closer. It was more than gloomy. It was dark. The grass needed mowing. It was a motel alright, but it was very closed. I rode into the parking lot to stop and think. That's when I noticed light coming from the unit closest to the office, which was also dark. I heard music. Hmm. I got off my bike and walked it over. I listened. Rolling Stones, "Sympathy for the Devil", playing pretty loud. I knocked, also loud. I heard a voice inside.

A woman said, "Get it." I waited. The door opened a few inches. Two faces, a man, and a woman behind him, and a powerful blast of high-octane liquor.

I figured this door could slam shut quickly so I said, all at once, "I'm a cross-country cyclist. I need a place for the night. I'm all out of options. It's dark." I could see the guy heard this.

He hesitated, "We're closed."

"That's okay," I said. "I just need a roof. It doesn't matter if it's a mess. I've got my camping gear. I'll pay. I'll be gone first thing in the morning."

He looked at me. Looked at my bike. Then said, "Hang on." The door thudded shut. I waited. Then it opened.

"What will you pay?"

"Twenty dollars?"

"Twenty-five."

"Deal." I gave him the money. I'd gathered some bills from my bag. He handed me a key.

"Unit 5. It's a mess. You sure you want it?"

"It's fine. I'll be gone first thing."

The guy shrugged, *Whatever*. The door closed. I heard the deadbolt.

The room lived up to its description. I spread my ground cloth over the bare mattress. The toilet worked. A few bugs skittered into the shadows when I twisted the faucet for the shower head. Water came out. Cold. It stayed cold. I took a shower. Without planning to, I'd ridden 100 miles today. In bike lingo, that's "a century." It's seen as a kind of landmark in your development as a cyclist. Good for me. I was dead tired.

I slept poorly. It rained during the night. There was no heat, but my sleeping bag was warm enough. First light, I gathered my stuff and was gone, feeling like maybe stealth camping would not be a thing for me, and feeling grateful for the room, as bad as it was. Clipping into my bike, it occurred to me, I'd said last night to the partying couple in Unit 1 I was a on *a cross-country trip*. Maybe that's how such things come to be. You play around with an idea in your head, and because you've been thinking it, when an opportune moment arises, you try it out, out loud. Suddenly, you start thinking, oh, really? So, I'm doing that?

Back to Buffalo, after which, the next landmark is Erie, Pennsylvania. Still a ways off from Erie, riding Route 5 as it hugs the southern shore of the massive Great Lake that bears its name, I came upon a road sign. It said, "Erie 15." That's about what I was figuring, but it's always exciting to see it on a sign. I rode a mile and came to another sign. It said, "Erie 15." I gave a chuckle. I rode some more. Another sign appeared. It said, "Erie 16." That sign was not funny.

The stretch from Buffalo, southwest through westernmost New York State and then into Pennsylvania felt bleak. Maybe it was the weather, which was gray and maybe it was the landscape, which was also gray. It might have been a place whose glory days were past, only there wasn't any past glory in evidence. Powerlines crisscrossed the flat landscape that alternated between farmland, industry, and retail centers. Signs of decay were everywhere—barns caved in, rusted equipment, fields gone fallow, a warehouse with a "space available" banner across the front. The upper left corner had torn loose so you couldn't read the "spa" part. A manufacturing plant, maybe steel, that looked frozen with rust was surrounded by an enormous empty parking lot. I passed a strip mall that looked mostly vacant. A Dollar Store. Years later I read J. D. Vance's *Hillbilly Elegy*, the 2016 bestseller about his family, originally from Appalachia that sought a better life up north and didn't find it. I felt like I was riding around his hometown, a place that felt defeated and angry — likely what was behind the flying beer can episodes. This was rural, mostly White America, with high unemployment, dead or dying industries, and spiraling addiction; a place that felt profoundly left behind.

In the afternoon, the sun came out and the temperature rose into the 70s. I noticed a field planted with grape vines, then another. On the lake side of the highway were pretty houses with neat lawns and a marina that looked active with pleasure boats. Maybe it was just my mood that was gray. Twenty miles west of Erie, I called it a day. Virginia's Beach Lakefront Cottages and Camping was my chosen destination, a short ride off Route 5, toward the lake. There were wooded campsites and then a big meadow with converted trailers — the "cottages" — made to look rustic with a few lacquered, knotty pine trim boards and a screened porch at one end. Dinner was at the Tasty Twist up the road. The sign out front advertised "Garlic parmesan fries. 40 Frozen Custard Flavors." I'd missed my last chance for cold beer at a distributorship back in Lake City. So, I made up for it with grease and calories, dining on pizza, a large chocolate shake, and onion rings. While I ate, cars started to gather on the lawn adjacent to the Tasty Twist. They were old, mostly 1960s vintage with squared off corners and no headrests. Then a black Model A rumbled in. It was a car show. It turned out Wednesday was Cruise Night at the Tasty Twist. I bought a frozen custard and strolled among the vintage autos. Things were looking up. Tomorrow on to Cleveland!

I braked for the stop sign, feeling a little like I didn't need to. Residential neighborhood, quiet, gently winding road, big houses, big trees starting to leaf out, and few vehicles, except for the occasional landscaper's truck. The air smelled like mulch. I heard something and looked over. A bike pulled up on my left. A young guy, nicely dressed with a messenger bag and a helmet, was a little out of breath.

"I saw your panniers, and I admit I'm curious," he said in a friendly way.

I looked at him and smiled, pleased he was interested, and I was starved for conversation.

"I started in Massachusetts," I said. "Rode across New York, and now I'm finishing up. Hope to take the train back to Boston day after tomorrow."

I acted casual, but I was secretly thrilled to utter those words. I'd ridden my bike 600 miles in eight days all the way to Ohio and now I was on the outskirts of Cleveland. I'd left Virginia's Beach Cottages early that morning, knowing I had 90 miles to cover with a fair amount of urban riding. At day's end a motel room, reserved three days back awaited me, for two whole nights. What a luxury! My new bicycle friend turned out to be a commuter who worked nearby and was headed home to the Lakewood part of the city, where I, too, was headed. He rode with me, and, along the way, I learned the particulars of the Amtrak Station and how to cross the Cuyahoga River, not a simple matter as it cuts five oxbows through the city before it exits into Lake Erie. Some roads over the river are good for bikes. Some are not. He asked me why I booked a motel five miles from the train station. That caught me short, and I learned that, indeed, I'd way overshot. No matter, he said, Lakewood is nice, and, on a bike, it's just 20 minutes back to the train station and the Hall of Fame. He asked if I had heard about the Rock and Roll Hall of Fame. We chatted about this and that and he peeled off a mile after we crossed the river. I got to thinking about people I'd met in the last week. The thing is, or maybe it's not the thing, maybe it's me, riding solo, I don't like getting too friendly with anyone because pretty soon they might say, "Hey, we're headed the same direction, let's ride together." That will suit some people, but I like my freedom, I like my solitude. I like making my own schedule and sticking to it. Which means that my encounters with other people tend to be short, friendly, and thank-you-very-much-bye-now. There were the two college girls I met at an ice cream stop in Erie the day before. They said how they'd just graduated from SUNY Geneseo and were headed west, all the way to California. Fifty to sixty miles a day, they said. No rush. All their stuff was brand new. They were riding on the sidewalk, they said, to avoid being in traffic. I didn't want to tell them they don't have sidewalks most places along their way, and that sidewalks are not meant for bikes. There was Niles Fitzduff, who I met on a stretch of quiet road near Barcelona, NY. We were headed opposite directions on bikes with panniers. We waved and found ourselves both coasting to a stop. Niles, from Dublin, Ireland, said he started in Los Angeles 32 days ago and how he was averaging 100 miles a day and was raising money through a website for a project in Guatemala. He said he had $6,000 in donations so far. He also said his butt had been sore the whole way. He described in too much detail how to apply "those clear bandaids from Walmart, four to a box." I thanked him for the tip. My thoughts lingered on his fundraiser. Hmm. Fundraiser plus bike ride. There were the three teenagers I met in Newark, New York at a Dairy Stand. Two scruffy lads and a girl. A detour sign was blocking the road where there was supposed to be a bridge over a river. They were eating ice cream at the DQ. I stopped, asked them if they knew how long the detour was.

    The big kid in a Buffalo Bills cap said, "It goes 15 miles."

My heart sank, and I guess my face showed it because the red head girl, too pretty to be hanging with these two delinquents, looked at him and said, "Whaa?" Then she turned to me. "You go up one block and there's another bridge. Then you can turn back to the Main Road. Then she scolded him.

I didn't hear what she said, but then he said, "He didn't ask that. He asked how far's the detour."

There was the guy who came by the pavilion that night at Oneide Lake before the rain arrived. He was a large grownup on a kid's mountain bike. We got to chatting. He brought out two cold beers from his backpack and offered me one. I thanked him kindly, and we talked some more. He said he served in Iraq and spent time in Germany. He said he liked Germany because they have big toilets. Besides people, I met some animals along the way. For example, I got bit by a little yipping rat dog in the driveway of country gift shop where'd I'd bought a Sprite. I went back inside and told the lady her dog just bit me. She said he doesn't like bicycles.

At 5:50 a.m. on May 23rd, 30 hours after I'd arrived in Cleveland, I boarded the Amtrak Lakeshore Limited, bound for Boston, filled with excitement for an outcome to my adventure that exceeded expectations. My celebratory visit to the city had included a stop at the Rock and Roll Hall of Fame and not one but two dinners at Angelo's Pizza, where the manager said if I did a cross country bike ride fundraiser, he'd sign up as a sponsor. He gave me six chocolate chip cookies on the house.

Chapter 4
The Heroine's Journey

During an interview late in his life, Joseph Campbell was asked about the place of women in the hero's journey. Here is what he said:

> ... at the end of my last year there [teaching at Sarah Lawrence College] this woman comes in and sits down and says, "Well, Mr. Campbell, you've been talking about the hero. But what about the woman?"
> I said, "The woman's the mother of the hero; she's the goal of the hero's achieving; she's the protectress of the hero; she is this, she is that. What more do you want?"
> She said, "I want to be the hero!"
> So, I was glad that I was retiring that year and not going to teach any more [laughter].[7]

After the airing of Bill Moyer's *Power of Myth* in 1988, Joseph Campbell's "monomyth" became a cultural touchstone. With success, however, comes the inevitable backlash. It wasn't long before critics questioned the monomyth's universality, with some challenging the man himself. A posthumous assessment of Campbell appearing in the *New York Review of Books* in 1989 accused Campbell of sexism, racism, anti-semitism, and wanton materialism, placing him "somewhere well to the right of William F. Buckley."[8] The article provoked many letters, some defending, and others piling on the Campbell-bashing, calling him a "crypto fascist", and "mean spirited."[9]

To my way of thinking, Campbell's view seems just too simple. It is also too male, too White, and too privileged, presuming to speak for everyone. While the fact I've met up with very few women touring on bikes might suggest Campbell was right and adventure is a mainly male thing, it might, alternatively, mean that women feel fundamentally unsafe in a misogynistic culture or that some, at least, think about adventure differently from the way Campbell framed it. What if, maybe, while middle-aged men like me are drawn to pumping their bike pedals as part of a self-important quest, women tend to be drawn to something else entirely, something that Campbell wouldn't consider a real adventure, but which others might. That's an idea worth exploring.

Nearly pre-ordained, a feminist response to Campbell's males-only hero template appeared two years after the Moyers interviews. Working as a therapist in the 1970s, Maureen Murdock had found that many of her women clients between the ages of 30 and 50 were dissatisfied with their lives. They had achieved career success but felt empty. She concluded the reason these women were unhappy is that they "chose to follow a model that denies who they are."[10] That model was Campbell's hero quest. A quest at which they had succeeded but which left them unfulfilled. She wondered what a woman's journey is meant to be and how it relates to a man's journey. She was beginning to think that "the focus of female spiritual development was to heal the internal split between woman and her feminine nature" (location 280). She reached out to Joseph Campbell to get his view. They met in New York in September of 1981. Campbell's answer, which Murdock said she found "deeply unsatisfying" was as follows:

In the whole mythological tradition, the woman is *there*. All she has to do is realize she is the place people are trying to get to. When a woman realizes what her wonderful character is, she's not going to get messed up with the notion of being pseudo-male. (location 281).

This answer did not fit the striving and passionate women Murdock had come to know in her practice who wanted to be much more than the object of someone else's quest. Two years later, during the course of a back injury that immobilized Murdock for several days, an image of the heroine's journey came to her. Several years after that, it was a book, *The Heroine's Journey: Woman's Quest for Wholeness*. According to Murdock, a woman's journey begins with a rejection of the feminine and an immersion in the male hero's journey, a la Campbell. Having won it all, however, the woman feels unfulfilled and descends into a period of darkness during which she wrestles with her rejection of the feminine and emerges a new person who validates her female nature and integrates it with the male skills she has learned. Murdock's book was popular and became a template for screen writers, influential in the creation of strong female leads who are more than just women cast in male hero roles. Consider Katniss Everdeen in the *Hunger Games*, and Wonder Woman in the 2017 movie.

Critiques that appear in the immediate wake of a cultural moment, such as the Moyers interviews, are often polar reactions. To Campbell's **Hero** *with a Thousand Faces*, Murdock countered with the **Heroine** with a thousand faces, and a template that countered Campbell's. With time, however, the critiques become more complex, placing the person or moment in question in a broader cultural context.

Maria Tatar is an expert in folklore and was a professor in Harvard University's Department of Germanic Languages and Literatures for many years. The pandemic helped her summon the courage to re-think that vast terrain of myth and folklore and reconsider the place of women in it. She writes that she had long viewed Campbell's interpretations as "capturing the symbolic worlds of our ancestors"[11], but re-reading Campbell, she noticed something for the first time. The role of women, Campbell had written is, "one, to give us life; two, to be the one who receives us in death; and three, to inspire our spiritual, poetic realization."[12] It was the "our" that caught Tatar's attention and led her to consider that Campbell was not just capturing symbolic past worlds, as she had long thought; he was, in fact, advancing a distinctly male interpretation of those worlds. Over the course of the pandemic, she wrote a book with a very different interpretation, one that gives voice and agency to the girls and women of myth and folklore who Campbell and other men had ceaselessly silenced. In *The Heroine with 1,001 Faces*, Tatar shows us that woman heroes, by and large, are not centered on a journey, but a desire to mend the world, driven by curiosity, care, and compassion, marginalized and brutalized in most cultures. Tatar writes:

> [Women] escape domestic violence and abuse through storytelling. Rarely wielding the sword and often deprived of the pen, women have relied on the domestic crafts and their verbal analogues— weaving tales, spinning plots, and weaving yarns, to make things right, not just getting even but also securing social justice."

As Tatar explains later in her book, the heroine is less about a quest or a journey and more about a mission.

Tatar's re-thinking of women as heroines is a critical response to Campbell and his adherents, but there is a collegial tone to Tatar's narrative, as if Campbell is her sparring partner at the faculty club, where they may disagree, but still share a drink. A different tone is struck by Sarah Bond and Joel Christensen, an historian and a classicist respectively, in a piece they did for the *Los Angeles Review of Books* in 2021.[13] Bond and Christensen who are far too young to have been enjoying cocktails in the metaphorical faculty club with Campbell and Tatar, view Campbell from an historical distance—an artifact of a time and a place, a figure to be deconstructed. According to Bond and Christensen, Campbell's hero "projects a toxically masculine, heteronormative point of view that often marginalizes other voices and bodies." Furthermore, "it uses weaker people as instruments; and it has no room for collective action, for families, or for bodies that fail to conform: the aged, the disabled, the sick." Bond and Christensen also challenge Campbell's scholarship, accusing him of cherry-picking to create the illusion of a monomyth and failing to dwell on the darker bits of hero stories. As Bond and Christensen point out, Hercules went mad in the end, killing his wife and children. Odysseus killed over 100 of his own people and hanged the enslaved women of his household.

Overall, Campbell's reputation has not fared well in recent years. I can imagine him, today, shrunken and whimpering on the sofa, pleading, "Okay, so what do women want?"

A fair question.

Donna Little of Queensland, Australia has long been fascinated by the ways that women experience adventure. Her life and career reflect her passion. Growing up, she spent time outdoors in the Queensland outback. She taught secondary school early in her career and then embarked on world travel on her own, which included a stint of teaching at a U.S. summer camp for girls. Her love for travel and the outdoors led to an academic career in the areas of tourism and outdoor education. Her master's and doctoral theses both focused on women and adventure. In 2005, she published a study with Erica Wilson in the Canadian journal *Loisir et Societe* titled, "Adventure and the Gender Gap: Acknowledging Diversity of Experience."[14] For the study, they identified 82 women between the ages of 19 and 86, all of whom had substantial experience with some kind of adventure recreation, including rock-climbing, kayaking, sailing, cross-country skiing, mountaineering, caving, and solo overseas travel. Each woman was interviewed for her perspectives on the nature of adventure and her own experiences with adventure. Interviews were in-depth, lasting as long as four hours. What did they find? While all of the women in the study had engaged in activities that met the criteria typically associated with adventure—danger, uncertainty of outcome, physical challenge, skillful mastery—those criteria, it turned out, were not necessarily the defining characteristics of their experience. Several excerpts, including quotes from women they interviewed, help make the point:

- For these women, adventure was something outside the everyday life that provided them with new knowledge, new experiences, or unusual stories and was not necessarily confined to a pursuit or type of travel (p. 192).
- [Women] found adventure in exploring the self. "It's finding things out about me - the me who is scared, who is fearful, who can persevere. That's adventure and it's just as real as any expedition or tangible adventure you see in the news" (p. 193).
- "For some women, adventure could be raising their children: Raising my children now is an adventure into the unknown. It's an ongoing challenge to help them become positive people of the world" (p. 193).
- On the whole, the women sought to find adventure in experiences that were accessible to their lives, and adventure could be experienced when there was uncertainty, difference, and personal challenge (p. 193).

The women in this study were clearly not pursuing the hero's quest as Campbell describes it. While the surface features of their experiences bear some resemblance, their motivation, their quest, is something quite different. These women were after learning, growth, connection. Interestingly, Little and Wilson found that even though the women had all the adventurer

credentials of any of their male counterparts, they were hesitant to self-identify as adventurers. They explain:
> For these women, the public meaning of adventurer was located in socially constructed and media generated ideals of adventures performed by men who were physically tough, mentally alert and aloof, and who had the resources to leave behind family and friends to pursue their dreams (or were not tied to family expectations of marriage and responsibility). This image was fueled by both past and present representations of adventurers. An avid tramper and explorer felt her understanding was forged in "the adventure stories of my childhood - Biggles, Robinson Crusoe, Hillary even. Men who left the comforts, who were stoic and strong - these were the people living exciting adventures." (p. 194)

When it comes to how we think about adventures, heroes, quests, journeys, and the like, Joseph Campbell's contribution to scholarship and pop culture is large and lasting. He remains a pillar nearly a half-century after his passing, but a pillar inevitably becomes a pivot point. Thanks to the work of scholars, therapists, and journalists—many of them women—our understanding of adventure and our access to it is now much broader than it was in Campbell's male-centric, narrowly proscribed view. When we expose Campbell's flaws (the cherry-picking, the chauvinism), and give a fresh look at the source material (folklore, myth), and we add in the lived experience of contemporary women, we draw some very different conclusions about the nature of adventure. While it can certainly involve the adrenaline-soaked daring of a solitary superman, it can also be a shared search for meaning from new experiences, spiritual development, and personal growth. It need not take place at the far end of the Earth, away from family and friends. Instead, it could happen during a walk up the beach that goes a bit further than anytime before. And it does not have to include the cruelty and violence often associated with the male heroes of myth and folklore. It can be driven by curiosity, an ethic of caring, a desire to mend society and advance social justice. The feminist turn of the last 50 years has provided a new liberatory take on adventure, not only for women, for everyone. Whether this broader understanding is particularly female or culturally or biological rooted, or constitutes a binary or a spectrum, or something else, that discussion is for another day. The fact remains, it opens exciting new possibilities.

My adventure, the one about me taking on a solo quest across many miles on two wheels, was very much in the male, Campbell tradition. And it was privileged. I left Laurie and the kids behind for days, weeks, at a time. I wasn't trying to heal the world or build relationships. If anything, I was trying to get away from people. Maybe I was sad. My father and my father-in-law had died. My mentor and friend was gravely ill. . It wasn't like I was accomplishing some historic or athletic first. I was not ascending Mount Everest. I was not rowing single-handed across the Pacific Ocean. So, even by the male standard that seemed to drive me, my quest was less Norgay and Hillary and more Man of La Mancha. I'd recently been thinking I could name my bicycle Rocinante for the horse that Don Quixote rode across the Spanish Meseta, charging the armies of windmills. Might there be a way I could make this more than just a fun bike ride, more than a quixotic ramble? Maybe it was a feminine energy within me urging me to make it into something socially redeeming. Or maybe it was the woman I live with. Turns out, Laurie had something to say on the matter.

Chapter 5
A Proper Meal

It sounded like a freight train. That's what they always say, and it's true. The lightning started at midnight. My campsite near Long Prairie, Minnesota, was out in the open. No trees, no large structures, no hills or valleys. Just my tent in an open field dotted with a few RVs and a bathroom. I'd switched from hammock to tent two summers before. It was hard always having to find two trees to hold up the hammock, and the arrangement I had with a tarp stretched over it provided no protection from bugs or other pesty intruders, like the animal I woke to one morning, just before dawn. I'd felt hot breath and opened my eyes. I was staring in the half light at a dog's snout, I think. Its eyes regarded me, and as soon as my face registered alarm, it scampered off. To this day, I don't know if it was another camper's dog or a coyote, but it was one of the reasons I switched to a tent. A good call, as it turned out. My tent weighed under three pounds and all its parts rolled up neatly into a bag the size of a loaf of bread that I could bungie between my panniers over the rear wheel. Opened up, it was about the size of a coffin, only you could sit up, and it had a vestibule where I could set my gear. With my fluffy sleeping bag rolled out over my backpacker's air mattress inside, it was cozy. And with the netting that surrounds the entire interior, it was bug free. The waterproof fly over the top was amazingly effective in keeping me dry, even in a hard rain. It was about to get tested.

The wind was picking up, and, in Minnesota, where there aren't many hills to slow it down, I was learning it can get pretty fierce. Just before the lightning, the tornado siren had sounded, a long, steady three-minute blast just like the air raid sirens you hear in movies. Not a comforting association. Tornado sirens are triggered by an alert from the National Weather Service that either a tornado has touched down nearby or there are damaging winds of 70 miles an hour or the radar indicates conditions for either. The main thing you're expected to do when you hear a tornado siren is go indoors. As stalwart as my tent had already proven itself to be that summer, it was not the kind of indoors they have in mind. On the other hand, the bathroom was about a 60-second dash from my tent. It was constructed of cement block and would do if push came to shove. The rain was picking up and the lightning was getting closer. I'd pounded my tent stakes in as far as they'd go, and the soil was hard. They might hold. Either that or I'd spend the storm spread eagle inside my tent holding down the four corners with hands and feet, something I'd done more than once before. Just then there was a bright flash. I counted. One, two, three, etc., and got to 10 before the thunder boomed and rolled. Two miles away. I decided if I got to a count of three, meaning about a half mile, before the thunder boomed, I'd grab my essentials and run for the bathroom. I wriggled out of my sleeping bag, put on my raincoat and my camp shoes, set up my grab-and-go bag and then lay down on top of my sleeping bag. The air was getting cool as it does in a lightning storm. Just then a bright flash illuminated the interior of the tent. In the eerie silence that followed, I counted to eight before a mighty boom shook the ground, followed by rolling thunder. I've read that along the path of a lightning bolt, the temperature can reach 50,000 degrees Fahrenheit, same as the surface of the sun. Maybe I'd just count to five, to make a run for it. Two more lightning strikes. I got to six and boom! Close enough. I quickly set one pannier at the head of my tent and the other down by my feet. Maybe they would keep the tent anchored. Otherwise, I'd need to go searching for my tent somewhere downwind once this was all over. I unzipped the tent fly, stumbled out into the darkness, saw where the bathroom was, and made a run for it through the grass wet with rain and squooshy soil. I got to the door just as a double flash lit up the air and I ducked inside. It was a one-seater, and I made myself comfortable, noting that my feet were wet but the rest of me was relatively dry. I could wait it out, but I wouldn't get any sleep. That's when the wind suddenly picked up. It began to howl. Then it roared like the freight train everybody talks about. It was like I was standing right next to the tracks as massive rail cars loaded with freight roared past. I could even hear the swoosh of each individual car as it passed.

Wait.

I opened the door and peaked out. The noise instantly got louder and not 100 feet off, a midnight freight train was rumbling east on a set of tracks I hadn't even noticed. I let the door shut. The wind continued to roar and so did the freight train. Then the train noise receded and after about 15 minutes, the wind started to die down. The thunder was quieting down, too. I counted 15 seconds between lightning and boom. Then I peeked out the door. The rain was somewhere between drizzle and steady. I squinted into the night and found my tent. It was right where I left it, looking intact. I squoosh-squooshed back, shed my wet gear, climbed into my sleeping bag, and fell into a deep sleep.

Since my Pittsfield to Cleveland ride the previous summer, much had happened. First, I declared out loud to Laurie that I wanted to do a scholarship ride. That was long enough after Laurie suggested it that I could almost fool myself into thinking I'd thought of it. Then, I lost 25 pounds on the theory it was the best way to reduce my load for a cross country bike trip. Third, I decided I'd ride from Cleveland to Minneapolis as the next leg of the trip and then, the following summer, I'd do the massive final segment of the trip, across the massive stretch of Montana, up and over the Rockies, up and over the Northern Cascades, to be followed by a long descent to Puget Sound.

The idea of riding coast to coast, broken up into, smaller trips spread out over several summers, had been growing since the Pittsfield to Cleveland ride and just kind of bubbled out on various occasions. Casual referencing out loud provided the oxygen needed to turn it into a declaration of intent. But the idea of a scholarship started with Laurie. One Saturday morning in November, we were in the kitchen. I was suited up in my yellow and black stretchy bike clothes and Laurie was emptying the dishwasher. She was growing less and less enamored with my longer and longer bike rides away from home-bound responsibilities. She asked, ever so patiently, in between hoisting dinner plates to the upper cabinet, if I might consider biking for a cause, like maybe a scholarship fundraiser. It was like we were enacting a Joseph Campbell meets Maria Tatar script.

"You know, maybe then, I'd be okay with it," She said. She meant it as an opportunity to turn something purely recreational into something meaningful, but inside my male brain, it got quickly re-formulated. What a great idea, I thought, shifting Laurie's praiseworthy idea into transactional terms: If I raise money for a scholarship, then I get to ride my bike.

The really big thing that happened that year was when Ted passed in October. It was a long decline, during which he and Nancy focused on living as well as they could each step along the way. When the end got close, Nancy made sure Ted was as comfortable as he could be. Reflecting on Ted's passing, and my father, and Laurie's father, it struck me that Nancy, Laurie's Mom, and my Mom had all demonstrated remarkable courage, compassion, and patience--endurance that was equivalent to somebody running a marathon. Their husbands were all remembered lovingly in their memorial services and other tributes. The labor of these three women, although widely admired, was only quietly acknowledged. It deserved to be openly recognized, but it's not something you get a plaque for. That's when the idea of a scholarship ride connected to their quiet heroism started to come into view, inspired by Laurie's suggestion. Their heroism was not a quest, there was no uncertain outcome. The outcome was predictable. The heroism lay in the selfless care that had no chance to improve matters, only to lessen the pain and offer comfort. The uncertainty that defined their heroism was how they would find the strength to face each day.. They were all heroes, no less than the best examples Campbell might offer up, but heroes of a different sort. More along the lines of what Murdock, Tatar, Little, and other feminists describe. The scholarship this fund raiser would create could be in their names and given to a deserving undergraduate who demonstrates courage and compassion in some significant way. That felt just right. I shared the idea with Laurie. She liked it. We had several talks about it through the autumn and winter after Ted's death. By spring, I was committed, and Laurie was supportive. We agreed we would not say anything to anyone until after I'd ridden the next leg to Minneapolis. That leg would take me 1200 miles across some hot, flat country and would involve a fair amount of camping in remote places. It would be a test. If I could do that, then it would be reasonable to think I could do the final marathon stretch across North Dakota, Montana, Idaho, and Washington, over all those mountains, 2000+ miles to the Pacific Ocean the following summer.

Each year that I took an extended trip on my bike, I learned something and made changes to improve the next ride. Riding across New York and Pennsylvania, I'd been wondering how I could shrink my load. I'd read about extremists drilling holes in the handle of their toothbrush to reduce weight. But there are only so many trick moves like that you can make, and they generally don't add up to much. That's when it occurred to me that I hadn't always weighed 175 pounds. Back in the day, way back, I was closer to 140. I recalled, when I was a competitive long-distance runner in my early 20s, one summer, following a tough training routine, I got down to a steady 139. This was not about my toothbrush, it was about my butt. Instead of drilling holes in gear, I needed to go on a diet. Thing is, it would need to be more than a diet, it would need to be a change, overall, in what I eat and how much. It began on December 30th, a kind of New Year's resolution with a one-day head start. Plan was to cut all portions in half, stop eating late at night, and continue with an experiment I'd already begun in cutting out alcohol. I announced what I was doing to people in my circle because that way I'd embarrass myself to everyone if I gave up. I dropped a fast three pounds the first week, which is normal with diets as your body burns up available glycogen. Then the pace slowed, but I stuck with it, dropping about a pound a week. All diets boil down to one main thing: eat less. That's what I did. Six months went by, I got down to 149 and decided to stop. I wanted to keep a little padding in case I fell off my bike. Luckily, I'd adopted some better habits about food along the way and was able to keep my weight after the weight loss program ended. I was just being healthier. The fact that I was riding my bike 100+ miles a week during the spring to train for the Cleveland to Minneapolis ride helped.

    Halfway into my ride across the great Midwest, I realized I was averaging over 100 miles a day-- back-to-back centuries-- and I wasn't sore and I wasn't running out of steam. I'd started my training for this leg of the trip in February, and, by the time I boarded the Amtrak for Cleveland, I was doing at least one, fifty to sixty mile ride each week, with weighted panniers. Across these vast, flat states—Ohio, Indiana, Illinois, Iowa, Wisconsin, Minnesota—I was feeling like a warrior, like I could ride forever. My training was paying off big-time. But warrior-mode was about to get tested. Five days in, crossing Illinois, I was 120 miles from the Mississippi River, with Iowa on the other side. Could I cover that distance in one day? I'd be riding half the width of the state, the entire distance between two great rivers, the Illinois, just to my east, and the mighty Mississippi to the west. I set my alarm for 4:15 a.m. the next morning and was on my bike, ready to go at 5:20. It was still dark. I wore my headlamp and started down the residential streets of Henry, Illinois. I'd spent the night in the Town Park and swum in the town pool in the late afternoon. I was finding that many small towns open their park, meaning the one right in the middle of town, often with a gazebo, to touring cyclists, who set up camp and, the town hopes, will drop a few dollars into the local economy. People were universally friendly in these small towns, and it buoyed my spirits to be welcomed and supported. Strategically mentioning that I was working up to a scholarship ride got me extra bonuses, like a swim in the town pool after closing time or access to the locker room in the high school where I could take a shower. The principal himself showed up with the key when I let the local police know I would be camping in the park that night.

If I was going to make it over the Mississippi today, I was going to have to forego any plans for a sumptuous meal enroute, often the lure I used with myself to get my butt through the first 40 miles or so. There's nothing quite like the vision of scrambled eggs and pancakes to keep me rolling forward in the early morning. No, I'd have to make today's food a series of quick stops. I'd become quite the expert at sizing up the options available at most convenience stores across the country, almost all of which are cut from the same cloth (i.e., nearly identical inventory of food with questionable nutritional value). When riding a bike, loaded with gear, 80 to 100miles a day, all at-home eating habits go out the window. Although I worried I might backslide from my new healthy habits once I returned home, I decided that would be a problem for when I returned home. For now, the plan was eat like a teenager. I would eat what my body craved and in the quantities my stomach signaled to my brain. This generally works for minors but not adults at mid-life, unless you're burning 5000 calories a day, which I was. In that case let the *bon temps* roll!

It's strange sometimes what those cravings conjure from the shelves of a convenience store. For example, on the day in question, I was rolling along Route 1350N about 70 miles out of Henry, Indiana. It was early afternoon. I'd been zigzagging straight flat county roads with four-digit numbers for names, followed by an "N" or an "E". It was hot. 90+ degrees, and humid. At a stoplight a ways back, the front seat passenger in the car that pulled up next to me had rolled down her window. I felt a blast of air conditioning.

She said from under her unnaturally curled hair and many layers of make-up, "You shouldn't be out here riding your bike, son. It's too hot. You could have a stroke."

I thanked her, and she rolled up her window, maybe 80 and possibly on her way to deliver a casserole. The light turned green and off we went. I kind of liked she called me son. Despite the heat, the roadside scenery had been drawing me in all day with a field of dreams sort of magic. On a typical stretch of highway, one side of the road was all soy as far as you could see and the other was all corn as far as you could see, which wasn't too far because it was so tall, but every so often, there was a little rise in the road and I could look up over top and all those corn rows just shot out in diagonals nearly to the horizon where there'd be a silo or two. This relentless scenery went on all morning, into the early afternoon. It became meditative and lulled me into a kind of trance state. That's why after 70 miles of riding, I suddenly realized I hadn't been off my bike since Henry. The only stops I made, I straddled the bike, swallowed a granola bar or two with some watered-down Gatorade and hopped back on my pedals. It was past time for a genuine, get-off-the-bike-and-walk-around stop. The next town center was coming into view through the heat waves just up the road. Shortly, I came to the combo Shell gas station and Orion Mart, propane tanks for sale in a metal cage out front and colorful signs in the big window, showing a pizza slice, a hot dog, and a chocolate donut up close and three feet tall. I was craving a blend of grease and sugar woven together in something heavily carbohydrate in nature. After heading to the men's room to freshen up for my special meal, I began prowling the aisles. Candy bars blended into protein bars, blended into granola bars in one giant rack. Another was all chips. Cookies and donuts in another. There were aisles also for canned goods, kitchen supplies, phone accessories, magazines, all the usual. And then the grill. A dozen hot dogs lay between stainless steel rods, rotating noiselessly. Who knows how long any one of them had been there. Did anyone keep track? Thing is, they looked almost inviting. I don't eat meat, but it still sometimes looks good. The pizza slices, housed in a heated plastic box on top of the counter were all orange and dried out, completely unappetizing. I went back to the aisles, headed for the chips, and felt drawn to the Cheetos, right next to the Cheese Puffs, which are no good. They have no weight, no mass, all air. You bite into them and there's nothing there. Just the orange dust they leave behind on your fingers. Cheetos, on the other hand, offer a satisfying crunch with greater density. It almost feels like food in your mouth. I reached for the medium-sized bag, one size up from "snack" size which stated on the package that it would "curb" my hunger. I didn't want my hunger curbed. I wanted it granted a superhighway of flavor and a bottomless bag of cheese-like munching. The grease half of my food plan was all set. On to sugar. None of the sweets seemed right. The candy-protein-granola bar rack was too much like the utilitarian stuff I down when making miles.

Unfortunately, all the cookies—the Oreos and the Chips Ahoy, etc.—were all too small or too crunchy. The box of Entenmann's chocolate covered donuts was tempting, but, after I ate my meal portion of three, what would I do with the other five? But I liked their weight and density. Then, glancing over at the register, I spied the Grandma's Cookies in their distinctive clear plastic wrapper. You can see what you're buying. I walked over, aiming for the oatmeal raisin. There they were, six to a package. I'd have leftovers, like the donuts, but that didn't bother me. Oatmeal raisin felt a little like food going down and the chewy soft-style cookie meat was so much more satisfying than thin and crumbly Oreos. And large diameter meant it wouldn't be gone in two bites. You could linger over it like a hamburger. I rounded out my purchase with a 23-ounce mega can of Arizona Iced Tea, the kind that's half lemonade and has a picture of Arnold Palmer. Why him, I wondered. Shortly, I was seated at the salmon-colored, molded plastic bench right next to the Keno display. The thought of a cookie like a hamburger lingered. You could put one on top of the other, like a bun. You just needed to put something in between. Cheetos! What a great idea! I set a cookie on an unfolded napkin on the table in front of me, ripped open the Cheetos bag and carefully laid two layers of Cheetos crisscrossed on top. I then positioned a second cookie over the Cheetos. I slowly applied pressure, breaking the Cheetos and embedding the sharp edges into the cookie, which would help hold them in place and keep the whole composition from exploding when I tried to eat it. That was the next step. I picked it up with two hands, like a hamburger in a bun. It was a bit of effort, but I got my mouth around it, and bit in. I felt my teeth descending through the soft, thick dough of the cookie and then, just as the sweet was registering in my mouth, I hit the crunch and zesty cheesiness of the Cheetos. My mouth circled around it, and I pulled away my first bite. It took some chewing, as it should, to complete the process. It was a heavenly concoction of sweet and salty, chewy and crunchy, all in a sustainable, sandwich-like matrix you could work through as a proper meal. I popped the top on Arnold Palmer and took a long satisfying pull. Very cold. I had just invented the perfect road food, available at every mini mart across America. I could now travel anywhere, knowing a good meal was always at hand.

Soon I was back on the road heading west out of Orion, on Route 1300N, also known as 176th Avenue. I don't think there are that many avenues in Orion. Curious, but no matter, I had bigger questions on my mind, like how to cover 50 miles starting at 3 o'clock in the afternoon. I started riding with purpose. If I pushed a little harder continuously, ramped up my speed by two miles an hour, I could shave some time off the back end of my ride. Twenty minutes in, I thought about having a swallow of water and realized that in my Cheetos sandwich excitement, I'd forgotten to fill my water bottles. My bike was fitted with two very large water bottles attached to the inside of the two upright tubes of the frame. Until recently, I hadn't known such large water bottles existed. I'd discovered last summer that my two 16-ounce plastic bottles with the Gear Works logo, my beloved bike shop back home, did not hold enough water to carry me the distance between reliable sources of clean water. I'd have to add more water bottle holders for the upcoming ride across the scorching Midwest. I looked all over, online, in any bike shop I happened by, and saw options. The thing is, none of them would work with all the other gear I was carrying. Then one day I saw an ad for mega water bottles. Studying it, I observed the water bottles were the same diameter as what I'm used to, they just kept going up. Each one held 32 ounces. I took some measurements on my bike frame and saw there was enough clearance. I clicked "buy" and, voila, I doubled my water carrying capacity without cluttering up the bike with more holders.

I've noticed over the years I tend to drink less water than other people. Whether it's hiking or boating or biking, my companions will go through a quart and I'm good with a few sips. This is especially true of people my kids' ages. Even when they're not working out, just going to school, or sitting in an office chair, they lug around personal water cooler size containers, sucking down water continuously through the day. It was popular at one point to *drink eight glasses of water a day*. Everybody repeated this medical mantra and dutifully toted a gallon jug. Soon people had personal water backpacks with a hose that feeds continuously to your mouth. They looked like astronauts. For years, a string of doctors told me tea and coffee don't count, nor beer, tragically. Too bad, because until I switched to tea some years back, I drank coffee all morning and into the early part of the afternoon. Now I drink tea that way. But, good news. For the first time, a few years ago, a nurse practitioner said tea and coffee count! I suspect she would have added beer only she didn't want to contribute to my delinquency.

She said, "Any liquid."

At first, I thought it was just the as-usual, practical, sensible guidance I've come to expect from nurse practitioners. But soon thereafter, the sometimes stuffy doctors I see started saying the same thing. Nonetheless, I continued to observe that, when exercising, I drank way less water than anyone else. I checked online, and while eight glasses is a kind of guideline on some health websites, the more respectable ones say, drink when you're thirsty. Since I was already applying this advice to beer in the early evening, I adopted it for water on bike trips.

Even though I drink less water than others, I still need some, and those two, quart-size bottles, newly acquired for my bike, turned out to keep me in stock for even the longest stretch with no source. One such long stretch occurred several days back in fact, and the problem turned out to be not the volume of water, but the quality. I came into Zanesville, Indiana, around 8:30 a.m., 25 miles out of Monroeville where I'd started earlier that day. My map indicated that, after Zanesville, the next place likely to have drinkable water would be the Salamonic Dam Visitor Center, if it was open, 50 miles further on. I'd drunk half of one bottle, and in my haste to get under way that morning, hadn't filled the other one, currently empty. I really needed to fill up now. Even for a camel like me, one water bottle for 80 miles was not a good idea. Zanesville didn't have much to offer. Rolling through town on West 1200 North 90 — long name, short town — I observed three churches, a truck accessories store, an auto repair place, and lots of tidy houses. Everything seemed pretty closed up, and none of the homeowners were outdoors. The only place that showed a sign of life was the auto shop. The big garage doors were open, and I heard a metal grinder going inside when I rode by. I got to the end of town with no fresh water in sight, turned around, and headed there. I got off my bike and stepped inside. It was dark, including the walls, dark from grease stains.

I called, "Hello." After a minute, a guy stepped out of the shadows, well camouflaged as he, too, was covered in black grease stains.

"Help you?" he said, wiping his hands on a soiled rag that looked like it was giving more than it was taking.

"I'm looking to fill my water bottles and everything in town is closed. Any chance you have a sink I could use?"

He shot me a hesitant look. "Well, I guess you could try that sink over there." He half-pointed to an especially dark and smudgy corner at the back of the garage. There stood a slop sink that fully paid tribute to its name.

I said, "Thank you!" and threaded my way among the carts with car parts.

At the sink, water was dripping from the faucet into a plastic spackling bucket filled with some kind of oily liquid with a rainbow shimmer. It wasn't clear whether that's what came from the faucet. I ran the water 60 seconds. It looked okay. I filled my bottles, couldn't find the guy on the way out to say thanks, and was soon on my bike. Heading out of town, I took a swig. It tasted like burnt steak. Fifty miles later, approaching the Salamonic Dam Visitor Center, I'd sipped my way gingerly through a third of one bottle. Even I was thirsty at that point, which meant, according to the when-to-drink-water website, time for a drink. Hooray, the Visitor Center was open! I quickly made my way indoors. Air-conditioned! I spotted the water fountain nearby, in between the restrooms. It was the kind that chills the water. Double-Hooray! I bent over and took a long drink and it gradually dawned on me, the water was tasting like what I'd been sipping the last 50 miles, the same taste I got first time I took a sip after the auto-grease shop. Burnt steak. Apparently, a regional thing. Did that mean the whole county has contaminated water? I comforted myself with the made-up thought that, no, it's a harmless and naturally occurring mineral. A mineral found, apparently, nowhere else in the world, with a vein running between Zanesville and the Salamonic Dam in the middle of Indiana. Maybe it was extra-healthy. I filled both bottles with cold water and was on my way. I had to drink.

Meanwhile, I was making progress on my 120-mile day to the Mississippi River. With Orion in my rearview, it was going to be a 50-mile sprint to Muskatine Iowa, where I'd read in my map notes, there was more than one motel, where, on a Friday in August, in the middle of the scorching, humid Midwest, I figured, I'd have no trouble finding a room. Those 50 miles clicked by quickly. I dodged two thunderstorms, waiting out one on the porch of a friendly man and his young daughter who invited me up. They gave me a Coke and we chatted. I waited out the other on another porch with no one at home, thinking the whole time what I'd do if suddenly they pulled into the driveway and saw a strange person in a weird neon suit making himself comfortable on the porch furniture. What would I do to signal friendly intentions and desperate need, thus justifying my moving in without permission before they reached for the shotgun on the rack behind the front seat. Luckily no one came home, and when the storming stopped, I got underway.

I eventually crossed the Mississippi at 6p.m. and made my way to the first motel that looked any good. Plenty of rooms, and I settled in. They had postcards in the desk drawer in my room with a photo of the place that looked like it was taken in 1962, judging by the cars parked out front and the woman in a bright pleated cotton skirt leaning invitingly over the hood of one. I decided to make use of them and wrote several postcards as my entertainment for the evening. I'd mail them the next day. I then slept happily between crisp white sheets. Total distance for the day, 121 miles. A new personal record.

Because I was averaging mega-miles a day, I hit Minneapolis several days early and, like the summer before, decided to enact my unannounced plan B, or maybe it was actually plan A, riding past the official destination. Three days later I crossed the Red River into Fargo. I'd ridden my bike to North Dakota! In my mental map of the world, North Dakota is a genuinely far-away place. Minnesota is still technically the Midwest, and the Midwest is right next to New York where I grew up. But North Dakota is a place beyond. Big empty stretches of open country that's not farmland. Undeveloped, sparsely inhabited with the promise of mountains upon craggy, snow-topped mountains just over the horizon. Next summer, surely, the real adventure would begin.

Chapter 6
The Not-So-Great Outdoors

Every year, the Outdoor Industry Association conducts a survey to find out who participates in outdoor recreation. In 2020, the survey included 18,000 people across the United States, balanced for gender, age, income, region, and ethnicity. It confirmed what many have noted, namely, that participation rates by African Americans in outdoor recreation is proportionately much lower than other racial/ethnic groups and that outdoor activities remain dominated overwhelmingly by White people.[15] My ride across many states, on city streets and country highways, was certainly bearing it out. According to the survey, only 9% of all people who participated in some form of outdoor recreation in 2020 were Black. Among Black Americans, just 38% participated. Meanwhile White people made up 72% of all participants while constituting just 60% of the total population. More troubling is the fact that youth participation rates among Black Americans is the lowest of any group. According to the report, "adults who were not exposed to outdoor recreation as children are far less likely to become adult outdoor participants" (p. 13). This suggests the White-Black gap will only widen. Other sources show similar patterns. The National Park Service reported in 2020 that just 6% of all visitors identify as Black.[16] The Snowsports Industries Annual Report for 2020 showed just 9.2%

of skiers and snowboarders are Black.[17] In the world of cycling, for every 100 miles covered by White people, Black people pedal less than 6.[18] Why is participation by Black people in outdoor sports and recreation so low compared to White people? Why was it I encountered so few people of color riding a bike with panniers, like me, across this wide country?

Carolyn Finney began her career as a television actor. After 11 years, she left for a five year backpacking sojourn across Asia and Africa, including an extended stay in Nepal. Returning home to the United States, and inspired by her travels, she earned a Ph.D. in Geography from Clark University in 2012. Her dissertation focused on the relationship of Black people to National Parks and Forests. It became the basis of a book, published two years later, *Black Faces White Spaces: Reimagining the Relationship of African Americans to the Great Outdoors*. In the book, Finney describes how she grew up on a beautiful estate of twelve acres of woodland and meadow with a pond. For her and her brothers, it was their playground. Finney developed a love of the outdoors. But the estate did not belong to her family. Her parents were the Black caretakers on the estate of a wealthy White couple that lived in New York City and used their rural haven as a weekend retreat in an exclusively White upland area. Thus, for Finney, her place in the outdoors as a Black person in a sea of White people, was an early reckoning.

According to Finney, there is a deep, collective, inter-generational hesitance to engage with outdoor spaces for many Black people, which is rooted in a history of White terror. It's not that Black people have no relationship with the land and the outdoors. Under slavery and Jim Crow they surely did. The land is what enslaved people worked long hours, every day, under hot sun, and the threat of violence by their White overseers. Woodland is where some enslaved Black people sought refuge, escaping from their White owners. It was the moonlit pathway of the dangerous underground railroad. It is where they were hunted by armed vigilantes on horseback with guns and dogs. A big oak tree with broad limbs standing in a meadow was a place one might expect to see the lifeless body of an innocent man hanged by a violent White mob. Finney points to research by historian Leon Litwack that between 1882 and 1968 nearly 5,000 Black people were lynched.[19] It's not that Black people lack a relationship to the land, it's that the relationship is centered on brutality and fear. At the same time, Finney points out, enslaved Black people, more than merely victims, sought out opportunity, as they could, in the nature that surrounded them, through hunting, fishing, and the gathering of medicinal herbs. Nonetheless, the outdoors, as such, was and remains, a deeply troubling space for African Americans. Add to this intergenerational sense of fear, the residential circumstances of many Black people today. In low income, urban neighborhoods, parents and guardians, out of concern for their children's well-being, understandably restrict them from heading outdoors. That leafy park across the street may be a place of gang violence.

What Finney chronicles in *Black Faces White Spaces* is echoed by the experiences of Black people documented elsewhere. Aaron Jones, an avid hiker from Chicago, describes the first time he headed out to an outdoor recreational space, invited by a friend to join her for a hike. His account, published in *The Guardian* speaks to the ongoing anxiety of Black hikers:

> A few years ago, a white friend suggested we go on a hike. All the fears I had about being in nature hit me in the face. It's a very real fear for Black people, especially those from urban communities, that bad things happen to Black people in the woods, like lynching. It's something that you see again and again when you look at the history of the civil rights movement and slavery: Black people going into the woods and not coming back. My friend had grown up hiking. I talked to her about my fears and she respected my apprehension. I said to myself: "You've got

to do this now or it will never happen." I grew up in kind of a rough neighborhood on the south side of Chicago, so my mother kept us in a lot. Our house was across the street from a public park but it was rife with gang violence so we never went there.[20]

For many Black people, there are additional barriers just *getting to* a designated outdoor space that is nominally safe: lack of discretionary income, lack of leisure time, and lack of a car. In addition, getting there may require crossing White spaces and the ongoing threats they represent. Tiffany Tharpe, a Black woman from Los Angeles commented in the same *Guardian* piece:

> After Trump became president, I became a little nervous about traveling in the US. Racism became more overt. Just after the inauguration I went with a couple of friends to western Arizona. On the way, we passed lots of gun stores, some with Confederate flags, and I felt very uncomfortable. When we got there I mostly felt OK because I was with friends who blended in, but there was this one old man who stared at me from the other side of the street. He was eating an ice cream and wearing a Make America Great Again hat. I felt challenged and stared back until he looked away.[21]

The hazards of crossing White spaces in order to travel from one location to the next has been a powerful theme in African American history. With the rise of the automobile in the 1920s and 1930s, people began to travel longer distances. For a Black family traveling, say, from New York City to Georgia to visit relatives during the Jim Crow era, it meant driving through towns and cities where it was unknown which businesses would serve them. Also, they had no way of knowing in advance which places were "sundown" towns, where Black people were forbidden to be out after dark. Black people traveling by car over long distances faced potential harassment and violence. In the

1930s, a Black postal worker in New York City named Victor Hugo Green began to compile information about hotels, gas stations, and restaurants friendly to Black people in the New York area. He published it as *The Negro Motorist's Guide to Travel* in 1936. It was very popular and was expanded over time to include the entire United States. Nicknamed *The Green Book*, annual editions continued until 1967, three years after passage of the Civil Rights Act outlawed racial segregation. Violence and the threat of violence against Black travelers persists. Racial profiling of motorists by police and other hazards of *driving while Black* have been well documented.[22]

Lesser known but equally telling is the history of racism against Black cyclists in the United States. Before automobiles, bicycles enjoyed a brief heyday at the turn of the century, particularly with the invention of the safety bicycle. Early bicycles were impractical contraptions with an oversized front wheel, known as the "high wheeler," or heavy, wood monstrosities propelled by pushing with both feet, called the "velocipede." In 1885, a new kind of bike was invented with equal-sized wheels and a chain drive connecting pedals to the rear wheel. It was called the safety bike. It was practical to ride and greatly extended the distance and ease with which an individual could travel. Unlike a train, it could take you anywhere you wanted to go, and unlike a horse, required minimal upkeep. According to historian Nathan Cardon, professor at the University of Birmingham, by the turn of the century there were as many as 8 million safety bicycles in use across the United States. The bicycle was a path to mobility for many working-class Americans. As a technological innovation, the bicycle conferred on its owner an aura of modernity and civilization. For White Americans, the mobility and freedom that the bicycle offered to Black people was a threat, as was its association with civilized society. Black cyclists soon faced mounting restrictions.[23] Cardon documents police action and mob violence targeting Black cyclists. He also documents demeaning accounts of Black cyclists in the popular press, while White-controlled cycling associations restricted Black membership. Racist patterns from the early days of cycling persist today, and though less visible, continue to depress Black participation in cycling. A study published in the *American Journal of Preventive Medicine* documents lower participation rates and higher traffic fatality rates for Black cyclists. According to co-authors Matthew Raifman and Ernani Choma, for every 63 miles pedaled by White cyclists, Black cyclists log 3.5 miles. Meanwhile, the fatality rate for Black cyclists, per mile traveled is 4.5 times higher than it is for White cyclists.[24] They further speculate about potential causes of the disparity: "Possible explanations to consider include systemic underinvestment in pedestrian and cycling infrastructure in communities of color, disparities in emergency response, quality of care and outcomes, access to medical insurance, and economic constraints" (p. 165). In aggregate, they uncovered evidence of structural racism.

What is perhaps the greatest barrier to participation by African Americans in outdoor recreation is largely invisible and difficult to describe. It has to do with the way the outdoors are perceived or, metaphorically, *constructed* by the dominant culture—the ideas, values, questions, and aspirations it represents and which manifest themselves in myriad ways in what people say and do in their everyday lives, their literature, religion, art, and popular media (print and digital, text and image). Finney writes about *the great outdoors* in the United States, as a place constructed culturally by White people. She points, for example, to 19th century conservationist John Muir as an advocate for and popularizer of the dominant view of outdoor spaces as sacred, worthy of preservation, places of quiet retreat and reflection that inspire wonder and awe. Muir, who co-founded the Sierra Club, likened Yosemite Valley to the cathedrals of Europe. Muir was a force behind the National

Parks movement, Finney points out, which was fueled by an urgency to save such "sacred" places. President Theodore Roosevelt who championed the movement shared Muir's reverence. Try googling famous quotes from T. Roosevelt and you'll see many like this: "A grove of giant redwood or sequoias should be kept just as we keep a great and beautiful cathedral." There is nothing wrong with or culturally exclusive about the feeling of awe that a beautiful natural scene can inspire, but the movement to preserve so-called pristine natural environments disregarded the wishes, perspectives, and presence of First Nation people who had inhabited, protected, and revered them for millennia, until the often destructive encroachment of White settlers. Consider, also, Henry David Thoreau, another champion of the outdoors as constructed by the dominant White culture. Thoreau is revered for his willful rejection of the materialism of his day and the clarity of vision that resulted from his quest for personal meaning. For Thoreau, spending a year in a one-room cabin in the woods allowed him to strip back the material distractions of life to live simply. For a Black man in the mid-19th century, living alone, un-harassed and un-hunted, in a cabin in the woods would have been an impossibility in most parts of the United States. And for most Black people, particularly at that time, material goods were scarce. Possessing them was a sought-after dream. Only people surrounded with abundance, as was Thoreau, would have the opportunity and the luxury to temporarily remove it, knowing that it could be restored at any time. Likewise, Black people, a century ago, had little opportunity to experience quiet reflection and wonder in forests pursued by White mobs, or, today, urban parks where, in lower income areas, armed gangs are a menacing presence.

Culturally ingrained views about the outdoors run deep and they run along racial lines. The outdoor education movement, in its dominant form, is a good example. Jeff Rose and Karen Paisley worked as outdoor educators in the first decade of the

2000s. Both of them are White. They were formally trained as outdoor educators and had years of experience working at environmental education centers, university recreation programs and the like, teaching groups about leadership, environmental stewardship, social skills, and self-efficacy. In a remarkable essay, which they jointly wrote for the journal *Leisure Sciences* in 2012,[25] Rose and Paisley unpack a pivotal experience they shared leading a group of mostly young people of color. After an exciting three weeks of high adventure, woven together with expertly led discussions about the challenges everyone was experiencing, the two instructors felt exhilaration, confident they had scored a solid win with a group of students who could greatly benefit from the skills and dispositions that outdoor education teaches in such an intense and profound manner. After a closing activity on their final night, however, the activity took an unexpected turn:

> As our conversation began to wind down, one of the non-White male participants said to Jen and me, "So let me get this straight, after we go home, you'll turn around and do this again?" We acknowledged we would. After some laughing and head shaking, he replied, "I just don't get it, why would you want to do something like this all the time?" Jen and I explained that we enjoy helping people experience new things, explore new places, and gain outdoor skills. We then acknowledged we generally like camping, climbing, kayaking, and everything that comes with these experiences. The same participant then began to explain how he very much appreciated his experiences over the past three weeks but he would not be participating in something like this again. Others nodded. (p. 137)

Jeff then launched into a monologue extoling the bonds they had forged and the long-term benefit of the challenges they had faced and overcome together in the outdoors. It was a speech he was accustomed to offering, and it made him feel good about the work he does. He was sure he'd snuffed out the skepticism he sensed rising from the group. But the same young man spoke again.

> See Jeff, I don't think you understand. This isn't what I do. This is your thing. Why would I want to do stuff like this? Why would I want to come out here to sleep on the ground if I don't have to? Why would I scare myself on some ridiculous rock climb up a mountain in the middle of nowhere? Why would I work so hard to find water, to fix my dinner every night? I get that every day at home, and I hate it. I work hard to avoid those things, not to look for them. So why would I do that out here if I don't have to? (p. 137)

Why indeed? White, upper middle-class people who do not live with the daily, existential threats that are a constant companion for lower income people of color, feel a need to contrive such challenges. Two centuries ago, Henry David Thoreau contrived hardship with his cabin in the woods, which was a few miles from a home-cooked meal. Modern outdoor education is driven by the same bracketed, temporary experience of hardship. After three weeks of repelling and tenting in the rain, the typical White participant returns to their suburban home with plush carpets and a well-stocked kitchen.

Many White people are unaware of the racialized nature of their perception of the outdoors. The sacredness of a great-limbed oak tree in a meadow of wild grasses, for many White people, is a simple fact, presumably recognized by anyone anywhere. Consequently, someone who does not respond with awe and respect, well, there's just something wrong with them. Perhaps they are morally deficient. The failure of White people to understand that their view of nature is informed by their own privileged history, displays a profound ignorance of the fact that other cultures have their own culturally rooted perceptions of the outdoors. When John Muir called for Yosemite Valley to be "preserved," he ignored the fact that it was already designated by the Indigenous people in the area as a special place and that the threat to its status came mainly from White settlers, part of a culture of a White-defined "manifest destiny" to dominate the American west.

When Jeff and Jen encountered the skeptical responses coming from students of color, they could have easily dismissed it as an indication there is something wrong with *those kids*. Fortunately, Jeff and Jen chose, instead, to learn from the students' reactions. Organizations can learn, too. In the wave of racial reckoning that followed the murder of George Floyd, the Sierra Club's Executive Director, Michael Brune, posted a strongly worded letter on the organization's website during the summer of 2020,[26] condemning its racist history and ongoing practices. The letter came amidst growing charges of racist behavior within the organization that culminated in an internal report a year later calling for sweeping change. Brune resigned as executive director shortly after the report's publication.[27] In recent years, other organizations, such as, the National Park Service and the Union of Concerned Scientists have faced similar reckonings.

The reluctance of some Black people to engage with the outdoors in the ways and numbers that White people do is the outcome of a complex past. Talk of remedies that seek simply to increase the participation rates of people of color, while well-intending, are ultimately disrespectful of the cultures and histories behind such reluctance. The problem is not just the relatively low numbers of Black faces in White spaces, it is the way those spaces are constructed—by White people. Real change will not seek just to increase participation, it will require fundamentally altering the ways we perceive and shape outdoor recreation to reflect a range of cultural perceptions, values, and aspirations. Maybe, in the same way, but for different reasons that women often conceive of adventure differently from men, people of color will redefine, in terms they choose, kinds of adventure that just happen to be something other than riding a bike solo across the United States.

Chapter 7
Climbing

Dear Mom,

This letter is coming to you from "the road." I'm on my bike trip, and, at the moment, I'm in Minneapolis, Minnesota. This is turning out to be a great adventure. When I started it two summers ago, I didn't know if I could make it all the way across the United States, but now that I've passed the Mississippi River, I believe I can.

There's more to this multi-year bike ride than a grand adventure, and that's why I'm writing. Around the time that I started this trek in 2008, you were providing Dad with very intensive personal care. Long days and long nights, one after another. At the same time, Laurie's Mom and my friend, Nancy, were doing likewise for Don and Ted. I was amazed by all three of you, how you faced each day with as much good cheer as you could muster and helped your life's partner live as well as possible for his remaining days. All three of you showed a special kind of courage and compassion and, frankly, endurance.

I want to honor the courage and compassion I witness in all three of you by establishing a scholarship for a student pursuing a teaching career, at UMass Lowell, in your names. I want to call it the Mary, Joan, and Nancy Scholarship for Courage and Compassion. And I want to use the final leg of my cross-country bike ride next summer as the means to raise the money to fund the scholarship.

I'd like to do this for you and for all the people who provide long term care and support for their life partner or other loved one. You won't need to do anything — you've already done it all. I hope you'll consent to letting me do this. I'll be in touch soon to follow up.
      Much Love,
      Jim

Once I hit Minneapolis the summer of my ride to Fargo, I mailed three letters "from the road" to my Mom, Laurie's Mom, and Nancy. Then, shortly after my return from Fargo, via a 40-hour Amtrak train ride, I met with each of them. They gave their blessing to the scholarship idea and my preparations began. My goal was to raise $25,000 because that's what it takes for the University's Advancement office to open an endowment account. I'd never led a fundraising campaign, but I dove in, and the year flew by. I learned that if you want to fundraise, you have to actually ask people for their money. You have to look them in the eye and ask, "Can you please donate?" Sometimes you say, "How much can you donate?" And sometimes you even have to say, "Can you donate X dollars?" Asking for donations was not within my natural, comfortable zone, but it had to be done, and I did it. Approximately 400 people donated. I pledged to complete the remaining 2000 miles of my cross-country trek in one big go the following summer. There was no turning back.

Meanwhile, I needed to get ready for the ride. Two thousand miles across four big western states with mountainous terrain. I trained a hundred miles a week, starting in March. At work, I was teaching extra courses and consulting to help pay the bills for two of our kids in college. I was also putting together my portfolio for tenure. It was busy. In the midst of all the life stressors that year, the prospect of my nearly month-long trip-to-be, was feeling, frankly, like a terrific escape. I could leave everything behind for long days of monotony. By the end of May, I'd raised the money, much of it due to a very generous matching grant from two family members, and my tenure package was completed. Through June and July, I wrapped up several consulting projects and amped up my training to 150+ miles a week. Then, I boxed up my bike, got on a plane, and on Thursday, July 14th, I started pedaling west from Fargo. It was a sunny day, and I had a tailwind. Two days later, conditions changed.

"Have you heard a weather report?" I asked, stepping from the doorway of the barn into the driveway.

"Naw, I just been watchin' TV, had a few drinks," he replied. It was eight o'clock in the morning. He looked about 60 but, apparently a hard drinker with a hard life, I'd guess he was actually in his 40s. I'd watched him from the barn, where I'd retreated to get out of the rain. He'd stepped out his porch door, ambled down the driveway, a little wobbly. He wore blue jeans and a tee shirt on a wiry frame. A cigarette held loosely between his fingers sent up a smoke trail. He didn't seem to mind finding me, a complete stranger, standing in the open doorway of his barn. It had been storming with lightning, so I pulled off the highway into the nearest structure I could find, which happened to be a rundown looking barn on a rundown looking farm past Minnewauken, North Dakota. Having just pedaled through the Spirit Lake Sioux Indian Reservation, I was now headed due west on State Route 19. Passing through the Reservation, I thought twice about displaying that American flag off my rear pannier. I rolled it up and stuck it upside down in the outside pocket, just to keep it out of sight. That short ride constituted one of the few times I felt unprotected by the White skin that is generally my shield along lonely stretches of highway.

There'd been distant rumbling most of the morning, and then, lightning close by and rain sent me into the barn where I'd been the last twenty minutes. But now the rain was stopping and the clouds, still thick and gray, didn't look quite as threatening.

My farmer acquaintance and I exchanged a few pleasantries, I thanked him for the use of his barn, and I was on my way.

North Dakota is wheat country. Somewhere along the road in Minnesota, the farms had switched from corn and soy to wheat and more wheat. The soil and sparse rainfall in North Dakota is well suited to wheat and once the railroad arrived in the later 1800s, wheat farming took off, and the treeless plains got planted with a very profitable cash crop. I rode the highway up and down the gentle hills and dales, like broad ocean swells on a calm day. I felt like I was expanding my capacity for awe. Year upon year of long distance, solo cycling began to accustom me to a state of mind that was contemplative, meditative, deeper than anything I'd previously experienced. The endless landscape felt enormous, mysterious. It embraced me, and I was swallowed up by it.

I'd read harvest was just a few weeks off, which made sense as the fields were dense with grasses the color of a golden retriever and a good three feet tall. As I pedaled the nearly empty highway, with a farmhouse and silos about every two miles, it was all wheat front to back and side to side, as far as you could see to where the sky started. Distant breezes moving through distant fields would leave patterns like a vacuum cleaner makes on a rug—always the same color, just big swatches all shaded differently. Watching a wheat field wave is like the 2D version of a flock of starlings, moving as a great mass showing off subtle changes in color density and texture as the flock twists and turns, heads up and then down. It was a magnificent sight. The drama of the wheatfields contrasted with the drama overhead, one completely benign and the other an ongoing threat. A half hour past my barn refuge, the sky was flashing once again, the wind was picking up and the thunder was somewhere between distant and getting closer. In an electrical storm, the good thing about riding across a prairie is just how flat the land is. You can see a storm coming two counties away, and you can estimate whether it will cross your path and, if so, when. All that flat land, however, is also a bad thing. Riding a lonesome stretch of highway with nothing but wheatfields, a bicycle is likely the only metal object around, and running continuously, as it does, along a smooth elevated surface, offers itself invitingly to every lightning bolt looking for something shiny and conductive to take it to ground. In addition to being as hot as the sun, the average lightning bolt, I've read, is charged with 300 million volts and 30,000 amps. Just then a jagged line like the shiny edge of a broken piece of glass flashed to the southwest. I counted to twenty-five before the rolling rumbling reached me. Five miles off. More flashes, more counting, and it was clear, this electricity-bearing, black mass of sky was headed my way. Though I hadn't been looking for it at the time, I seemed to recall from my map review early that morning in the half light of my tent, a store of some kind between me and Esmond, the next town. By my reckoning, Esmond was too far off for shelter ahead of this storm, but maybe that store. Another flash and I picked up the pace. Over the next few minutes, I was able to track the path of the storm. It appeared we were on a collision course. One option was to get off my bike, ditch it by the side of the road, walk back from it 100 yards, remove everything on me that was metal, especially my shoes, which had big metal cleats, and then crouch in a ditch in the rain. I'd read about this somewhere. This option did not offer much of a guarantee, and it was not terribly appealing as a way to spend the next hour. A few more minutes and a few more flashes, the storm was nearly on me. I saw a Black squarish thing up the road, then I made out what looked like a sign in front. Just then, BLAMMO! The air lit up and a sound, like the earth splitting open and exploding, nearly knocked me off my bike. I've never truly ever felt life threatened. I haven't been in a plane on a nosedive. I haven't been in combat. I haven't been a Black person surrounded by a threatening White mob. But all of a sudden it felt like there was live ammo flying around me, and the enemy, not an enemy at all, something worse, an indifferent and all-powerful force of nature just moving through its day, following the laws of physics as it rides out the weather patterns, was, to me, a looming and lethal threat. As the possibility of sudden death flashed, literally, before me, I jammed my feet into the bike pedals and pushed with everything I had. I streaked through the rain, water shooting up my back from the rear tire, goggles fogging over from my breath in the suddenly cooling air. Several more flash-bangs. I pulled up to the store, yes, the black thing, thank goodness, was the store. A siren mounted on top of the building was wailing. I dropped my bike against the wall, threw open the door and ducked inside.

Girl from Ipanema was playing quietly on the store speaker. I looked around. A guy at the counter was reading the paper, mug of coffee in front of him. Another guy behind the counter had his hands in the sink. A woman at the cash register was casually watching the storm out the window, like a nice, easy Sunday morning. Bossa nova vibe on the radio. No one seemed particularly agitated by the world war going on outdoors. I shook off the rainwater onto the welcome mat. The guy with the paper turned the page, apparently not curious about my life drama of the last several minutes. I briefly assessed my situation. I was wet, but not cold. My synthetics would dry out fast. I dried my face, my head, my arms with a wad of napkins over by the Slushee dispenser. I noticed the menu, printed on the wall over the counter. It *was* breakfast time. I sat down, greeted my foxhole comrades casually, and shortly was enjoying pancakes and eggs and the relaxed vibe while rain pelted the metal roof and thunder continued booming nearby. The guy at the end of the counter offered me the front section of his paper.

Not all of my days out on the prairie were eventful. Some were dull as pocket lint. I'd ride for miles in decent weather, no hurricane-like winds, no prospect of imminent death by electrocution, no monster hills, a good shoulder with good pavement, and a reservation at the RV park 60 miles hence in a town likely to have a restaurant or two. Dreaming of food was entertaining for only so long. An occasional reverie of the previous day could offer a pleasant interruption—the cozy halo of my reading lamp in my tent, the cashier with a sweet face and a friendly smile. But periods with nothing but uneventful pedaling could go on for hours. And hours. Sometimes, I'd try to guess how many miles to some far-off object I'd make out down the road. That could give me fifteen minutes of low-quality distraction. Honestly, many hours I just can't account for. I don't know what I thought about. Maybe I thought about nothing, like when you're driving to work and suddenly you're there with no idea how you got there or what exactly happened with the last forty minutes. Or I'd fall into a meditative state.

But other times, I did think. For several days running, I thought about grief. Other people I'd observed seemed to feel it intensely. Me, not so much. Was there something wrong with me? Always a possibility, but it occurred to me that all three of the loved ones I'd lost experienced years of decline. Several years into Dad's increasing mental fog, I realized we could no longer engage in the deep interrogation of politics, culture, religion that was the staple of our adult relationship. That was probably three years before he passed. I used to consider the topics we'd discuss while driving to my parents house for a visit. But, gradually, there was less and less discussion to be had. My role became supportive son, cheerful presence, provider of small talk, helper to my Mom. I'd read Dad an article from the *Wall Street Journal* and he'd nod, implying the nub of an idea, but he had nothing to say. We enjoyed each other's company, but something essential was missing. It made me feel empty and sad. Is that grief? If it is, then the fact that I did not feel intense sadness when he passed could be due to the fact that I'd already grieved his loss. His final departure, after most of his mind and personality had ebbed, felt like relief.

Reflective thoughts aside, some days, my grand bicycle adventure felt like a job. One journal entry, penned at the tail end of North Dakota reads thus:

End of day routine so far: enter town, ride around to see what's there, find town park, go to someplace for a cold drink and interview the natives, set up tent at town park, take shower, wash laundry, organize stuff, get dinner, check maps for coming days, write in journal, clean and inspect bike, check tire treads carefully removing debris stuck in treads, check weather on radio, re-organize stuff (endlessly), keep moving freshly washed laundry into sun, get into tent, keep organizing stuff, lay there for a while, set cell phone alarm, fall asleep.

But then Montana happened. Back in New England, you can click off two, even three, states in a day. Crossing Montana took eleven days and 700 miles of hard labor. The first two thirds were a slow uphill into headwinds that rolled down from the continental divide, and the rest was a mountain range with no easy way around the long, knobby spine of western North America. By way of introduction to Montana's splendors, however, came the final bit of westernmost North Dakota, a boomtown called Williston. I'd been warned.

It was the most challenging shoulder I'd ever ridden. Not the worst, just the most difficult. I drew a diagram in my journal. Here it is.

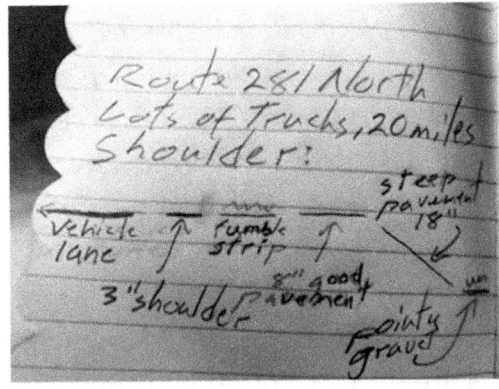

Starting at the right edge of the driving lane, there was maybe three inches of shoulder, then a rumble strip a foot wide. To the right of that was about eight inches of good, level pavement, and then it started to slope, not terribly steep but more than you could ride on without possibly falling over. The sloping pavement continued for a good 18 inches, ending in gravel. My choices were:

1) Ride the three-inch shoulder and look out for vehicles from behind. If they got too close, scamper across the rumble strip and, without overcompensating, re-center my wheels over the eight-inch bit of pavement on the other side of the rumble strip;

2) Ride the eight-inch bit next to the slope, watching carefully all the time that my front tire doesn't accidentally veer off the top, catch on the downward part and pull my whole bike down with it, where I'd likely wobble for a moment and then fall over. I'd fall beyond horizontal since it's a slope after all. It would hurt. It wouldn't kill me, but I'd rather avoid it if I could.

As it turned out, I experimented with both options. I had to because there was plenty of traffic to keep me vigilant. Williston was a boom town, and mad trucks were rolling everywhere. My journal from July 18 says it all:

Went through Williston, ND, today. Oil boom town. Was an oil town many years ago, but new technology allows more oil to be extracted from old wells. Every hotel chain is building, every fast-food place has moved in, lots of oil industry related business in new corrugated steel buildings on the outskirts, well sites under construction everywhere as much as 30 miles away, trucker bars, dust, and dirt everywhere, and trucks. Lots of trucks everywhere all the time. Big nasty gravel trucks, wide-load trucks carrying equipment and building materials, regular cargo trucks, etc.

The boom in Williston, I read later, was brought on by a new technology called hydraulic fracturing, in which proprietary liquid chemicals are injected into the ground under pressure to fracture stubborn rocks with locked-in natural gas. Williston had been an oil boom town decades before and once "fracking" became viable for oil companies, boomtimes returned to Williston to extract the remaining energy wealth underground. I was riding through Williston at the peak of the boom. Despite rosy projections of decades of wealth and opportunity to come, Williston went bust in 2014 when the price of oil plummeted.

Dodging big trucks on a roadside with a difficult shoulder was not my idea of a good time and I was glad to leave Williston in the rearview. I crossed into Montana twenty-one miles later, entering Mountain time, a kind of symbolic marker, and made it as far as Culbertson that day, having traveled 117 miles.

I'd been told since the start of my trip that I was going the wrong way, that if you plan to cross the United States on a bicycle, you should travel from west to east because that's how the wind goes. A tailwind to speed you on your way is a lot more attractive than a continuous headwind grinding you down. I did not find this to be true, traveling across the northeast, the midwest, and the length of North Dakota. Wind seemed to come from any direction it wanted on any given day. Sometimes it was a headwind, but there were plenty of magical days during which I sped along effortlessly at nearly 20 miles an hour with a warm tailwind caressing my back. Montana, however, changed all that. My journal shows a continuous string of headwind commentary:

- <u>Tuesday, July 19</u>, Wolf Point, MT: "Headwind most of ride today, but not fierce"
- <u>Wednesday, July 20</u>, Glasgow, MT: "Radio said 30-40 mph out of the west with gusts to 50! It was a *very* hard day of pedaling. Last 15 miles I rode in 3 lowest gears averaging 7mph in mostly level, flat terrain. Had to really concentrate to maintain control of bike keeping vigilant eye front and back. Felt safe but any more wind and I would have had to stop and pitch my tent by the side of the road."
- <u>Thursday, July 21</u>, Malta, MT: "Only a light headwind today. Thank goodness!"
- <u>Friday, July 22</u>, Chinook, MT: "Today's main course: Thunderstorm dodging w/ a side order of head wind ... last 15 miles was increasing headwind (20-25?) and a *very* small 12-inch shoulder with truck and RV traffic. Felt safe enough but had to keep alert in both front and back and be ready to bail – which I did a dozen times."
- <u>Saturday, July 23</u>, Chester, MT: "Long, lonely stretches through rolling prairie against moderate headwind."

But then the headwinds stopped, possibly because the mountains started. Quite abruptly, as it turned out. One day, all of a sudden, instead of pushing against an unfriendly continuous hot blast of air, I was climbing, and the air was still. Mountains out west, at least the ones I have experienced are different from the mountains of New England and New York. Back east ascents are short and steep. You struggle, but it's all over in an hour. Crossing the continental divide, on the other hand, was a full day affair, the first half of it spent climbing. But the rate of climb was gentle, very sustainable. This pattern held, for the most part, across Montana, Idaho, and Washington. In fact, the day I hit the actual continental divide, I kept wondering when it would get steep. I'd gotten an early start, 5:30 a.m., out of Cutbank, hit the town of East Glacier at 10 a.m. My plan was to follow Route 2 along the southern boundary of Glacier National Park, crossing the continental Divide at Marias Pass and then camp somewhere in the National Park heading down the other side. There was an alternative route that was longer, steeper, higher, and scarier, with switchbacks, tourist traffic, at least one tunnel, and a steep descent on the far side. Though I was tempted by the very cool name, *Going-to-the-Sun Road*, I passed it all up. I was starting to feel Stateline fever after riding most of the longest, wildest state I'd be crossing in the entire trip. Continental Divide? Get me up and over, please, with the least pain possible. And so it was, I cruised easily up toward Marias Pass, and somehow missed any signage for the top because I suddenly found myself gently descending. But then, after another mile, there was a sign "Marias Pass Continental Divide." Either the USGS needs to adjust their instruments or, accustomed to climbing as I was, when the road went from steepish-up to very-gentle-up, it felt, to me, like going down.

I was truly in the mountains now, where it became clear that many of the people here are a distinct breed, and the people who move here self-select. They're people who do what they want, even if it looks reckless. Or maybe it is reckless. For example, riding one early Sunday afternoon into Ione, Washington, population 479, at the end of a short fifty-three mile day, I was looking forward to some extra hours to loll around. I'd been following the Pend Orielle River north since entering the state at Newport, leaving my brief tour of Idaho behind. Idaho is tall and skinny, and I crossed it in a day's worth of riding, split over the second half of one day and the first half of the next. The top bit is kind of the Rhode Island of the northern border states. I was riding the east bank of the river and crossed into Ione at the Elizabeth Avenue Bridge and headed up Route 31 to the center of town. There was plenty going on business-wise for a town of just under 500 people, including, apparently, a racetrack. I could hear the engines roaring as I approached the town center. The sound was coming from the river. All of a sudden, the view of the river opened up and I saw mini speedboats, leaping across the water in a race that looked like it started on this side and went maybe a quarter mile to the other. I looked again. These were not speedboats. I couldn't believe what I was seeing. I left Main Street and angled down some side streets to the waterfront where there was a big crowd set up on lawn chairs and beach blankets at a riverfront park. These were funny looking speedboats because they weren't boats at all. They were snowmobiles. I stopped my bike with a good view of the starting line. A snowmobile up at the top of a wooden ramp revved its engine and, at the signal, cut loose down the ramp, at the bottom of which was the water's edge. Already moving fast by the time the ramp ran out, the snowmobile dropped onto the surface of the water and, instead of diving in, started to hydroplane at a high rate of speed across the river. Thirty seconds later it ran up onto the riverbank at the other side and the crowd cheered. This went on all afternoon. It was the town's annual Down River Days, and the place was packed. I was lucky to find a spot for my tent at the Cedar RV Park and Car Wash. I asked a local if a snowmobile ever sinks.

"Happens all the time," he said. "Long as you cut the engine before you go under. No problem. They got a barge with a crane. Pull it right back up. Dry 'er off. Fire up and do 'er again."

Another great example of the region's free spirit was Maddie and Neal Love of Wauconda, Washington. But first, I had to get to Wauconda. Starting the day in Kettle Falls, I rode over two high altitude Mountain passes, the first of which was a twelve-mile, slow-and-steady grind up 3000 feet to Sherman Pass. At 5,575 feet, it was literally the high point of my entire ride. But there was no time to celebrate as Wauconda Pass beckoned ten miles on, and then, I hoped, a cozy night just a few miles further at the high elevation town of Wauconda, which, according to the symbols on my bike map had a grocery store, a restaurant, and a campground. How such amenities were possible, in a town so tiny it didn't register a population count on the map, was mysterious. Part of its allure.

Coming up to the second of the two passes, I was making steady progress, when a half-ton pickup came up from behind and slowed. I looked over and could see the driver, who regarded me, waved sort of, and then took off up the hill. Fifteen minutes later, I crested the pass and saw a half-ton pickup parked by the side of the road just ahead. Same truck. Was this guy a creep? My plan was to give him a wide berth and just roll casually by. I got close, and the driver's door swung open. Out popped the guy, his arm extended in my direction. He had something in his hand. A gun? I slowed, ready for some kind of show-down. But it wasn't a gun.

"Hey," said the guy with a friendly smile. "These are for you." I pulled up. He was holding out a plastic bag. It was full of fresh cherries. "I saw you comin' up this mountain. Here's a reward, man. Great job! Bought these a couple miles back at the farm stand. They're delicious. Take 'em." I took them and thanked him. "Gotta go," he said. He piled back in his truck, pulled onto the road, and gave me a friendly wave out the window as he drove off. I waved back in between cherries that were golden yellow with a reddish blush, and sweet, and meaty. Yum! I learned they were rainier cherries, special to Washington State. I saved half the bag for later and was shortly on my way with just a few miles remaining to the town of Wauconda.

It turned out Wauconda, located between two grassy slopes right on Route 20, did indeed have all the things listed on my map, despite its size, and all in one building—combo store, gas station, post office, and restaurant. I parked my bike and entered what turned out to be the post office with a wall of P.O. boxes. I walked into the next room, which was the store, a couple aisles of food items, a refrigerated dairy case and, up against the wall, another case with cold beer. I passed through the store and the next room was the restaurant with a few tables, a counter, and a big guy with a beard and a bandana around his head cleaning the grill with a wire brush.

He looked over and said, "Welcome."

We had a friendly exchange during which I learned there was indeed camping available, consisting of a single large teepee up the hill, where I was welcome to spend the night for five dollars. Neal, was his name, said he'd be open for dinner. We stepped outside so he could point out the teepee, and I told him I'd be back around 5:30.

I was the only diner at 5:30, but Neal was there, ready to cook. He made me about the biggest omelette I've ever seen loaded with cheese, bursting with broccoli and onions with a mountain of home fries beside it. He knew a cyclist's hunger, and, while I ate, he told me his story. He and Maddie were living in Seattle. Maddie was a trade show coordinator. Neal was in the telecommunications industry. They both lost their jobs during the recession. They were both bikers (i.e., Harley-Davidson variety), and they had ridden through Wauconda in the past. After they lost their jobs, they learned it was for sale, meaning the combo store-PO-restaurant, and that it came with a zip code, 98859, which meant, in effect, the town was for sale. They sold everything and bought it. I told Neal it was a great story, at which point Maddie showed up, pretty and well-tattooed. She had a folded blanket in her arms and set it on my table.

"This is an Indian blanket," she said. "Wool. Please take it with you for tonight in the teepee. It's supposed to get down to 39."

I thanked her, said goodnight to both of them.

I ended up erecting my tent inside the teepee. It was that big, and I figured having an extra layer of tent might make me warmer for the cold night ahead. Soon, I was I lying under the comforting weight of the wool blanket, warm as toast. As I neared the end of my 4000-mile journey with just a few days left, I felt reflective. Waiting for sleep that night, thoughts darted around my mind. Crossing North Dakota, Montana, and Eastern

Washington was proving to be spectacular in every way—the endless land, the endless sky, the often-empty roads, and all the people, who were friendly enough, always ready to help a stranger, even if they were sometimes a little rough around the edges. It occurred to me though, all that ease of travel I experienced, as wonderful as it is, is not something everyone can enjoy. Would the friendly guy in the pickup who offered me cherries with a warm smile have thought to make that gesture were I a lone Black man pedaling my bike up that mountain? Maybe and maybe not. As a person of color, would I have made it safely all along those precarious highway shoulders, eight inches wide with trucks whipping past. Would some nasty White driver have tried to give me a scare? Would some *clueless* White driver simply not have paid me as much mind to give me a comfortable berth, sending me off-course down the sloping pavement to a crash in all that sharp edged gravel? Might I have been terrorized repeatedly passing through Williston, the boom town loaded with mostly White young guys, many of them likely raised in rural White communities with all the undisturbed racialized views such towns can breed. Would I have been welcomed in Wauconda, handed a warm wool blanket? Maybe and maybe not. Even if nothing bad had happened in any of these places, the prospect would have been there, looming, a continual threat. I don't regret riding my bike across beautiful landscapes. I just wish that other people could choose that option as freely as I do—if they wanted it.

In April 1992, an all-White jury declared police officers innocent in the beating of Rodney King, captured on videotape. Instantly, several neighborhoods in Los Angeles erupted in a riot. For nearly a week, fire and mayhem reigned. Sixty-three people died. Two weeks later, Time magazine ran a story contrasting life in the mostly White, leafy suburbs of the United

States and the mostly Black inner cities.[28] Spread across pages 38 and 39 is a street scene featuring charred storefronts in South Central LA as Black people make their way along a sidewalk littered with burnt debris, the remains of five days of rioting. When you turn the page, you see a companion spread of a suburban neighborhood near Seattle. A White family appears to be arriving home to a cozy enclave of colorful clapboard houses and green lawns. Shiny, late model cars are parked neatly in the driveways and just beyond the rooftops, stands a woodland of tall pine trees that enfolds a tranquil world. A banner headline above the first photo features the opening line from the famous Woody Guthrie song, "This land is your land." Above the second photo is the second line of the song, "This land is my land." With cutting irony, the composition captures what is still true 30 years after the riots. The land I inhabit as a White person is a land where I can feel safe. It's not a land really. It's more like a protective forcefield that surrounds and protects me wherever I go. It's a feature that comes with my skin color and my gender. If I were a Black man riding my bike cross country, it'd be a whole different story. It would be a different land. It would be different again if I were a woman riding solo on a bike in yellow spandex outlining my shape as I pedaled through places like Williston. Every male truck driver going by would check me out. How long would it be before one of them might stop a hundred yards up the road to ask me if I'm okay and then turn his fantasies into assault on the side of his truck facing away from the road where no one could see. It will take a whole lot of work and a whole lot of time before the green and welcoming land I get to adventure in is as welcoming to everybody. We may never get there.

Meantime, I had a cross-country bike trip to complete, and four hundred scholarship pledges pressing me on. It did get cold that night, but I was warm, inside my double-insulated tent, under that wool blanket. It wasn't lost on me that it was made by Native Americans. I slept like a rock. Slept through my phone alarm even, which was a good thing because, as it turned out, I would need extra energy for what lay ahead—Loup Loup Pass, Washington Pass, and the final mad descent to Puget Sound.

Chapter 8
Heroes and Adventurers

When George Mallory was asked by a *New York Times* reporter in 1923, why he was climbing Mt. Everest, he famously replied, "Because it's there." There's more that Mallory said in the interview, though it's not often quoted. The reporter asked next, "But hadn't the expedition valuable scientific results?" To which Mallory replied, "Yes ... but these things are by-products. Do you think Shackleton went to the South Pole to make scientific observations? He used the observations he did make to help finance the next trip. Sometimes science is the excuse for exploration. I think it is rarely the reason."[29]

Some people who love adventure don't need a reason. The adventure itself—the thrill, the risk, the uncertainty, the challenge, the discipline, the bodybuilding, the skilling-up, the bragging rights—is reason enough. Other things, like science, spiritual growth, personal development, societal benefit, when they are invoked, are often just the *excuse*, to use Mallory's word. Consider the recent accomplishments of amazing adventurers. For example, in 2013, Austrian mountain climber, Christian Stangl, became the first person to summit the three highest peaks on each of the seven continents, with no supplemental oxygen for any of his climbs, including Everest. In 2012, Erden Eruc, from Turkey became the first person to circumnavigate the globe solo by human power, using a rowboat, kayak, canoe, bicycle, and his two feet. It took him five years. In 2014, Christopher Strasser became the record holder for the fastest crossing by bicycle of the United States in 7 days, 15 hours, and 56 minutes. In accomplishing these feats, neither Stangl, Eruc, or Strasser rescued an oppressed person or gained enlightenment worthy of a new world religion. These feats were accomplished, principally, not to advance human knowledge, or for any other socially redeeming reason; rather, for the challenge they represented. Stangle, Eruc, Strasser, Mallory and others are adventurers above all else. They rise to the challenge because, in the language of the adventurer, *it's there*.

How does all this thrill-seeking square with the noble heroes of the *hero's quest*? Heroes rescue people and bring new understanding to humankind. Is an adventurer something different from that? *Adventure* and *the hero's quest* are used synonymously, but if you take a closer look, they're not the same. Moses, Jesus, the Buddha, St. George, and other heroes, were not after the record book or thrills. They were all serving a larger purpose. St. George rescued the villagers from a hungry dragon. Moses led the Israelites. Jesus died to save sinners. And Buddha brought enlightenment to the World. All noble deeds. On the other hand, Stangle and Mallory and the rest were after the thrill, the challenge, and no doubt, the bragging rights. In their purest form, heroes are selfless, and adventurers are all ego. Jesus and the Buddha were the epitome of humility. It's what they preached—death to self. Meanwhile, people who set records often relish the media attention, and fame that follow. But most heroes and most adventurers are, in the end, a hybrid. Adventurers sometimes offer nuggets of wisdom to the world, writing books about their experiences, and heroes are sometimes rewarded materially for their accomplishment. St. George got to marry the beautiful princess who lived in the village he rescued. Nobel prize winners get a million dollars in cash. Might it also be that the feminine aspects of adventure veer more toward the heroic, with socially redeeming features, often absent from male daring-do?

We've looked at different versions of the hero's quest from Campbell to Tatar, but what about adventure? What are the features that are unique to adventure? What are the elements of a *great* adventure? Are there different sorts of adventures? What ends are served by adventure? Popular definitions of adventure typically point to risk, danger, and an uncertain outcome as key elements. Matt Walker, a contemporary alpinist, adventure guide and "coach", writing for *Psychology Today*, says there are five elements which he calls, "high endeavor, total commitment, uncertain outcome, tolerance for adversity, and great companionship".[30] Walker's Adventure website (www.mattwalkeradventure.com) promotes personal liberation with catchy phrases like "Dismantle your limiting beliefs and take control of your life," and it offers edgy encouragement: "Let's fucking go." The adventure sports industry offers its take on adventure with popular slogans that urge impulsive action (i.e., *buy our stuff*) with the promise of limitless possibility (i.e., *what you get if you buy our stuff*). Consider REI's "Better is out there." Columbia Sportswear's "It's perfect. Now make it better." North Face's "Never stop exploring." Adidas's "Impossible is nothing" and, of course, Nike's "Just do it." To the extent that advertising slogans work, they serve as a rough barometer of what people want—breaking boundaries, new horizons, big thrills. But what if we want to know, beyond the popular adventure gurus and advertising slogans, what adventurers themselves see as the key elements? What if we could ask lots of adventure-seekers what they are looking for? It turns out, some people do. Adventure is an academic discipline pursued in university departments with names like *Adventure Studies, Outdoor Education, Recreation and Leisure Studies*. And there are professors who publish their research in journals with names like *Annals of Leisure Research, Journal of Adventure Education and Outdoor Learning,* etc..

Alan Ewert was an adventure educator with decades of experience leading groups outdoors. He served as an instructor for Outward Bound, the National Outdoor Leadership School and the United States Airforce, for which he taught survival. He also authored hundreds of articles and seven books on adventure, outdoor education, and related topics. He was a professor in Indiana University's Department of Environmental Health until his death in 2010. Much of his research focused on motivation. Why do people seek adventure? From an empirical standpoint, he was able to tell us, based on decades of research, the elements of a great adventure. For example, in one study from 1989, co-authored with Steve Hollenhorst at West Virginia University, 100 college students who were engaged in a variety of outdoor pursuits completed a detailed questionnaire aimed at understanding their motivations. Ewert and his colleague identified twelve motivational factors: socializing, excitement, image, novelty, skill development, career, status, friendship, awareness of self, self-control, self-efficacy, and challenge/risk taking.[31] Subsequent studies of adventure motivation corroborated and extended their findings. For example, in a 2013 article titled, "Beyond 'Because It's There'", Ewert and several colleagues, expanded their sample size to 800 participants engaged in several adventure sports, including rock climbing, whitewater kayaking, sea kayaking, and canoeing. They used an adapted version of the questionnaire from Ewert's (1989) study that allowed them to look for variations based on choice of activity, experience level, and gender. Overall, the top reasons for pursuing adventurous activities were 1) interacting closely with other people; 2) being known as... a sea kayaker, rock climber, etc.; and 3) "testing myself." Other big reasons were showing others my skill, being physically and emotionally challenged, and exhilaration. Looking across the variables, they found that more experienced participants in the high-risk sports, like rock climbing, did it for the thrill. Also, women more than men, across all activities, indicated the social aspect was important. Finally, they found that three big factors play major roles across activity, gender, and experience, namely, sensation-seeking, interacting with others, and self-image.[32] It turns out that people who adventure (new verb), do so for the thrills, the camaraderie, and a sense of personal empowerment. Not so far off the popular conceptions, after all.

Not all of the scholarship on adventure comes out of departments focused on empirical research. There's also the literary take. Martin Green was a cultural historian who taught for many years in Tufts University's English Department. In 1991, he published *Seven Types of Adventure Tale,* a book that looked at adventure in fiction.[33] According to Green, adventure as a genre is generally not accepted by the literary establishment and lives a fuller life in the realm of popular literature, where it represents shared cultural aspirations. As such, adventure tends to manifest broad cultural forces, which in the modern history of the west features nationalism, capitalism, patriarchy, and imperialism.

Green looked at literature of the west from roughly the 18th century onward, and rather than dividing up adventure tales into the usual groupings, land and sea, etc., his seven categories are based on the type of protagonist. Here's how he lays it out in *Seven Types of Adventure Tale: An Etiology of a Major Genre*. First is the Robinson Crusoe Story: a man cast away on an island ... who at first is in danger of dying but gradually learns how to survive, and later how to accumulate goods and crops and comforts until he is monarch of all he surveys (p. 48). Next comes the Three Musketeers Story — a band of comrades, their loyalty to one another, their rivalries with other groups, their romances, and courageous acts (pp. 70-71). Third is the Frontiersman Story — "The frontiersman is a hero who moves between civilization and savagery, in touch with but ahead of his countrymen as they advance their civilization across a continent or across an ocean ... " (p. 97). Fourth is the Avenger Story — An avenger, possibly a former victim, takes on the aggressor "to denounce the agents of injustice and oppression and to mobilize feeling for society's victims" (p. 123). Fifth is the Wanderer Story — a traveler whose journeying takes him to the far reaches of the known world, and possibly beyond. The traveler faces challenges and the story's interest lies with both the courage of the traveler and the exoticism of the locales through which he passes. Sixth is the Sagaman Story — A protagonist, set in a former age usually of heightened gallantry, virility, and savagery, engages in heroic acts. And seventh is the Hunted Man Story — Set in modern times, an unaided individual takes on large organizations and conspiracies that are subverting the state or the nation and can triumph over them" (p. 187). I note that Greene's adventurer is reliably "he." A book has yet to be written that identifies the variety of female adventurers in fiction. Categories would possibly include "the healer" and "the community builder."

It is telling that Green bases his work on fiction, to which adventure naturally lends itself. Real life doesn't always follow the formula of an adventure story with thrills and danger that end in success, just like real life doesn't always follow the formula of the hero's quest. Maybe that's why literary types steer away from adventure. It's formulaic, predictable, not terribly ground-breaking. When serious literature does veer into adventure it tends to be satire, which is the only enduring kind of adventure story in the literary canon. Think *Don Quijote*, poking fun at the wannabe knight who mistakes windmills for an army of giants or *Gulliver's Travels*, Jonathan Swift's classic critique of modern society wrapped in the outlandish adventures of Lemuel Gulliver, a surgeon turned sea captain. The other direction that serious literature can take adventure is with true adventure stories that don't turn out in the way a fictional adventure is meant to. Think Jon Krakauer's *Into Thin Air* about the tragic loss of life on Mt. Everest during the 1996 climbing season, or *The Perfect Storm* about adventurous Gloucester Fishermen who head out to sea and get stuck in a monster storm, never to return, or *Into the Wild*, the story of Chris McCandless, the young man, raised in suburban New Jersey who forsook his material life and worked his way to Alaska where, meaning to survive in the wild, wound up dead from poison berries.

Fiction is where we dream in writing. Both the hero's quest and the elements of adventure constitute wish-fulfilling dreams. People long to be the hero. People long for grand adventures — as long as they turn out okay. Both kinds of stories are deeply alluring. They are a kind of dream many share. Which is why they can so easily manipulate our thinking to, say, advance racist ideology or cultivate a militaristic nationalism. There is a vast adventure literature, both fiction and nominally non-fiction, that positions the agents of White European colonialism as heroes and brave adventurers, and everyone else as no more than the means to White colonial ends. War, too, is romanticized as adventure in the interest of advancing nationalistic goals, masking the carnage that is the essence of war, luring young men to enlist, and persuading a potentially hesitant populace of the nobility of their cause. Justin Livingstone, a lecturer in Literature at Queens University Belfast, has written extensively about Victorian era adventure literature set in Africa, for example. In an essay from 2018, he discusses fictional works produced by actual explorers Henry Stanley, Samuel Baker, and Verney Cameron. Livingstone writes, "Baker, Stanley and Cameron were all advocates of imperialism and used their fiction to provoke interest in sub-Saharan Africa and to provide legitimizing contexts for intervention."[34]

He writes that, according to a novel by Henry Stanley, "east Africa without European influence is ultimately a place of extreme violence and one that requires remedial intervention from the outside world" (p. 74). Such fictional accounts by real explorers were given legitimacy by the popular press of the times. A reviewer for London's *Morning Post* wrote that Stanley's work "has the advantage over most romanticists, who take their heroes into African wonderland; he has seen the places he speaks about for himself.".[35] The authors, themselves, advocated for the authenticity of their fictional works. Stanley, in the introduction to one of his novels, wrote, "The geography here described is correct" along with explanations of the "customs of the peoples around Lake Tanganyika."[36] Such tales of imperialist adventuring were enormously popular in an age of expanding literacy and available books and magazines, and they fed the popular mythology that White Europeans were meant to dominate and *civilize* people around the world—even if it meant sometimes killing them.

Tales of heroism and adventure also serve to valorize warfare. Historian Michael Paris, writing in *History Today*, examines fiction written between the World Wars that glorified Great Britain's "policing" of the Middle East.[37] With popular adventure stories about the Royal Airforce bombing rebellious Arabs, Paris writes: "the effect... was to reduce the conflict in the Middle East to exciting adventure and heroic escapades that captured the imagination of their readers and offered an explanation of why the British had undertaken the thankless task of acting as the world's policeman." (p. 34)

Perhaps, where popular adventure stories manipulate the public imagination to advance nationalistic causes, it is especially important for serious literature to expose the lies. Tim O'Brien makes the point emphatically in *The Things They Carried*,[38] a novelistic treatment of his service as an infantryman in Vietnam. He writes that, "a true war story is never moral. It does not instruct, nor encourage virtue..." Later, he tells the following war story:

Four guys go down a trail. A grenade sails out. One guy jumps on it and takes the blast, but it's a killer grenade and everybody dies anyway. Before they die, though, one of the dead guys says, "The fuck you do *that* for?" and the jumper says, "Story of my life, man," and the other guy starts to smile but he's dead. (p. 80)

Heroic quests and adventurous pursuits do not take place in a vacuum. They are conceived and enacted by people playing out culturally approved scripts. Heroic deeds can help some while harming others and adventurers can do damage in pursuit of thrills. One person's demise might be just a small background detail arranged for someone else's adventure. Both heroes and adventurers can enact scripts that advance toxic mythologies, or they can pause and consider. While impulse and bravado are essential ingredients to both the hero's quest and the adventurous pursuit, of equal importance, for White westerners especially, is a healthy dose of reflection.

Chapter 9
Into the Light

Entering that Black hole of a tunnel at the end of my descent from Washington Pass, I realized, as everything turned suddenly pitch dark, I'd forgotten to take off my sunglasses, which filled me with a double dose of dread. Accelerating hard to stay ahead of traffic, I needed both hands firmly on the handlebars. If I tried to pull off my sunglasses, I might wobble and fall. I couldn't see the road right in front of me, but after a second, I could make out the double yellow line, faintly, running down the middle of the tunnel. Then, looking up and to my right, I could see some glisteny stuff on what I guessed was the side of the tunnel, maybe some water weeping from the wall. A flash in my rearview mirror said headlights and the approach of a vehicle behind me. The headlights were low to the ground, which said car, as opposed to an 18-wheeler. Good. Another couple seconds and I could make out the tunnel wall to the right receding ahead of me. The double yellow was sharper. As long as there was no debris directly under me where I couldn't see a thing, I might make it out alive and uninjured. Shortly, faint light appeared at the other end, and a minute later, I was out. Hallelujah! I felt a surge of triumph, not just for surviving the tunnel, but accomplishing something I might not have been up to just a few years before. This tunnel seemed like a final test, after everything I'd endured on my bike. I'd learned I could withstand the challenges of urban riding in our Eastern cities, the wild weather and monotonous terrain of the Midwest, the endless climbs of the western mountains, the mad descent to the Pacific Coast. I could keep a steady pace — as much as a hundred miles-- day after day after day. I could manage every imaginable road condition. And though I was still not a big fan of speed, risk or uncertainty — some adventurer, huh? — when the situation demanded, I delivered.

The next two days brought me to my first view of Puget Sound and the Pacific Ocean. I was supposed to be thrilled, and I guess I was, but what I really wanted was a haircut, which I got in Burlington, WA. I told the barber my story and he treated me like a rockstar. "You're gonna be famous, man! And here I am giving you a haircut." Fame did not follow, but three days later — I had to stall at a state campground for family members to arrive from back east — I rode the final few miles to the waterfront in Anacortes where I was showered with daisy petals and dipped my front wheel in the gently lapping water. Best part was lunch at a Mexican restaurant in town with my family. But I felt melancholy, too. The end of this ride meant the beginning, once again, of sensible living. Flipping through my journal a couple days later, I was already getting nostalgic, like when I saw this entry from Whitefish, Montana, "Dinner at Taco John's (chain) 2 large burritos, 1 quesadilla, 1 soft taco, and massive fried apple tortilla thingy for dessert. Still felt a little hungry so I got a chocolate donut." I'd drawn a smiley face at the end of the entry, as if aware that a future self would read it, longing for the permissible gluttony of the open road. It only took two days. Clearly, more adventures were in store.

Chapter 10
Learning

I have several friends who are alcoholics. They've all been sober for years. Still, they think of themselves as alcoholics. They say they are "in recovery", or they say they are "recovering" alcoholics. That's because they know their lethal drinking behavior is a permanent condition, something about themselves they cannot change, only manage. They will never fully *recover*, which is why they say what they say. I wonder, sometimes, if I am a recovering racist. I am part of a culture where White people, and White men, in particular, and able-bodied White men with money and education and all the social capital that goes with it, get the advantages society offers. That includes being able to ride a bicycle along the highways and byways of America from one end of the continent to the other, without excessive worry about harassment, robbery, assault, you name it. I wonder sometimes if my own behavioral inclinations, part of a lethal cultural pattern, are a permanent condition, something I cannot change about myself, and which I can only manage. I believe that if other White people are honest, they wonder the same thing about themselves. When I see a White person walk into a coffee shop, the first thing I notice is maybe their hair, or their size, their age, their clothing, the way they're talking to the person they're with, their shoes, their smile. When

I see a Black person walk into a coffee shop, the first thing I notice, often, is that they're Black. This is due, in part, to the fact that the spaces I inhabit tend to be White dominated. That, by itself, is a symptom and a cause of the condition, but it's also because, when I see White people, I've been programmed to see them as individuals, even if I don't know them. When I see Black people, if I'm not being vigilant about my own imprinted tendencies, I see them as a group, until I've gotten to know someone. Even then, I have to work to overcome my categorizing. As a group, Black people, as they've been represented throughout my life, in much of my culture, are unreliable, uneducated, slow-witted, etc. You name it. Every undesirable attribute you can think of. Am I, like my alcoholic friends, "in recovery" from racism because I will never fully eradicate the cultural pathologies with which I have been imprinted since infancy, and which continue to surround me? My recovering alcoholic friends go to AA meetings. One goes three times a week. For me, it's diversity training at work, books and magazines, friends and colleagues of color who press me to be reflective and vigilant, and White friends who share my concerns. You have to work on it. That person who just walked into the coffee shop, what a warm smile. My effort to be a better person is a journey. Reading, during my sabbatical and beyond, was an important part of that journey.

Jose Maria Luna is a filmmaker from Colombia. I happened on a Youtube posting from him called, "De-colonizing Adventure: A Cinematic Road to El Dorado."[39] Luna does a great job exposing the Hollywood depiction of White people adventuring in other lands, where the people who live there are no more than the means to propel the adventure, whatever the cost is to them. He focuses on the legend of *El Dorado*, the city made of gold, which is the central idea to many, many adventure movies. For example, there's *National Treasure: Book of Secrets*, starring Nicholas Cage. Cage's character, Benjamin Franklin

Gates, follows clues to discover Cibola, a legendary city of gold. In *The Kingdom of the Crystal Skull*, Harrison Ford, as the iconic Indiana Jones, searches for Akator, a lost city of gold in the Amazon. In the Disney animated feature "Road to El Dorado", two Spanish bumblers, Miguel and Tulio, who are escaping from Conquistador Hernan Cortez, stumble onto a city of gold in Mexico. In all of these films, the indigenous people are either adoring admirers, uncivilized tribes, mystics, or victimized noble savages—wronged people of a simple uncorrupted nature. Luna points out they are "never the protagonist or the point-of-view characters … they reflect the very real erasure that these communities face in real life."

At about this point in Luna's movie, I started to get the feeling that adventure, the very idea of adventure, must be inherently bad. This thought has potentially catastrophic implications for someone who loves adventures and is writing a book featuring himself on an adventure. But here's the part of Luna's Youtube movie that really got my attention. After surveying the sorry genre of Hollywood adventure movies, he admits that he *loves adventure*, that he has loved it since he was a little boy, and that his love was inspired by the comic book adventure series *Tin Tin*, which, he acknowledges, is rife with the same pathological cultural tropes as the Hollywood movies. As the narrator in his own film, he states:

> But I love Tin Tin! Just as I love adventure in general. It's exciting, and as a kid it fired up my imagination and encouraged me to explore and learn more about the lost wonders of human potential. The earliest thing I wanted to be when I grew up was adventurer.

Hearing that, I felt like I wanted to shout, "That's me, Mr. Luna! That's me, too!" I stopped the video, moved it back and heard him say it again. I wanted to cheer. Here was an informed, critical voice of Latin America, from a country with a large indigenous population. Having just excoriated the genre of

White adventuring in film, he says, *nonetheless* he loves adventure! Many—most—of the adventure stories I grew up with, like *Tin Tin*, are problematic, but, like Luna, my imagination was fired up by them, and they encouraged me to explore. Perhaps we can salvage adventure. The rest of the excellent 43-minute video talks about the importance of transforming adventure, by centering indigenous people in their own stories, by letting indigenous people *tell* their own stories.

Luna's documentary focuses on White people adventuring outside their homeland, outside their culture, interacting with the indigenous peoples there. My bicycle trip took me across North America, culturally, my homeland. Nonetheless, there is still plenty of privilege and troubled history of which to be mindful. For example, the reason the land I'm traveling is not outside my home country and peopled with indigenous cultures is that the White settler societies from which I am descended, murdered or relocated them and then took the land. The reason I can travel by myself, on a bicycle, camping along the way, relatively free of concern for my safety is because I'm White and I'm a man and I have a credit card and health insurance and vacation time and all the rest of it. You pile up all those attributes and you end up peeling away most of the people who live in the cities and towns I was traveling through.

Where does this leave me? In as few words as possible, it leaves me chastened and still in love with adventure. It forces me to be mindful about what sorts of adventure I might pursue, and it demands that I consider what my adventure means to the people who are touched by it. Any White man pursuing adventure, should be cautious, given our history. Maybe the mantra should be *do no harm* or, better still, *lend a hand*.

The four years it took to complete my cross-country ride also gave me time to come to terms with the passing of three important people—my father, my father-in-law, and my mentor. I learned I was not a heartless person after all. Plenty of other faults, but I *am* capable of grief. It's just that, with all three men, I felt great sadness long before their mortal life finally ground to a halt. Several years before Ted passed, he stopped asking questions. Ted's signature role in conversation, solving problems, planning schools, was asker-of-the-right-question. After an hour of intense debate around a conference table, he'd quietly put a question in the air, and, as soon as it was out, everyone would stop, recognizing it was exactly the right question, the one nobody had asked. The whole conversation would shift. I noticed, after his sickness had taken a toll, that something was missing whenever I'd go for a visit. One day, it hit me. He'd stopped asking questions. That's the day my grieving began. Our conversations felt increasingly dull and one-sided. When he died, I'd already been feeling the loss for months. When the end came, I felt relief, as I did for my father and Laurie's dad, too.

A great by-product of this relentless cycling, sometimes across a barely changing landscape— pace of 80 strokes per minute gets you to 48,000 strokes in a ten hour day—was an appreciation for absence of sensory stimulus, a relaxed mind, and a simple, repetitive task. Stroke, stroke, stroke, stroke, stroke, stroke, stroke, stroke, stroke, stroke, stroke, stroke, stroke, stroke, stroke. I don't know if this is considered spiritual, but I place it in a category with people who sit in lotus position for twelve hours doing nothing more than breathing. It felt like I was strengthening a muscle group, which is, in contemporary society, generally under-developed. And, for me, it was way better than sitting motionless all day in a bare room with incense, because you get some exercise, see cool countryside slip by, and burn calories so that at day's end you get to eat like crazy, no guilt, then fall into bed and sleep like a rock.

My extended journey had also taught the value of a long term goal that involves physical challenge. Benefits accrue long before the finish line. Training on a weekly basis for the better part of four years meant I had something positive and important beyond my daily routines and grievances that made them feel not so big, lighter to carry. And the physical exercise flooded my brain with all those happy mood-enhancing chemicals that exercise produces.

My successful crossing of the great North American continent on two wheels, solo, no support vehicle, strictly human power, filled me with a new confidence. I didn't know yet what future adventures I would invent, but I knew there'd be more.

Part II
Row to Cape Hatteras

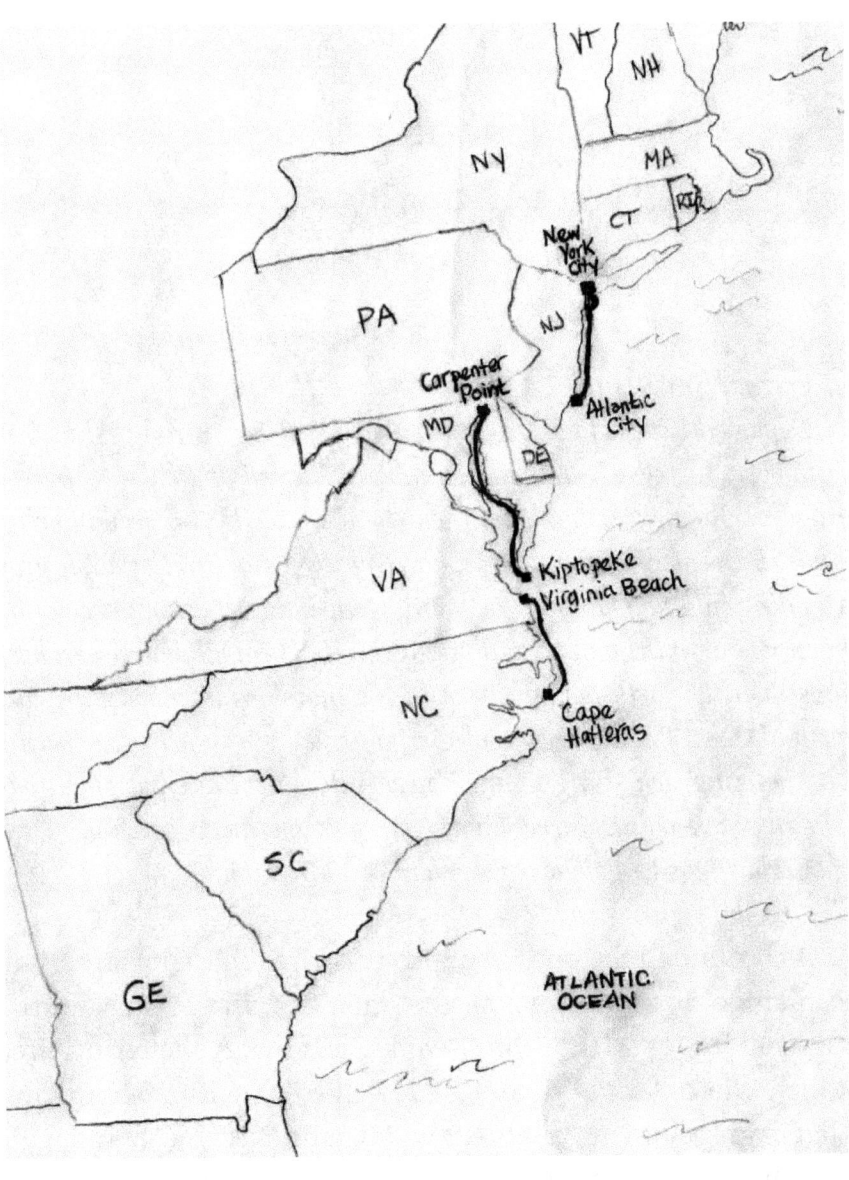

Chapter 11
Merrily

Journal Entry, June 22, 2021
Departed Kitty Hawk 7:05a.m. Swells 1-2 feet, strong wind from southwest, overcast. Wind and swells grew through the day. After big bridge at Roanoke Island, half-way point, swells 3-4 feet, howling winds. Extremely challenging. Shoreline almost entirely marsh grass extending inland a half mile or more. No way to get ashore. Very little shoreline out of the wind. Could not get out of boat all day. Several rest stops in little north-facing nooks in the marsh grass. Last mile, just north of Coast Guard station at Oregon Inlet, storm arrived – pelting rain, howling, whistling wind. Rowed into storm to cross small bay, then rounded point. Coast Guard station, on the point, flying two triangular flags (= gale warning, winds 39-54 mph).

As I rounded the point that protects Oregon Inlet Harbor, my destination for the day, at the moment where this journal fragment leaves off, the wind seemed to slow. A sheltering effect of the point of land, I figured. I'd been rowing for 10 hours into what had begun as a blustery day and became a full gale, officially certified by the two flags at the Coast Guard Station, defiant, atop a tall poll right at the head of the land mass facing the storm. Gusts to 54 miles an hour. I continued my 180 degree turn around the point, careful to avoid the shoreline reinforced with very jagged, boat-unfriendly boulders, but relieved that I would be able to rest, finally, in the lee of a peninsula, with a welcoming Coast Guard Station no less. I'd been unable to get out of my boat since I started at 7a.m. because the shoreline, until this moment, had been all sedge, meaning clumps of spikey grass growing in a swamp like mix of mud and tangled roots. No telling how deep you might sink, getting out of a boat before your feet hit something hard enough to hold you up, or your crotch lands on one of those spikey tufts. Normally, I might seek occasional relief from endless sitting by standing in the boat, but with all the turbulence in the water, I'd probably fall over. The other option would be to jump overboard, holding a line so the boat doesn't get away. That would feel good on my cramped muscles, jammed up backbone, sore butt, and stiff joints. But then, I'd have to climb back in, which can be done, but with all the wave action, I'd ship gallons of water and wind up with a half dozen bruises and scrapes. With all the possibilities of relief eliminated, I was stuck, in my rowing seat, and there I sat all 10 hours.

My mind drifted back to earlier in the day when a bucket-worth of tepid saltwater hit my back and splashed into the hold. "Stop annoying me!" I'd shouted. Silly because there was nobody within a mile, but it made me feel better. I'd been rowing for 6 hours, at that point, into a strong southwest wind. The wind and swell had been growing steadily through the morning and now, as I came from behind a sheltering sedge island that I'd enjoyed for a good 10 minutes, I was once again facing the full force of the wind. The swells were regularly three feet, occasionally piling up to four. My compass heading was 170 degrees, between south and southeast. The waves marched endlessly toward me. I cut through them at an angle. But it wasn't as neat as all that. These waves weren't like soldiers in steady lines. They were drunk and sloppy, coming from any compass point between south and southwest, with the occasional rogue wave appearing suddenly broadside and washing over the boat's combing. For the most part, my 18-foot expedition wherry, built by me in my garage, rode surprisingly well over the swells. When I'd first put it in the water four years before, I was pleased just to see that it floated. Despite my amateur boat-building skills, my sleek beauty with its striking, clear finish, had proven itself seaworthy time and again. But today was offering a new level of challenge. Occasionally, when the height of the wave was just too much for the bow to beat, water washed over the foredeck and got diverted by the enhanced combing that formed a protective semi-circle around the forward half of the cockpit. I bought this piece of rubber baseboard trim at Home Depot. Fitted upside down, and held in place with two spring loaded clips, it fended off 95% of water that arrived by way of the foredeck.

    I tried to figure out what sorts of waves would result in water coming inboard. First was the frontal foredeck wash, i.e., the 5% that were just too big and sent a flood over the Home Depot setup and *splash* on the middle of my back. Once in a while, the force was strong enough to yank the rubber strip out of place, sending in more water, which meant I had to speedily lift it back into place. That meant breaking my rowing stride, pulling oars inboard, turning around awkwardly in my seat, adjusting the combing, getting oars back in position, and pulling a hard five or six strokes on the port oar to get the boat back to 170 degrees. Thankfully, this issue only happened a few times. Another sort of wave was that rogue broadside wash, about which I could do nothing. The rest were mysterious. Sometimes, a wave would break 20 feet off my starboard bow, and I'd hear the boiling white cap rolling toward me. I'd brace for a bucketful on my back but then nothing happened as it dissipated harmlessly under the boat. All bark and no bite. Other times, I'd be stroking with a steady rhythm through the swells, just starting to feel like I'd figured it all out, and for no reason at all, I'd get hit in the back with a bucket full. It was as though I was the mark for some little, mischievous spirit. And because I was facing backwards, as one does in a rowboat, I had to rely on my peripheral vision and a tiny mirror attached to my cap to sort out what was coming at me. Because I couldn't figure out any scientific reason, some part of my brain assigned the over-the-top washes to an unknown agent, which is why I took to exclaiming, out loud, as the water would run down my back, "Knock it off!" I know now why sailors have invented gods and mystical beings since the dawn of boats. Hard-wired as we are to make sense of things, if we can't, we invent stuff.

Mostly, my little boat danced over the waves, but these annoying splashes inboard happened often enough that, about once an hour, I had to bail. I could feel the boat getting sluggish as water slammed back and forth in the hold with each stroke, looking more like a bathtub filled with floating toys. This procedure involved pulling in the 9-foot oars and scooping and tossing. Usually 15 to 20 scoops cleaned it up, but that meant nearly a minute of cut-engine and backward-drift, which took another two minutes of rowing to recover. I figured I drifted backwards at four miles an hour. In calm water and hard rowing, I could make six. Therefore, today, pulling hard, I advanced at an unsteady two miles an hour. But years of cycling, some of it across vast, empty landscapes had taught me the discipline of endurance and the quasi-spiritual practice of repetitive physical exercise. I could do this.

Back to the Coast Guard Station and the storm, four hours of hard rowing later, I rounded the point, and everything seemed to be settling down. But then, I thought, that doesn't make sense because the wind was blowing from the southwest, the direction this grassy point faced, which meant there was still nothing between me and the full fetch of this storm reaching all the way across Pamlico Sound. All the same, everything suddenly felt suspiciously calmer.

Then I get it. The wind hasn't changed. My direction of travel has. I'm no longer pressing my vessel into the wrath of this storm. I'm facing the other way. The storm is now behind me, and my relief shifts to dread. I'm not feeling the wind and waves any longer because I'm riding with them, and my speed is accelerating. As I enter this unknown harbor in search of the state boat ramp, I steal glances backwards and the scene comes into view. It's a complicated jumble of docks, pleasure boats, moored commercial vessels, abandoned pilings, a dredging rig, and more of the usual harbor clutter. It's the sort of very crowded space you want to approach slowly and carefully, especially in a boat with long oars sticking out from each side, and a very pointy bow made rock hard with a quart of hardened fiberglass resin jammed up into its cone.

I feel the push of the wind at my stern. It's driving the stern around, naturally wanting to push my boat broadside to the storm, rendering me unable to maneuver in close quarters, when I don't know where to go, and the rain and wind have just picked up again. It whistles a frightening chorus from the standing rigging of an armada of boats tugging at their mooring lines just ahead. I lean into my starboard oar, drop it into the sea, and pull with all my weight. It lifts me from my seat. The oar moves through the water, the boat comes around a few bare degrees, I finish the stroke, and, in the two beats it takes to lean in, slide my seat forward and drop the oar back into the boiling sea, I've lost three of the five degrees I won with the last stroke. I keep this up, each stroke pulling with everything I've got, while the peak of every swell makes a pivot on which the wind wants to spin me like a weather vane. Slowly, the boat comes around. With each stroke, I steal a glimpse of the harbor. A map I looked at yesterday showed two main branches to the harbor, the one nearest the point I just rounded is where the boat ramps are. My quick glances are not producing a clear picture of the harbor's layout. My boat, after many hard pulls on the starboard oar is now oriented stern to the wind, right where I want it. But this means it is also picking up speed as I begin surfing each swell. Stern to the wind is a hard point to hold because of the boat's natural tendency to pivot broadside. Every stroke counts. Miss one, and the stern will swing around, requiring 10 hard pulls to win back my delicate purchase on the sea. It's starting to feel like my second scholarship attempt and my dream of rowing 500 miles from New York City to Cape Hatteras is about to explode, three days shy of the finish line, in a splintering of fiberglass and plywood, when my boat smashes a hole through the side of a million-dollar yacht. I am now speeding ahead, propelled like a rocket on the downside of each swell. The tangled mass of boats and docks is just ahead, and I have little idea where I'm supposed to go or how to slow down this runaway locomotive.

Five years prior:
"And just how much does this kind of boat cost?" We're standing at the kitchen island. It's 5:30 p.m., almost dinner time. Laurie is sorting through mail at one end, mostly junk mail, that's been piling up. I'm chopping vegetables at the other end. The kind of boat we're talking about is a rowing shell. It is typically thirty feet long, super skinny, and made out of a kind of plastic that is the thickness of an eggshell and you race it on a river. It's fitted with a sliding seat, which means, the seat moves as much as the oars to produce a stroke of nearly 180 degrees, arcing from bow to stern. A single pull at the two nine-foot carbon fiber oars, each equipped with a massive blade, will rocket the fragile eggshell of a boat forward at lightning speed. I'd been introduced to this kind of rowing through lessons that spring. Then I joined the Merrimack River Rowing Association that sponsored the lessons, and I'd spent the summer rowing their boats. Getting out on the water at six o-clock in the morning, when the river is still, and mist is rising, and the only sound is the rhythmic gurgling of the oars and the boat sliding

swiftly up-river is magical. Now, it is September, the rowing season will end soon, and I'm thinking about next steps for my new obsession.

I wait a beat, then answer, tentatively, "$8,000 to $10,000."

"No. You are not buying a $10,000 boat," says Laurie without hesitation. I pause and look up. Laurie is tearing open a big white envelope that says, "You Are Already a Winner!" I resume chopping.

We rip and chop for a minute without speaking. Then Laurie says, "You know, if you were handy, like some of our male friends, like Graham, you might *build* a boat. That would be different."

Graham is more than handy. Graham is a genius with wood. He can build a house from construction scrap left at the curb. In fact, he did. It's the family getaway hidden on 30 acres of woodland in Maine, and it cost him almost nothing. He can build perfectly mitered cabinets and fit them magically into the kitchen of an antique house where nothing is square. He can design and build furniture on commission for an architect, which he also does. And, no doubt, he would be able to build a beautiful boat. I am not Graham. If I miter a joint, I'm lucky if the gap is less than a quarter-inch. Then it dawns on me. Maybe I could build a kit. Maybe there are people who sell boat kits. After dinner, Laurie and I each settle into the couch behind our laptops for a final hour or two of work before ending the day. Only I am not working. I am Googling "kit boats" and then "kit row boats." It quickly becomes clear, lots of people want to sell me kits from which I can produce boats—sailboats, motorboats, rowboats, made from aluminum, fiberglass, or wood. I click through several websites, until I get to Chesapeake Light Craft, "The best boats you can build." I like that motto. They have a list of all the kinds of boats for which they offer a kit, with a photo for each one. You can click on a boat in the list, and it takes you to a page with construction photos, detailed plans, action shots of the completed boat, and a price. They have a racing boat called the Oxford Shell. It is sleek and beautiful and the kind Laurie just shot down. But the price is $3,500, one third what I just quoted her. Right next to it is the Expedition Wherry. The photo shows a slightly more substantial boat, pulled up on shore, with a guy lifting camping gear out of a hatch near the stern. It reminds me that I'm not interested in racing so much as exploring on multi-day trips. I like that it has "expedition" in the name. I click on it. $2,700.

I heard the back-up beep and looked out the kitchen door. A big panel truck was pulling into the driveway. It stopped in front of the open garage and two big guys got out. I stepped outside to greet them. Shortly, they pulled four boxes off the truck. Two were big and flat, four feet by eight feet. They held all the pre-cut pieces of okoume marine plywood that I hoped would become a boat. Another box was short and stubby. It held the sliding seat unit, made of aluminum. The last box was the size of a laundry basket and held the fiberglass sheets, cans of resin, hardware, screws, and the all-important instruction manual. All I had to do was carefully follow the step-by-step instructions at a pace of six or seven hours a week, and, according to my new friends at Chesapeake Light Craft, in four months, I'd have an expedition wherry. Even Laurie was excited.

There was one problem. The garage, one side of which I'd converted to my new shop bay, was unheated, and fiberglass resin, an essential part of the construction process, requires an air temperature of at least 65 degrees in order to harden. It was December in New England. My first miscalculation. Undeterred, I spent the next two weeks conjuring a solution from the aisles of Home Depot, and, after some trial and error, had erected an insulated cocoon on one side of the garage interior, constructed of two-by-fours and rigid foam panels. There was even a door with duct tape hinges. For heat, I bought two oil-electric radiators. If I left them on, after a few hours, the former garage bay was transformed into a toasty, 70-degree fiberglass workshop.

Six months later, I had a boat, a mere two months behind schedule. The excellent instruction manual made it all possible. With clear descriptions of every minute step accompanied by a photograph, it carried me, all 143 pages, from start to finish. I began with a pile of cut plywood pieces inside the two big flat boxes that arrived that December day. The surface of the hull consisted of three 18-foot boards stacked widthwise on either side. Each of them was made of three shorter boards laid end to end and fitted together with precisely pre-cut puzzle joints. Step one was to assemble the 18 footers. Step two was to wrap them, one above the other, around six bulkheads running the length of the boat. The bulkheads formed the boat's ribs, around which the 18 footers were gently bent. Once the boards were glued to the ribs, I had something that looked a lot like a boat, all within the first two weeks. Then the process slowed down, much the way a new house gets framed up in a matter of days, but then it takes another four months to finish it. I plugged away evenings and weekends through the winter and spring.

I was serving, at the time, as the acting faculty chair for the College of Education, a six-month gig while the regular chair was on sabbatical. The job entails managing the master schedule, supervising junior faculty, holding the college to its mission, and keeping the trains running on time. It is stressful, complicated, emotionally fraught, and time consuming. It leaves you wondering at the end of a day whether you've actually accomplished anything. Meanwhile, the stepwise boat project laid out in the manual was straightforward, producing quick and visible results. Chair work was never straightforward and rarely produced visible results. The happy buzz of my warm cocoon in the garage became my therapy and retreat.

The most magical moment came when I fiberglassed the outside of the hull. The boat, 80% done at that point, was upside down on sawhorses. The kit included a massive fiberglass sheet, a kind of white blanket approximately 6 x 20 feet, which I was supposed to throw over the upside down boat and stretch tight. I did that, no problem. Then, according to the instructions, I was supposed to pour the liquid epoxy on top and spread it around with a paint brush. The result, promised by the manual, would be that the white fiberglass cloth would magically become translucent and the smooth, gently arcing, okoume surface underneath would reappear with a warm, shiny glow, showing off its beautiful grain. The manual said, "The entire hull, wetted with epoxy, is a thing of beauty." I was skeptical. How was this white cloth going to simply disappear? I mixed up some epoxy, held the container over the boat, and poured. It flowed out like pancake syrup, hit the fiberglass sheet stretched tight on the boat and, with a little help from the paint brush I held in my other hand, started to spread evenly over the hull. I kept this up, and, wherever the epoxy hit the fiberglass, the fiberglass disappeared. It just plain vanished, and, in its place were the beautifully patterned grains of the okoume with a copper and honey luster. Real magic.

The boat, overall, was formed from the okoume plywood, a fragile 3/16th of an inch thick, but fiberglass was laid over the entire surface, inside and out, producing a light vessel with a rock-hard shell and a beautiful natural finish. The completed, 18-foot boat weighed a mere 92 pounds. Near the end of the process came two scary steps. The first was sawing the hatches. At this point in construction, the deck of the boat, fore and aft, was completed with its fiberglass coating, a broad, gently curved surface sweeping to the bow and stern. Into this flawless surface, I had to cut two hatch holes, each one square with 16-inch sides. There was zero margin for error. The cut-out would become the hatch cover. My lines had to be straight and true. No false starts.

No wandering blade. No do-overs. I carefully drilled the pilot holes late one afternoon. Then I raised my jigsaw and with fierce concentration began to cut the aft hatch. I figured if I messed up the first one, better it be the aft. With surprising ease, the blade followed my pencil mark. The straightaway went fine, but then I had to negotiate the first 90 degree turn, a tight curve. The blade followed my command and made the turn. No doubt, the crisscrossed grains of the plywood layers, made it less likely the blade would fall into the grain of any one layer, which meant that, with nothing to distract it, it followed my lead. I finished the cut, and it was nearly perfect. The very small imperfections would be covered by the frame that would go around the hatch. Then I broke for dinner. During dinner, I didn't tell Laurie about the crucial step I was taking in the garage. One worried person was enough. After dinner, I headed back to the garage and started cutting the forward hatch. The jigsaw blade made its steady racket as I guided it along the pencil mark, around the corners and … Done! The forehatch cut was clean and sharp. Graham would have been pleased.

The other scary moment was cutting the bow eye, with the boat now flipped rightside-up on the sawhorses. The operation involved the most forward section of the boat, where the rising hull meets the forward deck in a sharp point. This is where, on a large sailing ship, the boat builder would place a figurehead of a mermaid or a warrior with shield and spear. No figurehead for my little boat, but the empty space inside that most forward section of the boat had been packed with fiberglass resin. Imagine the bow like an ice cream sugar cone laid sideways. The pointy bottom of the cone is the tip of the bow. Then imagine pouring molten chocolate into the bottom of the cone and letting it harden. That's the fiberglass that had gone into the hollow space at the bow. It made the bow into an uncrushable bumper. If ever I collided at full speed into a concrete bulkhead, the bow would bounce off, the entire boat would shudder, but no harm would be done. According to the instruction manual, the bow eye had to be cut in this spot. The bow eye is a hole drilled sideways, just a few inches back from the pointy tip of the boat, through that thick mass of chocolate/fiberglass. It's the hole through which you thread a rope that is used for the anchor, or a mooring, or pulling the boat up on a trailer, etc. Like the deck hatches, there was no margin for error. No do-overs. I'd been dreading this step for the last 10 pages of the instruction manual. Finally, I turned the page and there it was. After describing how to measure and set up the drill, the manual stated, "Take your courage in both hands and drill a 3/8-inch hole right through the boat." I measured, held up the drill, revved it, aimed it straight and true, and leaned in. A minute later, there was a clean hole through the bow, right where it was supposed to be.

In June, the boat was done. On Father's day, Laurie and I loaded it onto our pickup truck, atop a wood frame, which I also had to build, and we drove to the University boathouse on the Merrimack River in Lowell. In the parking lot, we unloaded and made the boat ready. Then I wheeled it down the dock on a dolly. Laurie was making a movie with her I-phone. At the end of the dock, I lifted the boat off the dolly, and then gently slid it off the dock and into the river, where the water was gently lapping just a few inches below. The stern hit the water and bounced up. The bow slid in, and, holding the line, threaded through the neat bow eye I'd cut, I observed my creation as it leveled itself in the smooth water, and rode high. Shortly, I set up the oars amidships, and climbed in. Laurie continued making her movie as I pushed off and took our first strokes as we glided away from the dock, upstream. It handled beautifully. It was a dream come true. I spent the summer rowing in the early morning upstream to Nashua, New Hampshire, and riding the current back to the Boathouse. Rowing further downstream was not an option. A mile past the boathouse was a massive waterfall that spilled onto exposed rock.

During the six months it took to build the boat, I had plenty of time to imagine where I might take it. It had been six years since I completed the scholarship bike ride so, maybe, in a few years, I could make an epic rowing journey and raise more money. Ten years between big asks from my circle of friends and family felt like enough time. But where would I go? The bike ride had taken me across the United States roughly to where my brother lives, north of Seattle. I had another brother, near Miami. I could row to Miami. That would be symmetrical. One trip west across the country. One trip south across the country. I could take the intracoastal waterway. Do it over four summers. Announce the fundraiser after the third summer, before the final leg. Do alligators eat rowboats, I wondered. But first, I had to see if my row-all-day-camp-out-at-night-row-all-day idea would work. After two months of rowing back and forth between Lowell and Nashua, it was time for an extended voyage.

The Merrimack River is made mostly of snowmelt from the White Mountains of northern New Hampshire. It starts where the Pemigewasset and Winnipesaukee rivers join in the town of Franklin. It meanders south, crossing the border to Massachusetts, where, shortly, it takes a sharp left turn and heads northeast to the Atlantic Ocean. In all, it is 117 miles, with long navigable stretches, such as my homebase in Lowell up to Nashua. In between, there are rapids and waterfalls. The waterpower within the Merrimack fueled the early stages of the industrial revolution in New England with mill cities like Concord, Manchester, Lowell, and Lawrence. The last section of river, before it spills into the sea at Newburyport, Massachusetts, is navigable as far upstream as Haverhill. From Haverhill to Salisbury State Reservation, which lies north across the unnamed bay from Newburyport, is 20 miles. It looked like a good two-day shakedown trip.

From my journal:

August 1
Hattie's Point Marina
Amesbury, MA

Day 1 of all future boating adventures. Left state ramp in Haverhill at 11:30 a.m. Arrived at marina @2.p.m. Appears to be 11.5 miles. Outgoing tide and river current helped. Followed red nuns and green cans the whole way. Swift current at bridge in Groveland got my attention. Didn't know how to land boat at dock with outriggers so I beached it. Checked in at office, got a slip near the boat on a protected side of dock. Went back to boat, removed sliding seat unit, readied fenders on port side, then paddled it to dock. Worked fine. Set up tent in cockpit. Fussed with stuff for an hour. Showered. Aah! Walked 2 miles to town for pizza. Yum. Looking forward to sleeping on the boat.

I was thrilled at the end of day one. I'd entered an unknown (to me) waterway, navigated over 10 miles by channel markers, managed swift-running currents, landed at a marina, and figured out dinner, and accommodations onboard. All I had to do was put consecutive days like this together for some number of weeks, and I'd find myself in Miami. Woohoo! I barely slept that night I was so excited. The next day was even better. *Merrily* turned heads. I have not mentioned, the boat was christened *Merrily*, like the song:

Row, row, row your boat
Gently down the stream.
Merrily, merrily, merrily, merrily.
Life is but a dream.

I'd wanted something playful, happy, and original. I don't know of another boat with an adverb for a name, which was decaled with fancy blue lettering on either side of the bow. The day I launched it, several people at the Boathouse remarked on the clever word play "Merrimack" and "Merrily." I smiled appreciatively, but in my head, I went *Wait. What?* I hadn't thought of that. I played it straight and took the compliment.

I slept poorly that first night tied to the dock. I woke up repeatedly, sometimes excited about all my future voyages, other times worried that I'd somehow gotten loose and was now adrift in the dark unknown. Finally, dawn came, and I was shortly underway under sunny skies, I rowed past a Boston Whaler anchored mid-channel. It looked official. I got closer. Big letters on the side read, Harbor Master. A man standing at the wheel called to me.

"That's a fine-looking vessel. You build it?"

"I did," I replied. "Thank you."

I pulled closer and asked him about the route ahead. He advised sticking to the channel to avoid shoaling, though it would probably not be an issue for my boat and, he said, to watch the currents around the bridges. I thanked him and was on my way. A short distance later, I came upon a large building on pilings at the water's edge. It was rambling and old looking, with an uneven roofline and rows of six over six windows, two stories of them, like it was an ancient factory or a mill. I got closer. It said, "Lowell's Boat Shop." I had to stop. Inside smelled like sawdust and fresh cut lumber. Work benches and hand tools were everywhere and here and there a wood boat lay in one stage or another of construction. A young guy, Nordic looking with a blond beard, was planing the top edge of the gunwale of a nearly completed dory. He paused when he saw me walk over. He had a curl of shaved wood in his beard. We got to chatting, and I learned that Lowell's Boat Shop is the oldest, continuously operating boat shop in the United States, having supplied small boats to the fishing industry over more than two centuries. He knew all about Chesapeake Light Craft and was delighted I was rowing my expedition wherry down the river. He took a peak out the window and declared it a beauty.

I made short work of the rest of the river, arriving, several hours later, at the boat ramp at Salisbury State Reservation, where I'd booked a campsite for the night. After just two days, I felt like I was part of a maritime community, admired for my hand-made boat and connected to a tradition of wood vessels going back centuries. It was heady stuff. I was riding high on the idea of a new adventure. But I also recognized that what lay ahead would include unknown hazards and uncertain outcomes. It would require skills I did not yet possess. It would challenge me in ways I couldn't know in advance. I would have to figure it out and just hope I was up to every test.

Chapter 12
Outward Bound

Hooligans, malingerers, and delinquents were on the loose in the early 20th century. Something was corrupting the character and moral fibre of youth. One observer commented on the times:

> Our young are today surrounded by five decays—the decay of softness due to our modern methods of locomotion, the decay of self-discipline helped by stimulants and tranquilisers, the decay of enterprise due to the widespread disease of spectatoritis, the decay of skill and care helped by the decline in craftsmanship and above all the decay of compassion, which [has been] called spiritual death.

Another observer, at the time, offered this frightening contrast between society and the well-run beehive, "... they [bees] are quite a model of community for they respect their queen and kill their unemployed." Spectatoritis, decay, and unemployment. The world was headed for a cliff! The two observers quoted came to the rescue, with their stark remedies. The first, a German émigré to Scotland, named Kurt Hahn, founded Outward Bound. The second, a retired British Army Officer named Robert Baden-Powell, founded the Boy Scouts.[40]

Adventure, since the end of World War II, has become the focus of educational programs that seek to accomplish more than strictly academic learning. No organization has been more influential in the field of adventure learning than Outward Bound. Its path from the early decades of the 20th century has been winding but, regardless, it has held to a core set of ideas. "Hooliganism" is no longer the target, but its origin—and that of Scouting—drew heavily on a conservative discourse of the times. Mark Freeman, at the University of Glasgow, who has studied the early years of outdoor education, writes there were "widespread concerns about the character of young men, and at the same time the emergence of 'hooliganism' and fears of moral decline resulted in the formation of character-building movements"(p. 27).[41] Outward Bound and the Boy Scouts became the most enduring examples.

I haven't participated in an Outward Bound Program, but my planned adventure on the high seas was starting to feel like what I imagined the program to be—taking on a challenge that was over my head, skilling-up to meet demands that would feel, at times, beyond anything I am capable of, and getting tested, with *live ammo*, so to speak. Would there be parallels between my personal, water-bound, outward bound program and the one with the registered trademark?

Kurt Hahn, born in Germany in 1886 was university educated, and, when war came in 1914, he worked in military intelligence. After the war, he became personal secretary to a high German official with whom he founded a school in 1920 that emphasized character development. Hahn was Jewish, and, in 1933, he was briefly jailed for his opposition to Hitler and forced to leave the country, settling in Scotland. It was there, in 1934, that he founded the Gordonstoun School, and in 1941, the first Outward Bound School in Aberdovey, Wales.

The philosophy behind Gordonstoun and Aberdovey was a curious mix of romantic ideals and conservative politics. Echoing Rousseau's romanticism, Hahn believed that children are essentially good, and society corrupts them. This view had been reinforced for Hahn through the horror of two world wars. The "five decays" he describes above, were central tenets to his philosophy. The work of schooling, he believed, was to draw out the child's inherent goodness and strength in order to build a good society. The motto of Gordonstoun was *Plus Est En Vous*—"There is more in you." But there was a flip side to the philosophy behind Hahn's schools. His collaborator in the founding of Aberdovey was Lawrence Holt, partner in a shipping company, who was looking to improve the training of seamen on his ships. He was part of a circle of early Outward Bound supporters representing a moneyed elite and something called "muscular Christianity." A Victorian era trend in religious thought, muscular Christianity taught that God meant for men to have strong bodies to subdue the Earth and protect the weak. Team sports, physical challenges, and a spartan lifestyle were seen as the means of character training and became popular in the elite English boarding schools of the era.[42] In addition, a professor at Gottingen University, named Bernhard Zimmerman, who advanced the importance of physical education for fit bodies, had been an early influence on Hahn, so the combination of the child's inherent goodness, the corrupting influence of society, and the restorative potential of muscular Christian ideals all made sense to Hahn. So much so, that, in response to the Five Decays, Hahn developed guiding principles for the development of youth, which he called the "remedy," summarized in a speech in 1958, many years after the founding of his first schools (Hahn, 1958). The first was daily physical training, often as a mid-morning break in sedentary study. Sometimes, the daily routine included a cold shower. According to Hahn:

> Every normal boy, also the sensitive and the vulnerable and the clumsy ones, can be brought to performances in athletics good enough to draw self respect there from,

provided the sedentary habits of the morning are interrupted by this health-giving break.

Expeditions were next. Hahn wrote, "I know few boys who do not draw strength, and retrospectively also joy, from an arduous expedition carried out to a definite goal." Then came skills and crafts. Hahn continued, "I believe every boy should learn a craft—should learn how to use his hands. It is particularly necessary for the sensitive bookworms." I wondered, when I read this, if Hahn might place me in the "sensitive bookworm" category, and though I take exception to "muscular Christianity," I admit I draw strength and joy from an arduous expedition. Finally was service, Hahn claimed that "...through active Samaritan service you can satisfy the thirst for action in an honourable way and at the same time link it to the Christian purpose of life." Hahn had converted to Christianity years after his emigration from Germany.

Hahn admired the character development that came from military training, but he lamented that war was seen as the only means by which boys could grow into men of character. He was looking for something else and wrote, "I refuse to arrange a world war in every generation to rescue the young from a depressing peace. Let us rather plan their life at school so that they can discover and test their hidden powers".[43] These ideas became the foundation of the Outward Bound course, first developed at Aberdovey, designed from the start as a short program, typically several weeks long. Mark Freeman summarizes the original Aberdovey program:

> a four-week course, in which trainees were given intensive athletics training, learnt seamanship, and prepared for a land-based expedition at the end of the course. Boys at Aberdovey were organised into groups known as 'watches', which were introduced to promote a spirit of teamwork and friendly competition. The development of character was the declared aim of the school. (p. 25).

Early literature described the training not "for the sea" but "through the sea."[44] I, too, faced a training *through the sea*.

Despite its framing in 19th century thinking from a White European elite, Outward Bound gradually became popular beyond its culture of origin. Because the principles focused on personal traits and not specific skills required for seamanship or other sorts of work, Outward Bound was adaptable to other realms of physical challenge, like mountaineering, trekking, and river expeditions. By 1963, there were six Outward Bound schools across the UK and, by 1964, there were over 55,000 alumni. Soon, there were centers in Malaysia, Kenya, Germany, and the United States. Today, there are 38 schools in 35 countries with 155,000 students completing a program each year.[45]

Over the decades, the conceptual framework for Outward Bound evolved, but the core elements of adventure, the improvement of personal traits, teamwork, and an ethic of care, remained stable. The program allowed itself to change with the times, a factor, no doubt, in its longevity. For example, Freeman explains that developments in the field of psychology in the 1960s and 1970s problematized the Victorian idea of *character-training* and led to the adoption of new terminology: *personal growth, individual development* (Freeman). More recently *self-efficacy* has been featured in Outward Bound (OB) literature.

From the beginning, skeptics wondered if such a short program—just several weeks in length—could produce a meaningful and lasting result. While the ongoing popularity of OB spoke for itself and while alumni testimonies of personal transformation abounded, there was little systematic evidence of OB's impact through the early decades. In the 1990s, however, the New Zealand academic John Hattie and his international team employed a new research approach to test the professed impact of Outward Bound programs. Meta-analysis is an analytic method that allows researchers to quantify results across widely varied studies. Using a kind of common denominator known as *effect size*, Hattie and his team analyzed 96 studies with over 12,000 participants to identify trends. Overall, they found that Outward Bound had a moderate impact on a range of individual traits, including independence, confidence, self-efficacy, self-understanding, assertiveness, internal locus of control, and decision making. This finding confirmed, empirically, that OB produced positive results. But, according to Hattie and his team, so did other educational programs of similar duration. There was, however, an additional finding that changed everything. Hattie found, in follow-up studies of OB participants, that the positive impact of OB participation lingered and even *increased* over time. Hattie wrote, "These substantial follow-up effects are unlike most educational programs, where the typical follow-up effects are negative or at best zero and there is quick fading" (p. 57). Hattie concluded:

> While the overall effects of adventure programs on the outcome measures are at least equivalent to those of other educational programs, the continued gains and longevity of the follow-up effects are the most impressive findings...leading to a combined pre-follow-up effect... unique in the education literature. (p. 70)[46]

There was now persuasive evidence for nothing short of transformative change—what alumni testimonies had professed all along and what skeptics had dismissed. Hattie's findings from 1997 have since been corroborated by another meta-analysis published in 2021 of short term outdoor education programs serving adolescents, conducted by Bin-Bin Fang at Quangzou Normal University with several other researchers in China and the United States.[47] In recent years, OB has partnered with the Institute for the Study of Resilience in Youth (www.ISRY.org) to create its own outcomes survey, which it administers regularly to graduates. Results, available on the OB website, show 81% have "gained the courage to face new challenges," 76% "have committed to making a difference in my world," 81% "say they can work more effectively in a group," and 74% "feel they are a better person." I've wondered, can I make those claims about my own adventuring? And, if I do, do they hold up?

How is it that a mere four weeks of programming can produce such dramatic results? And how is it that the results endure and even *increase* over time? Despite decades of research, empirically based answers remain elusive. As early as 1983, Alan Ewert was writing, "We have discovered an educational Blackbox; we know something works but we don't know why or how."[48] Forty years later, we still don't know, but there is a body of theory that is generally accepted. Jack Mezirow, a sociologist at Columbia University and an expert in adult learning, who died in 2014, is responsible for the main ideas, known as "transformative learning," which, applied to adventure, goes like this: learning begins with a "disorienting dilemma" that creates cognitive dissonance. For example, you are going on a trek that will involve scaling rock walls, descending into ravines, camping in the wilderness, and carrying everything you need to survive for two weeks on your back. But you've never done anything like it, and the prospect fills you with dread, violating core assumptions of what you believe you can do. Then, through activities that involve training, individual and group reflection, team building, and increasingly challenging tasks, you build confidence in your ability. You complete the two-week trek, with all the built-in challenges that just a short time before felt impossible. You experience a kind of euphoria from your accomplishment, your sense of self-efficacy has been transformed. You believe you can now take on other challenges by learning about them and then tackling them. Mezirow wrote:

> Transformative learning refers to the process by which we transform our taken-for-granted frames of reference (meaning perspectives, habits of mind, mind-sets) to make

them more inclusive, discriminating, open, emotionally capable of change, and reflective so that they may generate beliefs and opinions that will prove more true or justified to guide action.[49]

Given the long history of glowing alumni testimonies, its ability to translate across cultures and activities, and a growing body of research attesting to its power to produce positive, lasting results, outdoor education has become a movement. It is known by various names. In addition to outdoor education, there's adventure education, wilderness education, and, sometimes, experiential education. It includes large programs, like Outward Bound, Project Adventure, Nature's Classroom, and, in the UK, the Duke of Edinburgh Award. There are also one-offs connected to schools and youth development organizations. And it continues to evolve.

Outdoor education organizations have been criticized as inaccessible to urban youth of color from low-income families. While the movement remains largely White and middle class in both membership and orientation, there are signs of change. For example, Justice Outside, based in Oakland, California, is rooted in and committed to serving under-resourced communities of color seeking engagement with the outdoors in culturally relevant ways. Their mission statement captures the ambition of their work:

> Justice Outside advances racial justice and equity in the outdoor and environmental movement. We shift resources to, build power with, and center the voices and leadership of Black, Indigenous, and People of Color because the health of current and future generations demands it (www.justiceoutside.org).

Justice Outside offers a range of outdoor education programming for youth and community leaders focused on cultural relevance. They include training, grantmaking, and advocacy. What exactly does cultural relevance for low-income communities of color look like?

Bicis del Pueblo, located in San Francisco, offers one answer. Focused on bicycling in the city, Bicis helps low-income youth, and their families incorporate cycling into their lives. They provide used bikes along with training in repair and riding skills, building community in the process. Rock climbing and sea kayaking are not options in the city, but riding a bike is a great way to get outdoors, build confidence, community and combat climate change (www.bicisdelpueblo.com). In Charlotte, North Carolina, Camping with Cradle (www.campingwithcradle.org) introduces urban youth to nearby state parks, sensitive to the ways that youth of color from urban environments may experience outdoor recreation spaces differently from their White, middle-class counterparts. The organization's website states that it "focuses on creative ways under-exposed youth can experience the outdoors in their own way... [and is] dedicated to helping underserved youth discover the great outdoors and develop life skills that attach themselves to social mobility."

Educators during the last several decades have increasingly seized on outdoor adventure as a powerful resource for learning among youth and adults. There seems to be no limit to its adaptability across class and culture. At the same time, though, powerful crosscurrents within the education establishment are pushing us in the opposite direction-- sit in your chair, copy the notes, and take the test. One wonders, which side is winning? This is a topic to which we will return, but first, there is a rowing expedition about to get underway, my own outward bound journey.

Chapter 13
Here Be Dragons

After two years of prep, the 48 hours leading up to the launch of my big rowing trip down the East Coast were a blur. It felt like stuff I had to just *get through*. What I *wanted* was to be pushing my boat down the last two feet of wet sand into the water, climbing in, fixing the oars, and pulling that first full stroke out into open water, and the first leg of my epic row to Miami. But first I had to drive the truck to Chuck's house in Westchester, boat strapped down on a frame overhead (Yup. Chuck from the storm sewer. Still friends.) Then he followed me in his Prius, clear across Metro-New York through Friday afternoon traffic to the most southerly point of Staten Island. Leaving the boat and all my gear there at Conference House Park under the watchful eye of Park Director John Killcullen, we then drove to Rob's house in New Jersey (Rob = brother), left the truck in his driveway, and rode back to Westchester in the Prius. The following morning we drove to the West Village for brunch, wandered around Eataly with Chuck's chef friend, Derek, looking for ingredients to accompany a giant truffle, which he held, wrapped in a napkin. It was the size of a big orange. They were very excited about the meal they would build around it, and I might be, too, but, at the moment, I just needed to get away. I finally begged off and descended alone into the subway, riding it to Battery Park. Then I rode the Staten Island Ferry, then the Staten Island Railway straight down the full length of New York City's most southerly borough, and then a short walk to Conference House Park, where my new friend, the Park Director, let me crash on the floor in the mansion museum, where peace talks with the British had taken place 200 years earlier to end the war for U.S. independence. The groundskeeper, who lived in a cottage next door, was hosting a birthday party for his eight year old daughter and brought me a plate of barbecue. Normally, I don't eat meat, but seafaring men must sometimes accommodate local customs. The cheeseburger was really good.

Things finally slowed down Saturday at sunset. I love my friends and family. I am appreciative for the kindness of strangers. And what's also true is I needed to be alone. With my boat and the water. I walked from the mansion along a sandy path lined with beach grass to the waterfront facing the Arthur Kill. Across the river, the sun was going down over Perth Amboy, rows of two-story homes receding to the horizon. There was a warm breeze. Orangey sunlight glistened on the wet sand under my feet. A big cargo vessel was making swift progress down the river. Not far behind it was another. The first one moved steadily, plowing the water with its bow that rose like a hundred-foot cliff face to a deck laden with shipping containers. It moved like a force of nature, like an iceberg the size of an office building laid on its side, like nothing could impede its progress, and when it came abreast of me, it nearly filled the river as long as half the river's width. I'd read that the Arthur Kill is one of the busiest shipping channels in the world. Running up the back side of Staten Island, it bypasses New York Harbor, taking some of the largest ships ever built to Port Newark just west of New York City where consumer goods bound for box stores and Amazon distribution centers across North America are off-loaded to eighteen-wheelers with quick access to the interstate highway system. No sooner had the first ship cruised past, the next one was presenting its massive bow. Looking up the river, I saw cargo ships cued up to pass every several minutes. Tomorrow morning early, I would cross the Arthur Kill, then follow the western shoreline as the river emptied into Raritan Bay. Continuing along the perimeter of the Bay, I'd follow its curve until I reached Sandy Hook, a beachy finger reaching north that makes Raritan Bay a bay by closing it off from the Atlantic Ocean. Once there, I'd cut south and enter the Navesink River and follow it eight miles to Long Branch, New Jersey and Kelly's Landing Marina, my destination for Day 1. The Navesink, which is actually a tidal estuary, is famous for powerful currents, the kind you need a 20 horsepower outboard for a small boat to safely navigate.

At the edges of European maps of the world made during the middle ages, cartographers drew lions or dragons and other mystical beasts. This was because where the dragons began is where their questionable knowledge of geography ended. For all of us, unknown spaces often loom fearsomely: the closet door you've never opened, the basement you've never entered, the ocean you've never crossed, the woodland you've never walked. They fire our imaginations with thoughts of salivating, predatory creatures with big teeth looking to do us harm. Medieval cartographers, because they were good with a pen, rendered their fears as fantastic and ghastly illustrations, sometimes accompanying their drawing with a statement such as, "Here be dragons." When I finished my two-day shakedown voyage on the Merrimack River, I was as buoyant with optimism and confidence as an unloaded boat. I could do this! That feeling gradually sank as I spent the fall and winter months reading about small boat navigation, watching scary Youtube videos of ships in storms, and learning about things like tides, swift running currents, submerged hazards, shoaling, the interaction of wind and wave, thick fogs, windstorms, lightning storms, rogue waves, shipping lanes, and drunk-at-the-helm recreational boaters operating large vessels capable of serious damage. I had almost no experience with any of these things. Two calm days on a peaceful river with very little traffic and a gentle tidal pull under a bridge or two didn't count for much. What would it be like to cross the Arthur Kill while dodging mammoth cargo ships? What sorts of abandoned pilings and other hazards lurked inches under the surface of a gently rising and falling swell ready to punch a hole in my paper-thin hull? Just how powerful would that tidal pull be in the Navesink where the waterway narrows dramatically through the chokepoint of the Sea Bright Bridge. I'd read that each outgoing tide drains 95 square miles with a flow of approximately 98 million gallons, like a hundred-barrel beer vat, draining through a quarter inch hole.[50] I had not a clue. Ask me the myriad hazards available to the cross-country cyclist and I'll rattle off a long list, together with tales and advice to fill many chapters of a book. See Part 1, for example. But rowing a boat down the East Coast of the United States? I was at the bottom of a very steep learning curve, looking up with considerable trepidation. Was I about to experience "transformative education?" Was I going to get my own, singular Outward Bound version of intensive training that would equip me to do something that scares the daylights out of me, master it, and then become some kind of transformed, super-capable, adventuring god? Would that "follow-up effect" from prior adventures see me through? Or would I be found clinging to driftwood with my boat gone forever to Davy Jones' locker?

Here be dragons.

Sunday, August 5 dawned clear and surprisingly chilly. I gathered my few things from the night off the ancient wood floor of the Conference House and headed outside where I pulled the canvas cover off my fully loaded boat, which I'd locked to an iron fence. I rolled the boat several hundred yards down the hardened dune path, picked up speed before hitting the soft beach, powered through it, hit the firmer wave-lapped sand, freed the boat from the dolly, which got neatly stowed, and climbed in. Moments later, I was under way. There were no cargo ships in sight. I chose not to overthink it, counted my blessings, and scurried across to New Jersey. Soon, I was rowing contentedly along a placid shoreline. Within an hour, I'd entered the zone. The state of being I'd been learning to love—the repetitive physical task that frees you from the burden of rational thought. There I dwelled for the better part of the day. Until.

Seven hours later found me entering the Navesink estuary on an incoming tide. The morning had gone smoothly. No dragons. Yet. I'd followed my route as planned, hugging the shoreline, pushed by a gentle breeze, enjoying big strokes, gliding across calm water. At Highlands, I'd met up with the Navy Pier, a giant dock that sticks out three miles and blocked my easy-going shoreline path to the Navesink. Officially "Naval Weapons Station Earle," the pier was constructed to create a space far from populated areas where the U.S. military could off-load explosive charges. In my planning, I'd harbored the hope I might row underneath the dock, in between the piers. Fat chance. Signs posted in the bay a quarter mile off declared in big red letters, "NO TRESPASSING RESTRICTED AREA DO NOT ENTER." My backup plan had been that I'd find a boat ramp nearby and wheel my boat around on a local road and then push it back into the water. I bobbed in the swells for a minute, looking out to the end of the pier. It didn't look like three miles, and, even if it was, three miles isn't so far on a calm day. And the day was outstandingly calm. So calm, in fact, I might just row out to the end of this pier, out where the water was essentially Atlantic Ocean, latitude-wise, beyond the northernmost point of Sandy Hook and then circle back down the other side of the pier and slide into the Navesink. The weather forecast showed nothing scary in sight for days. The skies were completely clear for the next four hours, the farthest the radar on my phone's weather app projected. The heck with it. I started rowing. As I rowed, I met up with small boats and kayaks, people fishing casually. Clearly, the locals feared no Gilligan's Island style disasters. Why should I? As I reached the end of the pier and rowed the obligatory quarter mile beyond to stay out of the no trespassing zone, I felt the long slow swells of the ocean under my boat, like I was resting on the chest of a great sleeping beast breathing slowly and evenly in and out. I felt unexpectedly safe, like sitting in a well secured chair on top of a very tall flagpole. With a seatbelt. Nonetheless, I did not linger. You never know with weather or sleeping beasts, and besides, I had a date with the Navesink where the tide was now incoming and I had about a five-hour window to ride it, if I was lucky, all the way to Kelly's Landing Marina and dinner, and a shower.

I entered the Navesink at 1 p.m. Low tide had been 11:30 a.m., which meant I was now riding on top of that 98-million-gallon flood to Long Branch, the twice-daily tsunami that roars into this coastal canyon. It would take 30 swimming pools, each the size of a football field, 10 feet deep, to equal that much water. Imagine draining that volume of water every six hours, which puts the rate of flow at about 1 football field-sized swimming pool every 12 minutes. Even at the River's wide mouth I could sense the pull of the tide. I checked my gear while I still could, before everything got frantic, just to make sure all was in order. I was wearing my waist-band style personal floatation device (PFD), basically a fanny pack loaded with a CO_2 cartridge. Pull the cord when you hit the water and instant life jacket. Just push your arms through. The flagpole was in place with my United States ensign flying six feet up—mainly so I could be seen by bigger boats, but it was also a patriotic display that could endear me to potentially hostile others—a lesson I carried over from my cross-country bike ride. There was nothing of value loose in the cockpit and everything below deck was in waterproof plastic crates or dry bags. Theoretically, if the boat tipped over, I would float, and my stuff would stay dry, and I'd just kick my way, pushing the boat, to the nearest shoreline. What I like about theory is everything always works there.

Slowly, as the two opposing shorelines on either side of me got closer, the water got faster. I've read about rafting on the Colorado River and how the pilot of a raft uses the oars, not to propel the boat, because the wild rush of water is providing more propulsion than anyone could ever want, but instead the oars are used for braking and steering, but mostly steering. As the Navesink picked up speed I found myself steering more than pulling. My job with the oars was shifting from physical labor to finesse. I noticed also that the chop was building. Those big, majestic ocean swells I was riding at the end of the Navy Pier were gone, but it wasn't like the gentle calm of earlier that morning hugging the shoreline of Raritan Bay. It was like the wave action of a bathtub when you slide your butt forward and the space between you and the end of the tub shrinks, and because the waves can't expand laterally, they get taller and steeper, and closer. All of a sudden the top of the increasingly choppy waves was at eye level — which means about 3 feet — and my boat was riding swiftly downstream. At this point a police boat motored by. The uniformed officers on board eyed me. They gave me a long considering look like, does this guy know what he's doing? Does he know what's he's in for? It occurred to me, as I glanced around, I was the only non-motorized vessel in sight. I was the smallest by half of the next larger boat I could see. I must have passed the police test because shortly they gave me a friendly wave. I nodded back. At least *they* thought I could do this. The first bridge was coming up. The chop was wild — tall, steep, eye-level, and moving in every direction at once. The river was a boiling pot with boats everywhere. I set my sights for a space right in the middle of two bridge stanchions, knowing I would not get a second chance. Steering with my oars, looking alternately over each shoulder and checking my mirror, I guided my little wooden boat toward and then…Whoosh!… through the gap. I was out the other side. No sooner was I through and the river suddenly got narrower, the water faster, the chop wilder and the second of the two bridges was upon me. The narrow passage was crowded with boat traffic. The steep swells had grown and were now sometimes above eye level. Also, there was no shoreline. Everything was bulkheaded, a fortified shoreline of corrugated steel walls, which meant no escape path. I didn't have time to worry about it. I lined up two stanchions under the bridge, aimed my bow for the middle, gingerly managed my oars and whoosh! I flew under the second bridge. Almost immediately everything calmed down by 20%, which made no sense because the water wasn't any wider. Nonetheless, I was grateful. Then I had a crazy idea. What if I turned my boat around, just to see if I could row against this current and beat it? I thought for a moment. Whether I could beat the current would be important knowledge for future escapades, like I'm running down a stretch of fast-moving water and suddenly I realize there's a spillway ahead. Would I be able to turn around and row away from danger? I decided to give it a try. I rowed over to the side of the channel, near the bulkheaded shoreline. I looked around. No traffic in the immediate vicinity. I pulled on my port oar, and the nose of my boat started to come around. Soon I was broadside to the current, a place I fear, so I pulled extra hard, while reverse rowing with my starboard oar. The boat came around slowly, and the bow was now facing directly upstream, and, noting the nearby bulkhead on my left, I could see we were drifting rapidly downstream. I leaned forward, dropped both oars in and pulled hard. I completed one big stroke and repeated. I pulled again. And again. The rapid passage of the bulkhead slowed, then stopped. With hard, full-body strokes, I was holding the boat in position. Three more hard strokes and the boat inched forward. I kept stroking and the boat was moving upstream, now steadily, maybe one mile per hour. Now that the boat was moving, the inertia allowed me to ease off a bit and I found that with steady full strokes, I was able to move the boat upstream at a slow steady pace. When danger arrived, I'd be ready. Maybe.

The day calmed down after that. The water got wider and slowed. Traffic thinned out. At one point, there was an island with a sandy beach. I pulled in on the downstream side, slid my boat onto the sand, and unfolded myself as I stepped out. After holding a tense crouch for the last several hours, standing never felt so good.

The Intracoastal Waterway extends from Manasquan, New Jersey to Florida, where it runs around the southern tip of the Florida peninsula and then up the gulf coast, across coastal Alabama, Mississippi, Louisiana, and Texas, all the way to Brownsville at the border with Mexico. It provides mostly protected passage the whole way, cobbled together from bays, harbors, estuaries, and canals. For a trip that starts in New York City, 30 miles north of Manasquan, you need to navigate the first bit by other means. Leaving Sandy Hook, either you go "outside" into the ocean (i.e., not protected water), and duck back inside at Manasquan Inlet, or you ride the Navesink to Long Branch and then trailer your boat another 18 miles to Manasquan. The trip I had planned was to take me from New York City to Miami. I could have started in Manasquan, but for a fundraiser, it sounds a lot more exciting to say the starting point is New York City. People know where that is. Manasquan? What's that? But starting at NYC left me with a difficult choice. Either I go "outside" into the open Atlantic (scary) or I stay inside and figure out how to get my boat across 18 miles of dry land (puzzling). I felt that for my journey to be legit, any portion of it that I did not row, I would have to cover on foot, presumably pulling my boat on its dolly. That way I could say I covered the whole distance under human power. No free ride in the back of a truck. I was super-hesitant about committing myself to 18 miles of ocean rowing, especially when the only way to get off the water in an emergency would be to attempt a beach landing in the crashing surf. Because the reason for attempting a landing would likely be a storm, the surf would be riled up with huge breakers, making the idea of coming ashore especially daunting. The boat would most likely capsize and there's a good chance the outriggers would catch in the sand tearing the rowing unit from the boat, thus exposing the watertight compartments and making an awful mess that might be impossible to fix, assuming I survived. If I did make it the full 18 miles in the ocean without mishap, it would be exhilarating, but then I'd have to come back "inside" via the Manasquan inlet. I'd done some reading and learned it was famous for strong currents, heavy boat traffic, steep chop, dangerous rock jetties, and shifting shoals. Maybe not. Therefore, I turned my attention to the prospect of pulling my boat on its dolly a full 18 miles. It turns out there are boardwalks for much of the distance, and where there isn't a boardwalk, there's Ocean Avenue, which seems to pop up in almost every town on the Jersey Shore. On a weekend in April, before I made my trip, Chuck and I drove to Long Branch in the truck with our bikes loaded in back. We rode the distance and found that the boardwalks covered much of it, providing a decent surface for pulling a boat, and the additional mileage on all the Ocean Avenues didn't seem so bad. If I kept up a brisk walking pace of three miles an hour, I'd knock it off in a short six-hour day.

I hit Belmar at mile 10 of my portage and was completely spent. The temperature was hovering at 100 degrees, and I was averaging just under 2 miles an hour pulling a boat, which, loaded with all my gear, weighed 150 pounds. I'd started at 6 a.m. from Kelly's Landing Marina in Long Branch. It was now noon and I still had eight miles to go. It was also high summer on the Jersey Shore. The boardwalks were crowded with vacationers shlepping beach gear to the shore or out for a stroll with a cool drink, gawking at the honky-tonk souvenir shops, fried dough stands, burger joints, and Italian Ice carts—all colorful and lively. And then there was me marching slowly ahead of my 18-foot boat with a canvas cover, straining to pull it with a short lead while balanced on a single axle dolly, like some medieval penitent dragging a sack of rocks. Even with the deck covered, people still remarked the beauty of the boat, noticing the brightwork of its graceful flank and the elegant wineglass transom.

"Wow! That's a gorgeous boat!"

"Beautiful boat. Is it Italian?"

And then other comments like "You build that?" "You're gettin' your workout today!" and "How far you going with that?"

I enjoyed the praise and mostly ignored the questions as best I could. I didn't want to get sidetracked with an answer that could take 10 minutes to unpack with onlookers joining the conversation.

Earlier, at ten o'clock I'd been walking along one of the several Ocean Avenues amidst mansions facing the sea. I stopped for a short rest and a drink of water. I checked the dolly, which was designed to carry a boat short distances, like across a parking lot, down a boat ramp. It was not meant for an 18-mile portage. The axle was hot to my touch. Not good. A broken axle at this point would be a major problem. Maybe some lubricating oil would help. I didn't have any, but the gardener across the street who was fiddling with a lawnmower did, and happily lent me his oil can. When I checked the axle a mile later, it was just warm. No broken axle today. Crossing intersections, I gained a new appreciation for curb cuts, the little slope in a sidewalk when it meets a street corner that allows a wheelchair to cross the street. I've since read that the Americans with Disabilities Act mandated these for all sidewalks starting in 1990 when the law was passed. Thank goodness. Without them, getting my boat down and then back up a curbstone would have been a major undertaking with the very real possibility of upsetting the apple cart—boat tips over, stuff spills everywhere into busy intersection, cars honking, me running around chasing after rolling debris.

Back to Belmar where I was slogging along the shoulder of the fourth or fifth Ocean Avenue of the day, lost in thought.

"You want something cold to drink?" I look up. Across the street is a woman in a swimsuit with three young boys. They look like they've been on the beach all morning and are headed home for lunch.

"You want something to drink?" she repeats holding up a make-believe glass in her outstretched hand. I say I'm fine, thanks. She offers other things, and says she lives two blocks up. Finally, I ask if she could fill my water bottle with ice.

She says, "I'll bring you a whole thing of ice. I'm Kerry. You keep going. We'll catch up." She runs ahead with her kids, like she's on a mission. "Come on, Robbie," she shouts to the little one at the back of the line who's not keeping up. Half an hour later an SUV finds me a mile up the road. It's Kerry and the kids. We stop. I tell about the scholarship row I'm planning and why I'm pulling this boat eighteen miles.

"Eighteen miles!" she exclaims. We talk. She studied education and theology at Princeton, then worked fifteen years on Wall Street. They've brought fruit, power bars, ice water, and a 10-pound bag of ice. Oy. Really? I cheerfully and gratefully accept it all.

At five o'clock I was still two miles from Manasquan. I'd cancelled my lodging for the night early in the afternoon because it was based on a much rosier estimate of where I'd be by day's end, which meant I now had no idea where I'd be spending the night. Stealth camping by the roadside had vaguely been the backup plan but I hadn't seen a woodland or any kind of remote, undeveloped property all day anywhere along this very developed coastline. I checked Airbnb, Hotels.com, etc. Everything was $300 and up, this being the shore in August. Then I remembered momandpopmotels.com. It turned out, Twin Oaks motel was just one mile up the road at a rotary. $79 and they had rooms available. I spent the night, and when I woke up the following morning, I could barely get out of bed. My shoulders and back were stiff. My hips, painfully sore. My whole body ached. I spent the day recovering, paid for another night. No more portage, please. Next time, I'll hazard the ocean passage.

Following day, I was back on the water, merrily rowing the intracoastal waterway through New Jersey. I found, over the course of the next several days, that the logistics and scheduling of a boat trip are a lot less predictable than biking. Rowing Barnagat Bay, for example, I quickly learned that wind and tide have a huge influence on my progress, as much as doubling it or cutting it in half. On a bike, a good tailwind will get you further, but not that much. Also, on a bike, you can stop almost anywhere for a stretch and a rest. On a boat, the shoreline can be very unfriendly for miles, lined with sedge or bulkheaded properties, or commercial docks that are inaccessible. Also, with a bike, there are more options for where you can ride. If one road has no shoulder and a lot of traffic, there's sometimes an alternate route. In a boat, more often than not, it's just one option. And there is no parallel bicycle experience for a narrow channel with a swift running current. Okay, the Black-hole of a highway tunnel with no shoulder might come close.

Three days later, I was approaching Atlantic City. I'd successfully navigated Barnagat Bay, Little Egg Harbor, Great Bay, and Reeds Bay with Absecon Bay just ahead, where I'd use the municipal boat ramp to end this first leg of my trip. Atlantic City's casinos, clustered to the south stood out starkly against the otherwise flat horizon of marshland and open water. The final approach to Atlantic City was a narrow channel in the middle of a wide, and apparently very shallow bay. Here and there shoals rose just above the water's surface creating sandbars crowded with shorebirds. Some sandbars had tufts of beach grass suggesting a more permanent presence. Elsewhere, I could tell by the water's color that the bottom was no more than a foot down. Meandering through what constituted a minefield of shallows for large vessels were red and green buoys. Follow the red and green markers, and you'll be fine. Wander 10 feet beyond and you risk running aground. Even I, in my little boat that drew less than a foot, had to be mindful. In places, the shoaling was just under the water's surface, causing waves to break. If I got too close, I could get pushed broadside and then get pounded with breaking waves just strong enough to keep me from turning the boat on the shoal, which was just shallow enough, under the pressure of a wave, to ground me, until the tide rose 6 inches. In the interim I'd be battered by each wave coming ashore. Though there had not been much traffic on the bay this Friday morning, it was all squooshed into a 100-foot wide channel, and as the sun peaked and began to fall into the western sky, traffic was building. Two o'clock found me approaching a sharp S curve. Behind me and catching up were two 30-foot fishing boats and further back a hive of jet skis. Approaching the S curve from the other side were three outbound vessels — two more fishing boats and then a sight that defied gravity. Lumbering into what would shortly become a maritime traffic snarl was a four-story sport fishing boat, maybe 40 feet long, with layers stacked up like a wedding cake topped with a canopied tower. Partygoers were crowded along the rails, drinks in hand, generally whooping it up with different music pounding away at each level. Under the canopy up top stood the not so trusty looking pilot, a slick young guy, bare chested, beer in hand with his two best buddies, yammering away, and clearly not paying attention to the trainwreck about to happen. All vessels were converging at roughly the same moment onto this tight little turn. Being the smallest and most able to operate outside the channel, though that was questionable with the breaking waves here and there, I made for the far side of the red nun at the bottom of the S, on a heading that would leave it a good 50 feet to port. My plan was to round the nun, then turn with the channel but well outside of it to leave room for the larger boats that had no choice but to operate within the channel's confines. The bigger boats were getting closer now. All the skippers, as well as I could see were looking alert, slowing down to a no-wake speed, and sticking to the right. Except for tower man. He was full steam ahead. He showed no sign of turning inside the red nun. He was on course for a head-on grounding in the shoal just on the other side of the buoy. If he had enough oomph with his many ton vessel he just might push his big skinny V hull nose right into the side of my boat. I started evasive action. I rowed like hell, expecting the monster imminently to beach itself and roll onto its side, spilling partygoers from every level. But then, at the last moment, tower man seemed to all of a sudden get it. He threw the throttle into reverse, kicking up a storm of smoke, mud, and turbulence in the water at his stern, right in the faces of the two fishing boats behind him. Then he threw the throttle the other way, made a dangerously sharp turn to starboard and roared out toward sea. Jet skis scattered just ahead of him, narrowly avoiding getting crushed. Off he went. I looked around. Everyone seemed to be okay. Several shook their heads in disbelief. It was the only time in six days on the water that a fellow boater was anything less than courteous, and it was a *lot* less.

Six hours later found me stretched out in a hotel bathtub, soaking away the caked-on layers of sunscreen, bug repellent, deodorant, anti-chafe cream, and general grime. I'd landed the boat, as planned, late that afternoon. Rob showed up, also as planned, in my truck, which I'd left in his driveway. He then provided the unexpected and generous gift of a room for the night at a fancy hotel nearby. I noticed, after soaking a good 10 minutes that the water was turning a coppery color and the surface was shimmering the way a gasoline spill shows off rainbow colors. I drained the tub and rinsed off with a shower, noticing my bath had left a dull brown ring. Embarrassed, I scrubbed it hard for 10 minutes, got most of it to disappear, and then showered again. We enjoyed a festive dinner at the hotel and later that evening I settled into a big bed with clean sheets and slept like a rock. Next day, I dropped Rob off at his house and headed home. Driving I-95 back to Massachusetts, with Merrily strapped to the roof, I felt far more confident in my boating abilities than just a week ago. I'd be turning 60 in two short months. Not bad for an old guy, I thought. *Transformative* would be a stretch, but I was starting to believe I just might be able to do this home-made, Outward Bound journey. My mind raced with all the changes I'd make for next year's leg, where the plan was to row the length of Chesapeake Bay.

Chapter 14
Stuck Indoors

The world we have created in the 21st century is driving our children crazy. According to the National Institute of Mental Health, just under half (49.5%) of all adolescents, age 12-18, have experienced a mental health disorder. If you're a girl in that age group, the odds are slightly better than even at 51%. For 17- to 18-year-olds, your chances rise to 56.7%. More than one in ten adolescents overall have a severe mental disorder. The study on which this information is based concludes, "Approximately one in every 4-5 youth in the U.S. meets criteria for a mental disorder with severe impairment across their lifetime."[51] These numbers are from 2010 and are based on more conservative diagnostic guidelines than are in use as of 2023, which means that by more recent standards, the numbers would be higher. And the Covid-19 pandemic made matters worse. Sixty-six percent of adolescents ages 12 to 17 reported that the pandemic negatively affected their mental health, with 1 in 5 reporting the effect was "quite a bit or a lot."[52] How can it be that, conservatively, over half of our teenagers have a "disorder," without even accounting for the further impact of Covid? How is it possible that, pre-pandemic, the mental health of 20-25% of our youth was "severely impaired?" It's hard to say with certainty, but if you look at a number of well documented factors, you begin to get a picture. Let's start with physical activity.

According to the United States Department of Health and Human Services, children and youth ages 6 to 17 should engage in one hour or more of moderate to vigorous physical exercise every day.[53] Moderate means activities like brisk walking, casual bike riding, baseball, and softball. Vigorous, according to the same guidelines, means running, physically demanding dancing, hard bike riding, soccer, and similarly intensive activities. If you've ever watched a raft of children take the playground at recess, this seems like a low bar. Kids race to the monkey bars, streak to the swings, and scramble over pavement and lawn with balls, jump ropes, and frisbees. Or they just chase each other around. Kids naturally want to run and jump and climb. They want to move, sometimes endlessly it seems. But it turns out that most children and adolescents, these days, fail to meet even this modest one hour a day expectation. If Kurt Hahn, the founder of Outward Bound, had a really bad nightmare, it wouldn't come close to the epidemic of inactivity that presently surrounds us. It is genuinely possible, given present trends, that outdoor adventuring, like taking a bike or a rowboat on a multi-day trip to a remote destination, or maybe just an afternoon walk in the woods, will become a quaint, antique pastime, something grandma and grampa did. I'm no fan of muscular Christianity, but I am a huge fan of challenging physical tests, matched to whatever one's abilities may be. They stretch us, they hold the potential to make us better people. Opportunities for such tests, abundant in years past, especially for young people, are growing scarce.

The Physical Activity Alliance is a national organization that promotes policies and systems to advance physical activity for children and adults. Since 2014 they've been publishing a "report card" on physical activity among people in the United States. Drawing on a host of national studies, the report card indicates that 72-79% of children and adolescents fail to meet the guideline of 60 minutes of physical activity every day. They also report approximately six in ten children and adolescents do not walk or ride a bike for travel *at all* in a given week. This latter statistic is part of a trend. In 1969, according to the Report Card, 41% of children and adolescents walked to school. By 2017, that number had shrunk to 11%. Predictably, the increasing inactivity of children and adolescents is negatively impacting physical health. The Report Card reports that approximately six in ten 12- to 15-year-old youth (58%) have inadequate cardiorespiratory fitness levels, and that by 2018, the prevalence of childhood obesity had reached 19.3%, nearly one in five, while the prevalence of severe obesity reached 6.1%.[54]

Another set of national studies has looked at how children spend their time and found that between 1981 and 1997, the percentage of children age 3 to 12 who regularly spend time outdoors during the school year (i.e., not including summer months), was fairly stable at 17-18%, already a distressingly low number.[55] But a follow-up study that looked at the same information for the years 1997 to 2003 found the percentage of children ages 6 to 12, participating in outdoor play (not organized sports), as one of 21 weekly activities, outside of school and attending to physical needs (eating, sleeping, personal care), declined from 16% in 1997 to 10% in 2003.[56] A slightly more encouraging fact is that approximately 40% of children and youth ages 6 to 17 engage in some type of organized sport.[57] The bottom line for all of this research is that recent decades have seen a dramatic decline in physical activity and, in particular, unstructured outdoor play with a resulting decline in physical health. Given the well-established association of physical activity and mental health, it is understandable that the dramatic decline in physical activity has resulted in a general deterioration of mental well-being. But why the decline in physical activity? What has changed in American society in recent decades to cause these significant shifts?

Richard Louv is a journalist who says he'd rather hike than write. When he was a young father, his son, who was 10, asked one evening at dinner, "Dad, how come it was more fun when you were a kid?" His son was referring to all the stories his father would regularly tell about unstructured outdoor play when he was growing up, like using "string and pieces of liver to catch crawdads in a creek" (p. 1). At first, Louv dismissed the question, thinking he'd given his son a romanticized version of the childhood of a generation ago with lots of fatherly embellishments. But that encounter and others like it got Louv wondering, and he decided his son was right. In the space of a generation, childhood had become boring, maybe worse, because kids were spending far less time outdoors in unstructured play. That thesis became the basis of a book by Louv, published in 2005 called *Last Child in the Woods*.[58] It was an international bestseller, chronicling how, as a society, we have become deeply alienated from the natural world. Louv attributes our separation from nature to a number of societal shifts. We've moved from an agricultural to an urban society in the space of three generations. Our urban and suburban planning with indoor shopping malls, big box stores, and housing developments without sidewalks focus our activity indoors while promoting travel between locations by car as opposed to walking or biking. Our schools have, over time, reduced opportunities for direct contact with the outdoors with increased emphasis on testing and academic subjects. And what our society offers children for recreation is often sedentary, involving a screen, finger-tip controls, and a chair — for hours on end. Louv characterizes our lack of connection to the outdoors as a "nature deficit disorder."

Think about the way small towns and commuter suburbs of a century ago were laid out compared with suburban developments of the last half century. The first house that Laurie and I owned, which we bought in 1986, was built in 1930. It was on a 100 X 100-foot lot on a street with similar houses on similar sized lots. It had a front porch that faced the street, and if you walked down the front stairs of that porch, in a few steps, you found yourself on a sidewalk. You could sit on the porch and talk with a neighbor on the sidewalk without shouting. If you followed the sidewalk two blocks, you came to a main street, which, in the space of a half mile included a hardware store, a post office, a library, the town hall, a luncheonette, three churches, and our favorite Chinese restaurant. We lived in what was called the "old" part of town. Meanwhile, two miles outside our pedestrian-friendly town center was a warren of modern developments. These developments featured houses approximately twice the size of our cute, and very functional three bedroom. Houses were typically set back from the road by at least 100 feet on lots that were approximately a half-acre. There were few sidewalks, most of which ran the distance of the circular street that defined the neighborhood. But you couldn't really call it a neighborhood because neighbors were kept physically quite distant from one another. And because the few sidewalks that existed were circumscribed by residential development, and because the entire development was two miles or more from the commercial center of town, and because each house came with a two-car attached garage, travel was almost exclusively by automobile. And when the Walmart was built a few miles in the other direction, car travel into town declined, which became an existential threat to the retail businesses in the town center. I am sure this story is familiar to many readers, either because you've lived it, observed it, or read about it. The bottom line is that suburban planning in the latter half of the 20th century isolated us from our neighbors, our town centers, and the outdoor world in our daily activities.

Trends in schooling have also diminished physical activity and our contact with the outdoors. In 2002, the No Child Left Behind Act (NCLB) became law. It was meant as a grand compromise between Democrats, who wanted more funding for public education, and Republicans, who wanted greater accountability for results in schools. The law required that for a state to receive federal education funding, it had to administer standardized tests in reading and math to all students, each year, in grades 3 through 8 and at least once in high school. Schools that failed to make progress risked losing funding and faced other sanctions. The impact of the law on K-12 education has been enormous. In response to NCLB, schools re-focused the curriculum on test preparation. Subjects like math and English that were tested received more attention, those not tested received less. Since schools have children for only so many hours per day, the importance of a subject translates into how much time it gets in a day. Jennifer McMurrer at the Center for Education Policy at George Washington University found that five years after the law was passed, many school districts nationwide had shifted their priorities by re-allocating where children spent their time each day. Based on a sample of 349 representative school districts, McMurrer discovered that nearly half (44%) had added time for English language arts and/or math (test subjects) at the elementary level while shaving time from other subjects (not tested), including social studies, science, art, music, physical education, recess and lunch. The biggest cuts occurred in social studies and science, but one in five districts that made reductions cut back on recess. One in 10 reduced lunch and some reduced physical education.[59] School increasingly was about success in two subjects. Everything else got pushed to the margin. And because success in the era of NCLB, meant high scores on tests that were mainly multiple-choice items, lessons that sparked imagination and curiosity and took time were replaced with test prep: drilling facts, test taking strategies, and practice tests. Trends in residential planning (car-based developments), education (test-driven teaching), and leisure time activities (phones, video games) are producing a sedentary lifestyle.

What have all these shifts in education meant for the daily school experience of children and adolescents? Over the years, Gallup, the national polling organization, has conducted a number of surveys of students in grades 5 through 12. The surveys have focused on engagement, a topic sometimes considered soft and squishy. It conjures the image of a curmudgeon barking that school isn't meant to be fun, its work! And since there's a touch of curmudgeon in all of us, "engagement" can indeed seem a little indulgent. But here's the thing, engagement is a significant factor in school success and one's overall outlook on life. According to Gallup's surveys of over 5 million children and adolescents, students who are engaged are 2.5 times more likely to report excellent grades and they are 4.5 times more likely to report that they are hopeful about the future. So, what is the state of student engagement in the era of school as test prep? Tim Hodges, writing for Gallup in 2018, reported that more than half of all public-school students (53%) in grades 5 through 12 are either "not engaged" or "actively disengaged" in school. If you look closer at the data, you see a steady decline in engagement as students advance through middle school and high school. By the time students reach high school, two thirds are disengaged with school.[60] Bear in mind, engagement doesn't just mean having fun or being entertained. As Hodges defines it, engagement is a measurement of how "involved, enthusiastic and committed one is to an organization". Involvement, enthusiasm, commitment. Those are really important traits for overall quality of life, and the schools we are offering our kids fail to build those qualities. In fact, going to school, over time, gradually sucks these important qualities away, leaving us with two thirds of our high school graduates—assuming they haven't already dropped out—utterly lacking in enthusiasm, involvement, and commitment for their education.

It gets worse. The remedy that we, as a society, have concocted for this toxic combination of reduced physical activity, reduced contact with nature, and a school experience that is generally dull as mud, is worse than the illness. Imagine for a minute it is you, not a 12-year-old you know, who is sitting at a desk for six-plus hours a day, five days a week, doing worksheets with computational exercises or fill-in-the-blank reading exercises. How would you cope? Is it possible you might get restless and fidgety? Might you find it hard to pay attention to the teacher, follow instructions, stay in your seat? Might you feel a little impulsive, become forgetful? Might you start talking out of turn to other kids seated near you? Might you make a little mischief just to inject some imagination and creativity into the equation? If that is how you would respond, you would not be alone. It is exactly how millions of school children have responded to the thin gruel we serve up as school every day. The problem is these natural responses run counter to the kind of behavior required for a smooth-running test prep operation—compliance, silence, and a super-human ability to focus on repetitive, non-demanding tasks. In the modern classroom, these behaviors would be viewed as a problem. Your teacher might consider you a troublemaker or, if your teacher has a more social scientific mindset, you would be called *disregulated*. In either case, messages would filter home via your casual reports on how the day went. *It was boring, my teacher yelled at me.* And, perhaps, more official notices from school. *[Insert your name] has been assigned detention six times this quarter. May we schedule a parent/guardian conference?* And then the report card would come, and, assuming it is not straight As, any grades less than superlative would be attributed to your restlessness. Your parents or other caregivers would reach out to their social network and shortly you would be scheduled for behaviorial testing, the result of which would be a diagnosis of attention deficit hyperactivity disorder (ADHD). You would be prescribed a powerful stimulant. It would make you feel strange, but it would change you enough so that you would be able to sit still for worksheets.

I am closely acquainted with serious health challenges related to brain chemistry, and I offer this commentary aware of the pain and suffering that sometimes results from the extreme gap between the neurology of individuals and the demands of society as we have chosen to construct it. I do not imply criticism of any individual choices. I do, emphatically, wish to point out the general trends, which are alarming not just to me but, in many respects, the medical community.

The Diagnostic and Statistical Manual of Mental Disorders of the American Psychiatric Association (DSM) is generally considered the Bible of mental health. What is called ADHD today first appeared in the DSM in 1968 as hyperkinetic reaction of childhood. In 1980, it was renamed attention deficit disorder (ADD). In 1987, the name was changed again to attention deficit hyperactivity disorder (ADHD), and in 1994, three types of ADHD were identified.[61] In 2012, the DSM underwent a controversial revision in which many diagnostic thresholds, including ADHD, were lowered, making it much easier for a child's natural tendencies to be pathologized by the medical community.[62] The Centers for Disease Control reports that in 1997 roughly 5.5 million children were diagnosed with ADHD and, as of 2012, depending on which study you read, the number stood somewhere between 9 and 11 million with the trend line continuing at the same rate or an accelerated rate since then.[63] A review of several studies, published in the Journal of the American Medical Association, shows similar numbers and reported that 10.2% of all children ages 4 to 17 having an ADHD diagnosis, including 14% of all boys and 6.3% of all girls. The authors warn, "ADHD is overdiagnosed in children and adolescents. For individuals with milder symptoms in particular, the harms associated with an ADHD diagnosis may often outweigh the benefits."[64]

In summary, our society has made life for our children dull, sedentary, and isolated from nature. Because children are naturally inquisitive, active, and excited to be outdoors, they have rebelled in entirely innocent ways. In response, we have drugged them into submission.

Chapter 15
Half Moon Island

There's a scene in the movie *Apollo 13* where Tom Hanks, as Jim Lovell, is steering a crippled command module toward a docking with the lunar lander—an unplanned and unwieldly coupling intended to rescue a damaged ship. In the scene, Hanks' character is watching the gimbal—a special compass for pitch, roll, and yaw, which are three kinds of motion. Pitch is when the ship goes like a teeter-totter, rocking front to back. Roll is when it goes side-to-side, the action of a baby's cradle, and yaw is when the ship spins right or left. Hanks, as Lovell, must drive the tip of the command module, straight-on, to a precise point at the tip of the very fragile Lunar Lander, a difficult and high stakes operation. He gently nudges the joystick this way, then that, making micro-adjustments to the ship's attitude and rides it to an amazing, bulls-eye landing.

I'd started the three-mile crossing to the mouth of Chesconessex Creek in light to moderate wind and one-foot chop. Easy peasy. I was eight days into my nine-day voyage running the length of Chesapeake Bay from its northernmost navigable arm to its southernmost point. It was the summer after my row to Atlantic City. About a mile in, the wind picked up and the bay rose to four-foot swells. First the wind howled. Then it started to whistle across the tops of white caps. Because my direction was 45 degrees off the swells, and because the waves were irregular in their direction, the boat rocked unpredictably — front to back, side to side, as it climbed earnestly to the top and then surfed down the back side of each powerful swell. The bow would heave to the right or left with little warning, sending the compass swinging 15 degrees one way, then, the other. I was managing pitch, roll, and yaw, much like Jim Lovell, except for the fact I wasn't commanding a multi-billion-dollar rocket ship, a million miles from Earth, with the world looking on. I was in my home-made rowboat in the middle of Chesapeake Bay. A few family members had a rough idea of my location, and in case of disaster, I could always swim ashore. Nonetheless, in my own way, I felt, like the Apollo 13 crew, right at the edge of my ability to cope, even if the stakes were nowhere near as high. With each wave, I had one chance, with a single oar stroke, to correct the deviation produced by the last wave. The compass would veer east, so I'd pull hard on my port oar to get us back to south. Meanwhile, the wildly uneven water surface meant I had to quickly judge how deep to bury each oar so each blade would catch and lever me with another strong stroke toward my destination. Sometimes I misjudged, the oar was too shallow in the water, and wouldn't grab, skipping across the surface. Other times, I'd drop the oar deep into the bay, too deep as it turned out, and the oar would start to crab, meaning it would get pulled under the boat, a dangerous event in rough water. So, I'd quickly twist the oar, sharp side up, to eliminate resistance, and shoot it to the surface. Misjudging in either way would yaw the boat further in the wrong direction. Each stroke was a chance to get the boat on course or make matters worse. In this manner, I clawed my way to the far shore at what turned out to be half my usual speed.

    My original plan for this boating adventure was row to Miami. After a slow, six-day trudge from Staten Island to Atlantic City, and the realization that, at that rate, I might make

Miami by the time I was 70, I decided to re-calculate. What could I do in four summers? I picked four summers just because that's what it took for my cross-country bike ride. It was a goal I knew I could meet because I had a track record. Next question: What is a destination that would be recognizable and, therefore, appealing for a fundraiser, if not Miami? The answer was Charleston, South Carolina, iconic city of the American South, an even 800 miles from my starting point, and a little over 200 miles for each of the next three summers. So that was settled. Next question was how to proceed from Atlantic City the following summer. Directly to the south are mostly tidal estuaries and marshland. If the similar waterscape I'd encountered just north of Atlantic City was any indication, it would be a ride in the company of many, many green head flies, the biting kind, the kind that get bigger the further south you go. And marshland is what the map showed all the way to Cape May. Once I reached Cape May, I'd have to back track northwards up Delaware Bay, then, partway up the Delaware River, to the Chesapeake and Delaware Canal. Narrow passages, such as canals, I was learning, are notorious for traffic and swift, dangerous currents. The Canal is 14 miles long, and only after navigating its full length, would I find myself, once again rowing south as I entered the northernmost branch of Chesapeake Bay. It would be a summer of mostly detouring, and the detour would turn my nice, round-numbered 800-mile journey to Charleston into a much more complicated and longer trip closer to a thousand miles. There had to be a better way. That's when I noticed, looking at my east coast map, wishing it was different, that the northernmost point on Chesapeake Bay is slightly north of Atlantic City. If I started there, then, in terms of latitude, I'd be approximately where I left off the previous summer. It was a way around a nasty leg of this trip without cheating. Very quickly, that became the plan. Logistics were similar to the previous summer. I'd drive the truck with the boat on top to my starting point in Maryland, leaving the truck there. Nine days later, Rob would hitch a ride with his wife, Mary Jane, from New Jersey, to my starting point, where he would hop into the truck and drive to my journey's endpoint, hopefully, the southern extreme of Chesapeake Bay. There, we'd have a celebratory camp-out for a couple days before returning north.

During the winter in between, I spent a lot of time staring at nautical charts of Chesapeake Bay. The thing that stood out mainly is it was big, and the shoreline was bumpy with coves and inlets, meaning that, unless I wanted to add a huge number of miles to my rowing experience by following the shore, I'd have to plan some open water crossings. I'd have to leave the comfort of my accustomed shoreline hug, with its (sometimes) quick and easy escape path, and venture farther from land, maybe as much as three miles out, rowing from one headland to the next, which made me nervous. What about things like fog where I could get lost, big waves that could knock me down, and big boats that could crush me without noticing?

Here is where I must pause and acknowledge that, in comparison to your typical book-worthy, death-defying, global-class adventures, my rowing jaunt down the coast is preposterously out of their league. No matter that, to me, at the time, it all scared me quite a lot. I'd recently read Tori Murden McClure's *Pearl in the Storm* about her 1999 solo crossing of the Atlantic Ocean in a rowboat, the first woman ever to do so. It took her two tries and much of her 300-page tale is a gripping description of the harrowing circumstances aboard her frequently storm-tossed little boat. She'd spend days locked up in the little, water-tight aft cabin while gales, and, at one point, a hurricane, threw the boat around like a cork, capsizing it multiple times and even sending it end over end with monster waves. It was the worst hurricane season on record. Inside the cabin, Murden was thrown from port to starboard, floor to ceiling and fore to aft. She endured a dislocated shoulder, an injured back and arm. For hours at a time, she languished in a swill of vomit, urine, and feces unable to open the hatch to the passing storms. Eventually the boat started to crack open and only when it became mostly submerged did she finally issue an electronic call for help. She was rescued by a passing container ship. Undeterred, Murden headed out the following year and this time, she made it. Hardship makes for better storytelling and so it was that the second, successful attempt took just 30 pages to tell. If you look her up on the web, you'll see that in addition to her rowing record, Murden is also the first woman and the first American to ski to the South Pole and to summit a famous mountain in Antarctica. She holds a master's degree in divinity from Harvard, a J.D. from the University of Louisville and serves as a university president.

So out of my league.

Having now offered up these ego-flattening admissions, I will say in defense of the adventurousness of my clearly not-world-class adventure that were I to tip over in the middle of a five-mile crossing through a stormy chunk of Chesapeake Bay, I would truly be a vessel in distress. More to the point, I would be a person in distress (i.e., something approaching mortal danger). Would my overturned boat continue to float? How long before water would seep into the storage areas under the hatch covers? How long before my cans of beans, Velveeta log, and mini bottles of merlot would send my boat to Davy Jones' locker (even if it was just 10 feet down). Would I be able to swim to shore? Maybe. Or, actually, maybe not. Therein lies my slim shred of true adventure! Is a roller coaster ride an adventure? No. The outcome is certain, unless something truly bizarre happens, like the rail breaks and all the coaster cars go flying into the wide blue yonder. My outcome, in my little rowboat, was not certain, and, though humble, the scale of my mini-adventure, to me, at certain moments, was all I could muster to manage, stay focused, overcome my fears, and get through.

And isn't this the essence of adventure? It's not the height of the mountain or the breadth of the sea, it's how a person, in this case, me, experiences the challenge they've chosen. And the wonderful, democratic truth at the heart of the adventure idea, is that it is available to anyone. We should advertise this. I suppose that's what this book is meant to do. We know adventuring and exerting ourselves physically in these ways is good for our individual mental health and, surely, our societal well-being. What a colossal tragedy that our institutions—school, residential real estate development, gaming and recreation, medicine—are pushing us the opposite way.

Before heading out onto Chesapeake Bay, I bought a compass. About time. Given the Chesapeake's size, irregular shoreline, and the fact that I'd be crossing open water for the first time ever, it seemed like a good idea to know my direction. The nautical charts I was looking at always had a compass rose in the corner, and I was aware, from movies, that with a funny looking ruler that walks across a map, you could plot the direction and distance of a course: "three and a half miles on a heading of 170 degrees, from Highland point to the northwest corner of Barley Neck." Like that. Shortly, I was the owner of a Weems and Plath 15-inch marine parallel ruler. Course plotting works like this: you draw a pencil line on your chart from your starting point to your ending point. Then you lay the edge of your parallel ruler along the pencil line. Then you "walk" the ruler across the map to the compass rose. The ruler is actually two rulers connected by two strips of metal acting like a hinge, which allows you to step the ruler across a chart while maintaining the direction of the pencil line you lined it up with. Once you get to the compass rose, you position the edge of one of the rulers at the center and you can read the precise compass heading of your original pencil line. I decided to break my trip down the Chesapeake into segments of two to five miles. I spent many happy hours during the winter months, locating features on my maps that would be visible from the boat—a water tower near the shore, a headland, a rock jetty, a marina—and then connecting them to make a continuous pathway of pencil line segments from start to finish of my planned voyage. My starting point was to be the Craft Haven Campground and Marina just off Carpenter Point in a very northerly section of the Bay known as North East River. My ending point was set for Kiptopeke State Park, approximately 225 miles south at the southern extreme of the Eastern Shore. Along the way, I noted campgrounds, marinas, and RV parks on the shoreline where I might spend a night. I estimated I could average 25 miles a day, completing the trip in nine days. I made a reservation at Camp Haven for one night and another reservation nine days hence at Kiptopeke State Park for two nights. That way, if I got delayed by a day en route, I'd still have one night reserved. I ended up relying heavily on my course plotting. Those pencilled line segments became my guide, and with the compass mounted at the foot of my rowing station, I was able to continuously monitor where my boat was pointed. There was just one problem: I was looking backwards at my compass. Because, as a rower, I face backwards, I end up looking at the wrong side of the compass, which means I have to subtract 180 degrees from whatever heading I read. Compass makers sometimes account for this by printing reverse headings in smaller print on the compass. My compass showed reverse headings but, unfortunately, the print was too small for me to read while rowing. Subtracting 180 quickly became second nature. My compass became an essential tool. Its value was highlighted in one particularly vexing segment of the trip. My journal entry from Sunday, August 4 tells the story.

Today, I felt lost in the middle of a big sound. It was a 4.5-mile crossing on a hazy afternoon with many fuzzy land masses on the horizon all the way around. My bearing set me on course to a land mass appearing, in the far distance, to be well more than the 4.5 miles it was supposed to be. Looked more like 10. Afternoon wind was picking up. Following sea of 2 feet. I checked the chart, checked bearing, checked compass. Felt panicky but realized, worst case — barring storm that swamps boat — I come safely to shore at the wrong place. Tried GPS on my phone but couldn't read it in brilliant mid-day sun (no shadowed area). I decided to trust my course plotting and follow the compass heading. Two miles in, the far shore still looked too far. I kept on. At 3 miles, I saw something long and low in the water maybe a mile off. Was it a sun line at the far edge of a cloud? I rowed another half mile. Then I figured it out. It was a shoreline backed by low lying marshy land. Several miles beyond it, across the next body of water, was a taller land mass. All I could see when I started was the taller land mass, which as it turned out, was the next crossing, my last of the day.

For most of my Chesapeake trip, the weather and the tides cooperated. I made steady progress from day to day averaging 25 miles as I'd hoped. Figuring out my camp arrangement each night added some adventure to the mostly humdrum — with notable exceptions — of endless rowing and landed me in some varied and interesting locales, starting with the very first night.

Camp 1 - July 30

I arrive in the truck at 1:30 p.m. No one around. I wonder how to get boat off truck. I'll need help. Two older people with canes are coming down the lane. One more, not old, but very large and slow moving stands in a doorway. . I decide to try again later, closer to check-in time. I retreat to nearby Northeast (name of town) for a couple hours. Return. No one around. Woman drives up in golf cart.

She asks, "Can I help you?" I explain about the boat.

She says, "Let me see who I can find." Several minutes go by. I notice sea gull poop coats the top of a picnic table nearby. Beefy guy shows up in golf cart. Danny, he says. I explain about the boat.

He says, "Where ya goin' with this?"

I say, "Cape Charles," expecting his jaw to drop since Cape Charles is 200 miles away.

He says, "I mean right now. Where do you want to put the boat?"

"Oh, right," I say. He helps me lift it off the truck.

Later, I've got the boat all loaded up on its dolly and my tent set up next to it. A couple shows up in a golf cart. I know from the earlier golf cart person that I've set up my tent in the wrong place near the boat ramp, the right place being a half mile up the road. I figure, here it comes. They're gonna make me move. I stroll over. The guy driving the cart has a Hawaiian shirt and a titanium leg. We make introductions.

He says, "You gonna sleep in that little-ass tent?" I turn my head to look at it hoping it will suddenly look big. It doesn't. I look back at him.

"Yesssir," I say. He chuckles. We both chuckle.

Camp 2 - July 31

Arrive at marina exactly at noon. Killer current in tiny channel at mouth of Fairlee Creek. Whips my bow around 90 degrees just like that. I work hard to re-align boat, then pull super hard a dozen strokes and am through it. Excited to spend the afternoon getting settled, hanging out at the beach and then getting a drink at Jelly Fish Joel's Tiki Bar (reason I chose this marina), which I spotted on way in. Set up camp in grassy grove of giant trees. Excitement builds through afternoon. I imagine beach music, tiki torches, grass skirts, big red sky. I stroll over 4 p.m. Bar closed. In bed 8:30 p.m.. At 10:49 p.m. I wake to a loud ragged cracking overhead. A falling tree? But no tree hits the ground. No matter, I move my tent to a freshly mowed field, well away from trees. Leave 6 a.m. Strong incoming current at Jelly Fish Joel's. I fight my way out.

Camp 3 - August 1

I am sleeping aboard *Outnumbered*, a 30-foot cruiser belonging to John Harris, owner of Chesapeake Light Craft and designer of my expedition wherry. John was following my progress with the boat kit over last several years and offered to shoot a promo video as I approached his local waters. Met me as I entered the Kent Island Narrows, and shot footage while circling me in his boat. I felt briefly like a movie star. Then he offered to let me sleep aboard for the night, told me where to find it. His boat has padded bunks and A/C. It rained overnight. I'm dry.

Camp 4 - August 2

From the pictures online, Taylor Island Family Campground is an oasis of cold beer, convenience store-level grocery offerings, and showers plus toilets. I arrive via bulkheaded channel, inches wider than my boat with oars out. I tie up and disembark. Friendly guy in lawn chair nearby offers to watch my boat. I thank him. Says he has a license to carry. I say I'll mind my manners. In camp store, where I check in, manager asks me what I'm doing rowing a boat. I explain, using too many words, about the whole scholarship thing and cycling and rowing and, etc.

He says, "So you're rowin' a boat to send kids to college?" At that moment he leans toward me on his prosthetic leg, which hisses.

I say, "Yessir."

He says, "Well your campsite is no charge."

Camp 5 - August 3.

I row 36 miles. Last bit is a long crossing with three kinds of weather all at once, spread out and circling overhead in a gigantic sky, the whole way. One place full sun, another, dark clouds, another, rain. I come to land at a primitive shoreline of coves with small trees right to the water's edge. In places, land meets water like the apron of a swimming pool with a wall made of clay and a shoreline just inches above water level. I pick a spot with some overhanging trees and a small beach nearby. I park, tie up my boat, and step onto land without getting my feet in the water. No people, no buildings, no roads. I set up camp and make my plan: swim and bath at 5 p.m., hors d'oeuvres at 6 p.m. Then dinner, map planning for tomorrow, journal entry for today, and lights out. My Velveeta brick, despite scorching temperature in compartment under hatch—I estimate 140 degrees based on memories of restaurant cook summer job—is intact and excellent on Trader Joe's Multigrain crackers.

Camp 8 - August 6

Halfmoon Island tonight. Population 1. It's three football fields long, skinny, more like a crescent moon and two feet above high tide at its highest point. We just had high tide, so I know. Just to make sure, tent is tethered to boat with 50-foot rope. If the sea wants my boat it'll have to take me, inside my tent, with it. I feel free. Walk around naked. Sometimes a bird makes a call that sounds like a person. "Hey, you!" You can't camp on that island!

It wasn't all storms with big waves and howling winds. In fact, more of the time it was calm water and the only thing to occupy my mind, besides staring at the shoreline and occasional passing boat, was navigation logistics, like this: From the grassy point I just rounded at 1:56 p.m. to the headland to my south is 3 miles with a compass bearing of 190 degrees, which, because I view my compass from the wrong side, reads 10 degrees. I estimated it would take me 45 minutes to reach it based on an assumption that my cruising speed is 4 miles per hour. That assumption was based on several years of journeying in my boat and dozens of point-to-point passages with nothing to do but enjoy the scenery and count strokes. I've also learned from several years of rowing that when I am focused, well hydrated, not exhausted, and not fighting three-foot swells, I pull at the oars at a rate of 17 strokes per minute. So regular is my rowing pace, you can almost set your watch by it. During a typical day on the water, rowing for, say, eight hours, I will perform what I have named an "index row" probably a dozen times. For an index row, I check my watch, waiting for the seconds to come up on a new minute, mark the time in my head, then start counting strokes. Sometimes, when I get to 85, I'll check my watch, and sure enough, most of the time, it shows 5 minutes has passed, plus or minus a few seconds, and then at 170 strokes, I check again, and, as if by some unknown regulator, the watch shows 10 minutes has passed, almost exact. I've gotten so I can let my mind wander while doing an index row, but my brain keeps counting on its own in the background. I can admire the birds, swooping and soaring against the blue sky, I can look at the waterfront homes I pass and think about which one I would choose. Meantime, my mental counter keeps going 67, 68, 69, 70, etc. One day when I was bored, I figured out how many strokes to get from New York City to Charleston, South Carolina. Here's the math: 170 strokes per minute. Fifteen minutes to a mile. That's 2550 strokes in a mile. Times 800 miles equals 2,040,000 strokes to go from New York City to Charleston.

Some days, it's calm, but then, all of a sudden, it's not. The day after my Half Moon Island adventure saw me making steady progress along a shoreline of coves, inlets, marsh, and beach. Windy but not daunting. Mostly cloudy skies but not threatening. Around 2:30 p.m., I was passing along a three-mile beach with good, deep water just offshore. Ideal conditions. My marine radio suddenly came to life. I didn't know it was on. I recalled it had happened before. Radio off, and then, suddenly, it's on, broadcasting some kind of alert. I've read since that weather radios can be programmed to do that. I never programmed mine. Thank goodness some friendly sea nymph, apparently, with access to my radio, did. It crackled: something about emergency storm alert and lightning and hail and multiple counties, but it was fuzzy. I couldn't quite make it out. Anyway, I'd learned to take weather alerts with a grain or two of salt. Riding my bike across the Great Plains, I got scary-sounding alert messages pretty much anytime I tuned in a NOAA weather channel: "Chance of THUN-DER-STORMS!" Weather announcers have a flair for delivery, unless maybe it's just the same bot on all channels. "Thunderstorms" always rolls from the announcer's mouth the way the sonic boom of thunder rolls across the heavens, with a pronounced stutter-skip. "Thu-u-u-under storms!" like somebody about to sneeze. A-A-A CHOO! I looked around. Sky was gray but no more threatening than it had been all day. I could do without the alarmist messages. I went to turn off the radio. It was already off, part of the sea nymph program, I guess. I kept rowing. A half hour later, it was time for a break. I pulled the oars inboard and reached behind me for my bottle of 50/50 water and Gatorade. The bottle was warm, as usual. No matter. It would hydrate me just as well as if it were cold. As I reached around, I caught a glimpse of the sky off my bow.

Wait. What?

I pivoted around fully on my rowing seat and faced the bow, which pointed due south, the direction I'd been heading for the last several hours. I gazed in disbelief at a scene not just in front of me but enveloping me, slowly swallowing me and my boat. The entire southern sky, fully half of the dome of heaven was blue black, and it was starting to close around the other half of that dome. Just then, a puff of wind came from the south, then another, and then it was a steady wash of hot air pushing what looked to be the mother of all storms right at me. Still looking, I saw a bright flash diffused by atmosphere that suddenly illuminated a big patch of that black dome. Hold a beat and there was another. I didn't hear anything, but who's waiting. I turned around, got back into rowing position, picked up my oars and pushed them through their gates, blades to the water's surface, leaned in, dropped oars, and pulled! Just then the radio came back to life. The wind was picking up and I was concentrating on getting my boat moving so I didn't really hear the message, but I did hear the part that said, "THU-U-U-UN-DER-STORMS!" I don't know if it actually said, "Take cover immediately" but that's the message that ran from my brain down to every muscle in my rowing core. Rowing full tilt, I scanned the beach for a good place to pull in. Shortly I saw a spot, protected by a little sandbar with some beach grass and a big log on top running parallel to the shoreline just 50 feet offshore. I rowed past it, turned the boat, and pulled into my protective cove. I looked south and saw a line of rain coming my way. I hopped out—maybe more like hobble out because I'd been sitting for the last five hours and was scrunched and cramped as usual. I yanked the boat as high up the beach as I could, threw out the anchor (never really knew if it would do anything were the boat to find itself afloat), yanked off the hatches and started grabbing essentials to make camp for the night. Within minutes, I was inside my tent with everything I needed for the night, looking out at the gathering darkness. It was only 3:30 p.m. Then the wind and the rain hit all at once. My trusty tent bowed slightly but held. I was snug and dry. It stormed for the next four hours. I enjoyed hors d'ouevres, dinner, and journaling. At 8 o'clock the sun, low to the horizon, appeared. The black dome opened, retreating north, revealing a blue, bright sky as it went. I checked my phone. Three bars! I sent seven limericks I composed the day before on Half Moon Island. The seven limericks were for our daughter's 27th birthday on August 7. Today.

The other calm day that suddenly turned frantic occurred my very first day on the Chesapeake, shortly after launching from Carpenter Point. I was taking a short break from rowing merrily toward my presumed date with Jelly Fish Joel's Tiki Bar, under a blue sky and bright sun, when something caught my eye. A boat, in the distance. Gosh it seemed to be going fast, and, hey, right at me. It was getting bigger fast. I slid my oars into the water, mounted my seat, and off I went. I looked at the big boat.

Bigger again. Coming into view now, I could see it was a giant private yacht. The kind where you find a helipad on the aft deck. A few more strokes and I could see I was pulling out of its path. Thank goodness. But wait, it was changing course. Right at me again. And it was getting closer. I could make out the bowsprit. I rowed frantically and sloppily. Then, all of a sudden, the bow of the yacht dropped. It was slowing down. I pulled hard to clear out of its path. It held its course and soon I was out of harm's way.

Through calm weather and stormy, smooth water and choppy seas, hours of tedium and moments of high anxiety, Merrily carried me ably down the Bay to my destination, Kiptopeke State Park. There I spent a celebratory evening with Rob who arrived with fresh food and single malt whiskey. We shared a Cuban cigar I'd been saving, cut it in two, we each got half. When we were little, Mom would tear a napkin in half for us to share. She would have approved. She also smoked a corn cob pipe now and then. We slept that night in a yurt.

Driving home, I was exultant. The Chesapeake leg of my row-to-Charleston adventure was a glorious success. The question now was, would my luck hold as I headed, next summer, to North Carolina's Outer Banks and Cape Hatteras, graveyard of the Atlantic?

Chapter 16
Saving Recess

If Outward Bound is so good, why not just make it the model for public schools? Adapt the sea kayaking and mountaineering to cycling, walking, bouldering, stair climbing, ziplining, neighborhood exploring, a ropes course, or whatever else a school's surroundings offer up, and deploy the Outward Bound principles in whatever way you can.

In 1987, Paul Ylvisaker was wondering the same thing. The former Dean of Education at Harvard University, and a longtime admirer of Outward Bound, he'd been invited to keynote an Outward Bound Conference in Cooperstown, New York. The more he wondered, the more convinced he became Outward Bound was the direction to take public schools. His speech wound up as a fiery call to action.[65] Three years later, a team put together by Harvard's Graduate School of Education and Outward Bound International wrote a grant proposal to establish a network of public schools based on Outward Bound principles. School reform groups around the country had been invited to send their ideas to New American Schools, a public-private venture with its origins in the George Bush Sr. administration. The idea behind New American Schools was to take the most promising school reform ideas and help them scale up as national models. With funding to the tune of $130 million, the venture attracted nearly 700 proposals, of which nine were funded. The Outward Bound-Harvard plan was one of the nine, launching the very ambitious Expeditionary Learning Project. Shortly, Expeditionary Learning was a program with curriculum, professional development teams, and schools around the country clamoring to sign up. The basic element of the model was the "expedition" a 6-12 week project-based, interdisciplinary learning experience designed by the school's teachers. Kurt Hahn would have been thrilled, a mighty blow against hooliganism! Students would have a high degree of freedom choosing the content and products of their work. The focus would be on real-life issues and students would regularly be out and about in the community beyond the school's walls, interacting with adults in a wide range of professions and sectors.[66] There would be no standardized testing. Instead, students would collect evidence from their real-world learning in portfolios and their performance on the job would be monitored and evaluated as part of a system of performance-based assessment. Maybe there was hope afterall for the outdoors, for adventure, for the natural inclinations of childhood to find expression in the place we call school. Outward Bound, customized by and for diverse communities, was about to become the radically new American education.

Fast forward several years. The RAND Corporation, which had been hired by New American Schools to evaluate its progress, released a series of reports. At the 10-year mark, one report noted that implementation across all the school designs, including Expeditionary Learning, varied widely both within schools and between schools. In other words, in any given school, some teachers and some departments embraced the reform idea while others did not.[67] At the same time, some schools overall adopted the design vigorously, while others gave it only passing attention. Another report from RAND, around the same time noted that, in many locations, the original design had been compromised. Standardized tests replaced portfolios as the main form of assessment. District practices around testing became the norm.[68] It turned out most schools lacked some combination of freedom, time, and experience to develop and enact such a radically different kind of education. Competing priorities in the form of state and federal regulations, local school board wishes, other school reform ideas brought in by superintendents and principals, and public sentiment, muddied the water, making it very hard for anyone to act on a singular vision.

If you look at the Expeditionary Learning website today, the progressive ideals and free-spirited approach of the expeditions is barely visible. Fully developed curriculums fit neatly within the edges of the current public education cookie cutter with "Learning targets" "alignment to standards" and "lesson sequences" made of two hour "modules." Instruction is coded to precisely scripted learning outcomes. The code for one lesson plan, two hours long, is "LS G5:M2:U1:L10", which is based on "NGSS 5-LS2-1." Assessment of what students will learn in this lesson has two components, one of which is described as a group "performance task", the other, likely the one that actually counts, is an "on-demand summative assessment", otherwise known as a test.[69] No doubt, there are some schools where expeditionary learning, as originally envisioned, is thriving. These are schools that have managed to break through and hold consistently to a singular vision for learning. Good for them! May they continue to thrive. By and large, though, they are the exception. One of the last RAND reports in the series that studied the New American Schools initiative concluded:

> A danger in educational reform initiatives — especially those within urban settings with many complex economic, political, and social challenges — is that the whole-school designs may be another "program" that is turned on and off at selected times during the school day, week, and/or

year. As time goes on, the designs may be at risk of being turned off altogether, especially if districts and schools lose their focus on schoolwide programs such as NAS and turn to some other reform effort.[70]

Some people believe that educational change happens like this: smart people invent an innovation. Policy leaders craft funding schemes and regulations to scale up the innovation. Staff developers create engaging workshops. Classroom teachers attend the workshops, and the innovation is "implemented." Researchers then study fidelity of implementation and recommend technical refinements to the process. In 1973, long before Expeditionary Learning was imagined, a young researcher at the RAND Corporation tested this idea about educational change by studying the implementation of four federally funded school innovation programs. Five years later, she concluded that plans do not dictate practice. Local context matters, and many players exercise agency in the shaping of classroom learning, through a process she called "mutual adaptation."[71] Milbrey McLaughlin became a professor at Stanford University and *The RAND Change Agent Study*, published in 1979, has stood the test of time. Other observers of organizational change have drawn similar conclusions. Donald Schon at MIT wrote in the 1980s about the fallacy of the "technical-rational" theory of change, the linear approach just described.[72] Kevin Dooley, at Arizona State University, has written about the nature of complex adaptive social systems that defy linear logic. An entire field of study — complexity science — corroborates McLaughlin's findings.[73] It is widely acknowledged today that organizational change is multi-directional and non-linear. Still, policy makers, curriculum designers, textbook publishers, and education leaders act like it's not so. Scan the articles and ads in education magazines: technical trainings, teacher-proof textbooks and software, state boards creating curriculums dictating what will be taught. Strategies, driven by a simplistic view of change, are initiated regularly and wind up influencing the system in ways that are wholly different from what was anticipated. Imagine an 8-year-old climbing into the cockpit of a commercial jet and pressing the shiniest button, thinking, *I bet this button makes the jet go fast.* To be clear: funding mechanisms, government regulation, textbooks, and central office mandates DO impact the classroom, but often not in the ways imagined by those at the top of the system. Human agency has a way of asserting itself all along the path of influence. Any organization is an array of semi-autonomous individuals each of whom can bump an innovation this way or that ensuring the final outcome is nearly unpredictable. Organizational change is never a simple matter. An intentional change effort, from a single source, no matter how powerful, almost never works as planned, even if it's a great idea that transfers the powerful learning of adventurous experiences from the outdoors to the schoolhouse.

The disappointing story of expeditionary learning as a national model is only the most recent example of powerful learning principles, attuned to the naturally curious, adventurous spirit of children, stalling at the schoolhouse door. You would think schools should be all about inspiring a child's curiosity, fostering their ability to solve complex problems, working cooperatively with others, and gaining confidence as they take on successively greater challenges to their physical, intellectual, social, and emotional abilities. That is the rhetoric that surrounds many schools, but in practice as we've seen, schools are so deadening, that by the time young people reach high school, two-thirds are no longer interested. Why do schools regularly spit out initiatives driven by the very principles people generally believe in?

I've spent many years working in progressive schools, the chief characteristic of which is that they are not traditional. Or so we say. In fact, the schools I have worked in and admire are mislabeled. And so, too, are the "traditional" schools with which they are unceasingly compared. So-called progressive schools are the legacy of a long and proud tradition of thoughtful school practice stretching back centuries, while so-called traditional schools are the mostly unintended consequence of decades of politically driven and sometimes misguided school reforms, regulations, and school board policies issued decades ago, the purpose of which no one can remember. All these things accumulate like layers of wallpaper on old plaster. The schools we call progressive are, in fact, not new. They have appeared again and again in the history of American schooling. What is ironic is that each time they emerge, they are termed (sometimes, and unfortunately, by their advocates) as innovative, experimental, break-the-mold, or, well, progressive—and are frequently dismissed on those grounds. They have familiar features: a curriculum driven by questions, respect for the mind and imagination of the student, a focus on intellectual skills and habits, adventurous outings into nature and the world beyond the school, working with others to solve problems, and the driving conviction that students are not merely empty vessels into which knowledge is poured (the test-prep vision of so much state and federal regulation), but powerful thinkers, whose abilities are best nurtured through artful teaching and real world experiences.

Consider just a few examples.[74] In 1834, Bronson Alcott (father of Louisa May Alcott, the author of *Little Women*) launched the Temple School, on Tremont Street in downtown Boston. Alcott's school did not stand "for the inculcation of knowledge, but for the development of Genius—the creative attribute of spirit," wrote Elizabeth Peabody, an early advocate of Alcott's work. The children kept reflective journals and were encouraged to express their opinions. Unfortunately, such encouragement of original thought proved too much even for the Boston Unitarians who ruled the city's intellectual life. Alcott was increasingly criticized by William Ellery Channing, the great Boston preacher, for encouraging "too much analysis" among his pupils. The critics grew louder, pupils withdrew, and soon the Temple School was no more, a casualty of "innovation." A generation later, in nearby Quincy, Massachusetts, a Civil War veteran and New Hampshire schoolmaster named Francis W. Parker was hired as the superintendent. Shortly, Parker won over the town and the school committee with his child-centered approach to education. School committee Chairman Charles Adams wrote in a widely distributed article in 1879:

> In place of the old lymphatic, listless 'school marm,' pressing into the minds of tired and listless children the mystic significance of certain hieroglyphics, ... young women full of life and nervous energy found themselves surrounded at the Blackboard with groups of little ones who were learning how to read almost without knowing it.

Parker's notoriety grew, and his work in Quincy was soon described as "newfangled," an innovative "method." Parker vocally and wisely resisted such characterizations, insisting that what his teachers were doing in Quincy was simply common sense. But critics managed to sway public opinion through fear of "experimentation," Parker left Quincy, and the schools eventually returned to a sad normality. A third example, one generation hence, is the Beaver Country Day School, founded by activist mothers in the Boston suburb of Chestnut Hill. The prospectus of the school from 1923 reads like a manifesto of progressive ideals:

> The teacher will guide and use the interests and impulses of childhood rather than repress them. Much of the work will be founded on the pupils' real or imaginary participation in each situation, rather than on an

assignment of rote lessons to be subsequently heard in formal recitations.

The school flourished under the control of wealthy and influential Boston families, and by finding allies among prominent educators and within universities. But it fell on hard times during World War II, as anything perceived as experimental gave way to more conservative demands for rote learning. The school survived by moderating its approach. A TIME Magazine article of 1945 called the school "not quite so 'progressive' as it once was." Another casualty, it said, of "innovation." (Admirably, in modern times, the school has reasserted its original mission.)

This sampling of schools is just in one part of the country. Many others can be found elsewhere, as well as influential movements past and present that advance the same core convictions: Montessori; the kindergarten movement; Waldorf Schools; the Progressive Education Association of the 1920s, '30s, and '40s; and more recent beacons of hope such as the Coalition of Essential Schools and Expeditionary Learning. Examples abound; the tradition is long. The impulse for thoughtful—adventure filled—schooling goes back centuries. But sadly, a society that mass processes everything appears to be incapable of accepting the fact that it doesn't work with children.

If we can't rescue the whole system, can we at least preserve the parts of mainstream schooling that are good? Could we, maybe, save recess?

Tim Walker is an American teacher who lived in Finland for eight years, and for most of the time he was there he taught in Finnish schools. He has published widely on his experience.[75] He says that when he started, he taught his elementary students lessons for over an hour, and found they got restless. Meanwhile, all the other teachers in his school gave their pupils 15 minutes of recess for every 45 minutes in class, and their students were very engaged in the classroom lessons. Gradually,

Walker came around and realized his students learned better when they spent less time in the classroom and more time in generous breaks for free play. It turns out the other teachers in the school were following what is simply the Finnish national norm for elementary level students. To American ears, it sounds just plain wrong that less time in class equals better learning. For decades, American educators have relied on the simplistic view that more time-on-task equals more learning.[76] But, for years, Finland's education system has been at the top of international comparisons for K-12 schools[77] and generous recess appears to be part of the reason.

Anthony Pellegrini is a professor emeritus at the University of Minnesota. In the 1990s, Pellegrini and colleagues conducted a series of experiments with recess involving elementary school students. In each experiment they varied the length of time students spent doing seatwork before going to recess. They measured students' attention to classroom tasks before and after recess. In all the experiments, they found students were more attentive after recess than before. They concluded that providing breaks facilitates students' attention to instruction. Pellegrini also conducted a study to see whether the peer interactions associated with free play at recess can be positively correlated with academic learning, as opposed to the more constrained interactions between children and adults. They found in a two-year study that free play with peers, the kind of activity found in unstructured recess periods, was a significant predictor of academic achievement.[78] Given the research, the Finnish experience with recess, and Finland's overall academic success, we can start to see how the counter-intuitive logic of less time in the classroom really can equal more learning. Afterall, whoever said kids don't learn during recess? Recess, meaning free play, outdoors among peers, is probably the closest that many schools get these days to adventurous learning. There are unknowns and uncertain outcomes, the potential for social and physical risks, opportunities for cooperative problem solving, and situations that call for both leadership and followership. It should come as no surprise, given what we know about ADHD and American schooling, that in Finland the incidence of children medicated for ADHD is approximately one half the U.S. rate. Recent studies show 3% of Finnish children compared with 6% in the United States[79]. While, no doubt, many factors influence these statistics, it is easy to imagine how 15 minutes of vigorous free play would deliver up a child ready to sit for a bit and take in a lesson. If we value our children's health and learning, instead of subtracting recess minutes from our children's school day, we should give them more.

Chapter 17
Isaias

Through the open windows I hear syncopated rhythms of crickets and cicadas, only, here in the swamp country of southeastern Virginia, where the wide, flat land is a bare two feet above sea level and the trees are thick with vines and foliage, the chorus of night critters makes a wildly different sound from back home. To my ear, outer spacey. Something you would have produced on a Moog synthesizer, back when people did that. I lie awake under the truck cap in the back of the pickup. It is the summer after my Chesapeake row, and the eve of my departure into unfamiliar waters. Ahead lies a 10-day journey that will take me south through three sounds: Currituck, Albemarle, and Pamlico. Then I will follow the inner shoreline of the Outer Banks, a string of fragile barrier islands that arch southeast fending off the mighty Atlantic Ocean and then curve gently back southwest toward the mainland to my destination for this summer, Surf City, North Carolina. Buoyed by the success of my Chesapeake passage the previous summer, and my growing confidence as outdoor adventurer, I anticipate an average 25 miles a day. Ten days should be more than enough time. I lie on top of my bed roll, an old sheet folded over itself and made snug with a few safety pins down the side and across the bottom. The night is somewhere between warm and hot, and I'm still awake, several hours after clicking off my reading light. I've tried the usual tricks like visualizing sheep jumping over a stone wall, counting them slowly—I know, silly, but it sometimes works. Do sheep even jump over stone walls? How would a sheep jump? My eyes search the ceiling of the truck cap for the tear in the aluminum skin where it is prone to leak. I hope it doesn't rain tonight. It's not supposed to. I wonder if I can patch the tear with duct tape. I reach for my phone to check the weather. I'm not sure where on the boat I stashed the duct tape. My expedition wherry rests beside the truck, fully loaded, trimmed out with its neat and tidy canvas cover. Mounted on its dolly, I have only to roll it 100 feet to the boat ramp at 6 a.m., and I'll be on my way. I'm already dressed in my shorts and neon tee shirt. I tap the weather app which all week long has been showing an improving forecast for my first day on the water. A week ago, the app showed a lightning bolt. Not a welcome icon for boaters. Before I went to bed, the icon was a happy yellow sun with a white puffy cloud. Ideal conditions. The 10-day forecast pops up. Today is happy sun and puffy cloud. Hooray! Maybe now I'll sleep, and I won't have to search for my duct tape. I'm about to click off my screen when I see a notice at the bottom. "Alert," it says. "Tropical storm Isaias slamming Hispaniola, headed for Bahamas. Projected to track for Florida Atlantic coast and southeastern US to Eastern Carolinas."

Wait. What? But I am too exhausted to deal with it. Alerts come and go, I tell myself. I will deal with the weather later. Whatever storm might or might not travel up the coast is still several days away. Eventually, I fall asleep.

My alarm goes off at 5:30 a.m. and at 6:00 a.m. my boat is in the water. I pull through shallow canals surrounded by tall reedy grass and come, after a while, to the relatively open water of North Bay. I row into the morning through still air and calm water, arriving eventually at a narrowing of the bay and a confusing collection of small, sedgy islands. They are not accurately depicted on my maps, probably because they change from year to year. According to the chart, it should be a straight shot to the mouth of Currituck Sound if I hug the shoreline of Knott's Island, a substantial land mass and the most significant feature on my route. That will bring deeper water, and, I hope, at least occasional patches of beach where I can come ashore and get out of the boat and off my butt, which is starting to ache from three hours of continuous rowing.

North Bay, the northernmost body of water in the system of bays and estuaries that run south toward Currituck Sound is super shallow, in many places just 2-3 feet, and marshy, which means that the shoreline is all grass. In three hours of rowing, I haven't seen a single patch of beach either around the perimeter or on any of the numerous reedy islands that dot the Bay. At the moment, however, it's those islands not my sore butt that concern me. What I see around me doesn't match what's on the chart and because some of the "islands" are actually peninsulas, going off course could mean rowing miles into a dead end and then spending precious time and energy correcting the error. Such a misadventure of 2 miles would mean a 4 mile mistake since I'd have to row all the way back, in total about an hour of lost time, and a significant blow to my mental state. Imagine you're running a marathon and, several miles in, you realize you made a wrong turn down a dead-end road 2 miles back. Like that.

The wind is picking up as the sun ascends toward midday, baking the land and the sea. My boat's bright, lacquered surface reflects heat. My arms and legs are slick with sweat and sun block. I stare again at my paper chart, pulling it up from the combing, where it is duct taped and encased in a plastic sleeve, to get a closer look. Doing so means I need to be hands free, which means I need to take my oars out of the water, pull them inboard so the blades don't steer the boat crazy as they rest cockeyed on the water's surface. Because the wind is from the south, it means slowly my boat begins moving backwards. Loss of time and energy, a regrettable cost, especially in all this heat. I look to my left and right. Big headland on the left, which is the northern tip of Knot's Island, or should be, but the fingertip of land that juts out, according to the chart, isn't supposed to be there. To the right there is something that could be the fingertip, but if that's true, then I'm traveling down the inside of that finger to where it joins the hand. In other words, a dead end. I look ahead, but it's impossible to make out the edges of the open spaces between the grassy masses on the near horizon. I start to get annoyed at myself for not being able to figure this out. I decide that the potential cost of a dead end is worth pulling out my phone and using the GPS (i.e. Google Maps) to settle the matter. This is a project because it means opening up my grab-and-go dry bag to fetch my reading glasses, then pulling my phone out of its touch-sensitive watertight case—not touch-sensitive enough as it turns out—and trying to find some small bit of shadow on my open boat where my phone screen won't be blasted with sun glare. Meanwhile, I'm drifting backwards again. I'm losing valuable forward progress with all this navigational business.

That's when it hits me. Did I skip one of the legs of my route? I look at the zigzag pencil lines I've drawn on my chart that constitute today's route. For each one, I've calculated distance and compass heading, and beside it, the carefully rendered pencil line. I just completed the fourth leg and then, as I look at the third leg and the number beside it, it feels like the number is not fresh in my mind, as it would be if I'd just spent a chunk of time using it to read the compass and count the minutes. I think, did I skip the third leg? Now I'm really confused, super-annoyed at myself, and maybe a little panicked. Meanwhile the boat is drifting backwards. Google Maps is not much help. Same problem as my charts. I wonder how often Google updates its information. I decide to just row south and hope for the best. I do this the next two hours, following what I hope is the eastern shore of Knott's Island and wondering the whole time if I am making a cataclysmic mistake. As I round each grassy tuft, a new view unfolds as I try inconclusively to make sense of the road ahead. Right at two hours, the water opens up, and I can see, maybe a mile south, what looks like a headland jutting east from Knott's Island. If it's what I think, it means I've traversed the narrows and beyond that headland lies the open water of Currituck Sound. Encouraged, I pick up the pace. The further I go, the more the visuals make sense, and, as if a reward for my troubles, as I approach the headland, I see three little patches of sandy beach near the tip. I row straight for them. Ten minutes later, my heart suddenly feels light at the sound of my hull sliding onto the sand. I climb out and stretch. On the other side of the beach I can see the huge expanse of the sound.

I rowed hard all day, 25 miles, through a level of heat I am not accustomed to. I made my destination and penned the following in my journal late in the afternoon at the campground's waterfront.

July 30, 4:40 p.m.

Big, orangey-red dragon flies are swarming my picnic table and the rack of kayaks next to me, 50 feet from Currituck Sound, big and flat and a steely blue. The dragon flies are curious and fearless. Today, I saw a bald eagle take flight from a tall tree right on the shore of one of the many, many islands, mostly sedge, that I passed working my way south from North Bay past Knott's Island into the open water of the sound. Wildlife I was glad not to see were the copperheads and water moccasins I was told to watch out for. They swim in the shoreline grass, and since the entire shoreline – I mean entire, except for the bulkheaded front yards of the shoreline homes – is grass, that's a lot of snakes. Doug, last night's campground host said there used to be a Boy Scout summer camp on the Bay, but they closed it in the '70s because of snakes. He also told me to check in with the local fire department just so they would know what I'm doing. I did, and Suzie the Assistant

Chief said, in case of a bite, keep it below my heart to slow the spread of the poison and call 911. We practiced how to state my location on my marine radio should any of this happen, which, first she said was hours, minutes, seconds, but then she googled it. Degrees, minutes, seconds.

A dragonfly just landed on the head of my pen and seems to be enjoying the ride as my pen wiggles and jerks from my writing. I also saw a great blue heron this morning in the marshy area before I got onto the bay, around 6:45 a.m. I must have surprised it. Herons, as I've observed them, typically plan their flight, then take off without haste. This one fluttered and fumbled, and when it emerged fully from the grass and overhanging branches, it was huge, six-foot wingspan.

The flora and fauna in this part of the world are just different enough from back home that it can spook me. I'm especially nervous about the bugs. Setting up my campsite that evening, there was a thing the size of a bumble bee with stripes to match but with the segmentation and legs of an ant. And it was bright red. And it kept following me. It didn't fly. It crawled—with speed and determination, re-routing itself toward me every time I moved around. Later, I found the camp store was poorly stocked. I bought an "extra-cheese" pizza that the guy at the counter pulled from a freezer case and slid into a machine with a conveyer belt. Two minutes later it came out the other side. Not a microwave. Not a pizza oven. The extra-cheese saved it. I feel I'm in a foreign land. Everything's a little off from the world I know.

Lying in my tent that evening, I checked on the storm. News was it had ripped through Puerto Rico and Hispaniola and was headed for the Bahamas. Reports said it was intensifying and on track for Florida. When I checked my phone at midnight, a new alert was waiting. The National Hurricane Center had reclassified Isaias as a Category 1 hurricane. Something that had been merely looming felt suddenly like a direct threat to my travel plans. If the storm came up the East Coast, as Caribbean hurricanes often do, it would arrive in maybe three days, just when I would be rowing the outermost islands of the Outer Banks with no easy access to shelter. Could I wait out the storm in—a motel? Elementary school evacuation center? Where would I safely stash my boat? What about Covid contact? I was headed at the end of my next day for an Airbnb. Maybe their other guests would cancel, and I could stay on for a few days. Expensive proposition. I wouldn't really be able to advance further than tomorrow's destination because it was the last stop before I was truly on the Outer Banks and far, as a rowboat rows, from the presumed safety of mainland. If I waited at the Airbnb, say, four days for the storm to pass and enough clean-up, I would not have enough days left to reach my destination, Surf City, North Carolina, but I *might* have enough days to complete the arc of the Outer Banks and touch base back at the beginnings of the mainland. That could work. That thought was encouraging. But here's the thing: something inside me didn't want to feel encouraged. I realized the idea of stopping felt like relief.

Why? The answer was ready at hand. I was exhausted. After just one day of rowing, I was questioning whether I could keep this pace up for another nine days. Covering that many miles a day was really hard physically and mentally. When I arrived at my campground at the end of that first day, I quickly made my way to the camp store and downed two quarts of lemonade mixed with water. I was almost immediately thirsty. I drank more. In the course of the evening, I drank easily a gallon of various beverages. I also had a headache. I took two Advil at 4p.m., another two at 8:30 p.m. I felt nauseous. During that first day on the water, I had deliberately managed my water intake to align with the one gallon per day maximum I would be able to consume if, at the most remote portion of my trip, I did not have access to fresh water for as much as three days. This had been an important consideration in my planning. A gallon of water weighs 8.34 pounds, which means 25 pounds total that I'd have to carry with me. But what if I actually needed two gallons a day, rowing for eight hours in 100+ degree heat under an intense Carolina coastal sun that made everything more intense as it reflected off the water and my shiny boat? Could I manage 50 pounds of extra weight? Would it reduce my boat's freeboard to the point where, instead of dancing merrily *over* 3-foot swells, the boat would dive into them, sea water would rush over the bow, breach the combing, and pour into the cockpit, swamping my small vessel when I'm a mile offshore? I was very possibly headed for conditions not intended for my boat's design.

I was awake as the light started to come up on Day 2. The night had not provided relief from the heat. I lay on top of my sheet, on my back, with limbs spread apart, and I was sweating. If I stopped after just two days, it meant that next summer, I would have to row the 450 miles remaining to Charleston in one marathon effort, something for which I had neither the time nor strength. Or heart. Then a thought appeared. What if I chose a different final destination, one not quite so far down the coast? I had yet to announce the fundraiser, so I was free to frame the journey as I wished. Originally, I thought I would row New York to Miami, but, after learning just how slow a rowboat moves, I decided that was out of the question. So, I scaled back to Charleston, South Carolina. That seemed doable, and it was a recognizable destination. The question now was whether there is anything with that kind of cachet closer at hand. I ran down a mental map of the coast. Nothing presented itself. Then I thought, Cape Hatteras. Flat-out famous for shipwrecks. Rounding Cape Hatteras is regularly remarked in maritime adventure stories. But it was close, too close, just another three to four days down the coast.

Wait. I could finish off this whole bloody escapade in a smart 4 days next summer? The idea took hold. Later that morning, as I prepared to disembark for Day 2, I checked on the storm. It was barreling toward Florida, due to make a direct hit on the Outer Banks in 72 hours. I composed a text to family members saying I was likely going to suspend this year's trip after today. I read it to myself. Hesitated a moment. Then I hit send.

Since starting these multi-year adventures, first biking, then rowing, I learned to recognize a feeling of dread that hovered during the winter months and all through the spring as I prepared for the next leg of the trip. It was a fear of the unknown. How steep, really, are those mountains I'd have to cross? What would the road conditions be like? Would there be heavy traffic with no shoulder and blind turns? How many miles a day would I have to ride to get the job done? What if I injured myself just before departure? Just how wide are those bays I'd have to row across? Can I row faster than the current that wants to suck me out to sea? What happens when lightning strikes a boat? Is the 18 feet of carbon fiber in my oars a big welcome sign to lightning bolts? Will I be able to find enough fresh water? The dread of all the unanswerable questions would sometimes wake me up in the middle of the night or suddenly drop-in uninvited during the day in the midst of a happy thought. It was a mostly unwelcome feeling, but, on the plus side, it pushed me to find answers and solutions where I could. I read accounts online by cyclists who had ridden over the northern cascades. It didn't sound impossible. One spring, training for the next bike ride, my right knee started acting up in a serious way. I practiced riding with just my left leg and installed a false pedal on the right side of my bike where I could rest my right leg when necessary, and I got a cortisone shot in my right knee just before I started the trip.

For rowing, I read extensively about lightning and small boats and designed a small, floating, inflated ring with a metal pole sticking up in the middle that would follow behind my boat with a 100-foot line. The idea was the lightning bolt would choose the metal pole, topped with a nice, tasty hunk of copper plumbing pipe, over me. In the end, I left that contraption behind. It was too heavy and took up too much space, and, despite the dire warnings I read everywhere about small boats and lightning, I hadn't read any actual accounts of people in small boats getting fried by a lightning bolt. Through all the night sweats, panic attacks, and problem solving over the last few years, I developed a feel for the kinds of problems that were manageable and the kind that were not. I was confident this current problem was of the second kind.

I rowed that second day through Currituck Sound, 25 miles to Kitty Hawk, site of the Wright Brothers' first flight. I stayed at my Airbnb as planned. Meanwhile, Isaias was crossing Florida with devastating effects. We'd likely have one more day of calm before the storm hit. The couple running the Airbnb was very kind. He, 81 years young, offered to drive me back to my truck which was parked 50 miles north at the campground where I'd started. On the ride, we discussed boats and Donald Trump most of the way. He supported Trump and I tried to keep the conversation on boats. I asked him about tides at the Oregon Inlet, which I'd have to row past next summer on my way to Cape Hatteras. I'd heard they can be fierce, I said. He proceeded to tell how years ago he was in his aluminum skiff with an 18 horse Evinrude. He was fishing well into the sound, over a mile from the Inlet, when his boat got pulled and pulled toward the cut. He started up the outboard to get away but it was too late. He got sucked right through to the outside where he managed to tie up to a red nun until the tide changed, and he rode it back in.

The next day, the Governor of North Carolina ordered an evacuation of Hatteras Island, where I would have been in a couple more days. When the Hurricane hit two days later, I was just arriving back home with the boat strapped to the truck's roof. Down south, there was significant destruction. Boats were scrambled in marinas. Extensive flooding from the tidal surge damaged homes and destroyed vehicles. Winds reached 100 miles an hour, and six confirmed tornadoes touched down in North Carolina. Meanwhile, I was already starting to obsess about Oregon Inlet, where I'd be next summer, fueled by my driving companion's story, which I suspect was embellished but still scared me. At the same time, I was happy that the final leg would be just three to four days along a mostly smooth, beachy coastline with resort accommodations and a fun summer vacation feel. I announced the fundraiser in the fall. It had been 10 years since the first round on my bike, and the scholarship had grown to $35 thousand. The goal was to double the endowment. Again, two generous family members offered a matching grant that spurred on others, and, by the time, next summer rolled around, we'd met the goal, and all I had to do now was get in my boat and row.

I like success and I like having fun. I like them both too much, I guess, to be a true, world class adventurer. While I find the ordeals I read in books about Everest and ocean crossings thrilling, I also know the level of pain and the physically and mentally battering conditions such adventures entail is beyond me. Faced with the likely failure of a coastal row to Miami, I restored hope by simply scaling the trip back to Charleston, South Carolina. When failure at that goal loomed, I scaled it back again to Cape Hatteras. What if Tenzing Norgay and Edmund Hillary had decided it was too much to summit Everest and, instead, they decided to just go halfway up? What if Tania Aebi, instead of sailing around the world, decided to sail around Florida? What if Tori Murden, instead of rowing across the Atlantic, rowed from Cape Cod to Nantucket? There would be no book. Not the usual kind, anyway. Not the kind that celebrates the absolute scale of the feat. But where there is an adventure, there is a story. Where there is an uncertain outcome, personal challenge, risk, stakes, and conflict, there's a story between the challenge and the person who takes it on.

I make no claim to World Class. I enjoy a good adventure, and I like to challenge my abilities, and I'll push my limits, but I have other goals and commitments that I wish not to abandon in the singular pursuit of the apparently impossible. Tenzing, Tania, and Tori—I'm full of admiration for what you've accomplished. You inspire me. And I am not you. I also, quite frankly, want to have fun. Laying face down in a swill of vomit for days on end is not fun. Slowly succumbing to frostbite and losing several fingers is not fun. Sitting becalmed in the middle of an ocean for weeks with nothing left to do but desiccate in the equatorial sun is also not fun.

Chapter 18
Cape Hatteras

The last leg of what was now officially a fundraising trip from New York City to Cape Hatteras was shaping up to be both a solid physical challenge and a fun ride along a coastline of summer cottages and summertime vacationing. To my surprise, however, the physical challenge turned out to be more than planned, perhaps the greatest I've ever faced. But this summer there would be no turning back, no scaling back either. I had to succeed. I had no choice. Hundreds of people had donated to an important cause. I had pledged to row the boat to a named destination. The stakes were high. I simply had to get it done.

I've already described my harrowing first day of this final leg, rowing into a full gale. What I haven't told is how it ended and what followed in the days meant to carry me to my destination. Where I left off the tale of that first day, I was surfing a wild swell toward a certain collision with some expensive yacht docked in the harbor at Oregon Inlet. That's where we'll pick it up. As you may recall, the wind, with gusts to 54 miles an hour, was piling up the waves behind me and those waves were rocketing me into the tangle of docked boats. I recalled, from a harbor diagram I'd looked at the day before, that the state boat ramp, where I wanted to end up was to the left as you enter the harbor. That's where I steered, to the extent I could steer. I managed to pull the boat that way and where the harbor split, I took the left fork. Then something amazing happened. The wind dropped. I got a little farther and the wind dropped more. Soon I was rowing in a moderate breeze across water that was merely choppy. The state dock and ramp, several in a row, actually, came into view. A few minutes later I was disembarking, which is close to the word dismembering, which is how it felt after 10 hours, butt to seat, bending and pulling. The math says 170 strokes per 10 minutes for 10 hours come to 10,200 strokes. Imagine sitting in a rowing machine for 10 hours straight, pulling at a steady pace against maximum resistance. Imagine an earthquake continuously heaving the ground underneath. Oh, and it's raining the whole time, and somebody you can't see throws buckets of seawater at your back every few minutes. Like that. It was not days-on-end of vomit swill, but it might be the hardest thing I've ever done. I got the boat situated on its dolly and pulled it a half mile through cold rain at 7:30p.m. to the State Campground where I had a reservation.

I took my time getting started on Day 2. Sore everywhere from yesterday's ordeal, I slept in until 7 a.m., made a good breakfast of instant oatmeal with a cut-up apple and two crumbled, oatmeal raisin cookies added. Drank a mug of tea. It was still windy but no rain, thank goodness. The wind was blowing from the ocean-facing dune over my shoulder, out of the northeast. That meant it reversed overnight. I'd be rowing in a following sea, which would push me away from the inlet. Oregon Inlet, a half mile tear in the Outer Banks with shifting shoals, strong, clashing currents, and boat traffic like an interstate, or so I'd been told. I'd be crossing the mouth of Oregon Inlet on my journey south with the goal of not getting sucked in or crashing with a commercial vessel or getting flipped over by a breaking wave on a shoal.

I pack up and, by 10 a.m., I'm ready to roll. I look around the campsite for anything I've left behind, I look at the boat, where everything appears to be in order. I check for my oars. Wait. What? My oars. Where are my oars? Oh crud. Oh crud, my oars are on the dock where I placed them as I was preparing to disembark last night. In the wind and the rain and my brain-fogged weariness, I forgot to collect them. They've been there all night in a storm. There's no fence on those docks, just planks and then water. If an oar blade or maybe the nine foot shank of the oar itself were propelled by the wind, they'd drop into the harbor and who knows where they'd go from there. There's also traffic on those docks. No telling how many vessels have already launched this morning. A couple of nice-looking carbon fiber oars? What are the chances someone nabs them? On the other hand, they're no good unless you have a sliding seat boat. Someone seeing them might think the owner left them there for just a few minutes and will be back shortly to get them. Maybe someone saw them sitting there for a while and turned them in at the bait shop or the Coast Guard station. If my oars are gone, I think, this trip is over. I feel a little, guilty wave of relief, and then dread. I'd have to come back in August, middle of hurricane season, to finish. I'd have to worry for another month about crossing Oregon Inlet. I grab the PVC handle at the bow of my boat and start to pull. Shortly, I'm at the far end of the parking lot by the waterfront. I can make out the piers of the boat ramps. I pick up my pace and strain to make sense of the jumble of clutter at the water's edge. Now the docks themselves and the ramps are coming into view. Far as I can see from here, no oars. I get closer, I can make out the individual finger docks that separate each of the five ramps. No oars. But I can't see all the way to the end of each dock. Now I'm closer. I can see all five docks, all the way to the end. No oars. No, wait. What's that? At the very end of. Could it be? I get closer. Yes, there they are. Pushed by the wind to the end of the dock and somehow, miraculously, still there. I set down the bow of the boat and jog stiffly to the dock and out to the end. The oars are just sitting there, like no big deal. Here we are, right where you left us. What did you expect? I breathe a sigh of relief and turn immediately to the challenge ahead—crossing Oregon Inlet.

A sport fisherman with tanned leathery skin is pulling his boat, decked out with rods, and two big outboards, maybe 30 feet, with his pickup, out of the harbor. He clears the ramp and sea water pours off the trailer. He stops the truck, hops out and walks once around the boat to check. I catch his eye.

"Good morning," I say cheerfully. "Are you familiar with these waters?" He nods. "Any advice for me? I plan to cross the inlet in my rowboat. I'm heading south to Cape Hatteras on the inside."

He pauses, looks at me, looks at my boat. "You're gonna cross with that?"

I nod.

"Launch from the other side," he says. I process this comment. He continues, "Currents go miles into that sound, and the other boats won't see you. Drive it over the bridge and launch it from the other side." There's a dramatic, ribbon-like highway of a bridge that rises high over the inlet and goes a good 3 miles before easing back down on the southern side. He offers a few more scary prognostications, which I acknowledge, and thank him for his advice. Which I plan to ignore. Shortly, I am rowing out of the harbor. My plan is to use the gentle arc of the bridge and its shadow as my route planner. I'll roughly follow the shadow line, leaving it a quarter mile to my right. I figure I can't go too far wrong. The wind and waves are calmer this morning. I've rowed currents. As I enter the deeper water, swells are 2-3 feet. Steep but manageable. With the wind in my face, it's a following sea, but with less force behind it than last night, the maneuvering is not as hard. I wait for the pull of the inlet's current, ready to turn sharp west at the first indication of anything strong. No current I can detect. But, in the now deeper water, the waves are a mess, coming from all directions, and there are boats, big motorboats with towers, rocking back and forth, and fishing rods hanging off the stern and both sides. Enough boats that I need to keep an eye out where I'm headed and where they're headed. I have a near run-in with one. As I approach, the skipper is looking at me, waving his hands. Then he does a what's-your-plan gesture with his arms, scrunching his shoulders. His boat is in the deep water of the channel, near the edge. I see the lighter colored water of a shoal off his stern. I decide I'll pass off his stern between him and the shoal. That way I avoid rowing further into the channel where there's more likelihood of trouble. I look at him, I point to me, then I point to his stern, and I head that way. As I approach, he's waving his arms like mad. I pull into shouting distance.

"I've got fishing lines off my stern! Go around!" He points to his bow. "You're gonna mess 'em all up!"

I get it and wave my understanding. I execute a quick turn, pulling hard on the starboard oar and come around his bow. I can see he's shaking his head in disbelief at my stupidity.

I call, "Sorry 'bout that."

He waves an arm which looks like a combination of "Thank you" and "You're an idiot."

It takes an hour to clear Oregon Inlet. The main worry it turns out is shoaling. My boat can move through a bare six inches of water. Running aground is not the issue. It's breaking waves. If the water suddenly gets shallow, and I'm right there, and a breaking wave hits me broadside, it could tip me over. I keep a sharp eye, and gradually as I move beyond the inlet, the wind slows, the swells soften, and I find myself rowing placidly with a gentle following breeze. I notice ahead of me shallows that appear to extend pretty far offshore. I follow the line where the weedy bottom starts to come to the surface, which I start to notice is at an angle to the shoreline taking me further into the sound. Soon I find myself a good mile offshore. If I keep it up, I'll wind up, eventually, on the other side of the sound. Not a good plan, I decide, and turn my boat parallel to the shoreline, rowing into the expansive shallows, like many football fields covered with a few bare inches of water. There's risk that the tide will go further out, leaving me stranded a mile from the beach for the next 6 hours or more, but I notice the bottom is weedy. If it was exposed at low tide, it wouldn't have all those weeds growing on it. I spend the afternoon like this, rowing the shallows, wondering if I'll get stuck. At several points, the depth narrows to a scant five inches. My boat scrapes bottom. I have boots, I note. I put them on, climb out and, with the boat 150 pounds lighter, it no longer scrapes bottom, and I can pull it, walking dry-footed through the shallow water—a very pleasant break from rowing. And with my nearly knee-high rubber boots, I don't have to worry about sharp objects or stinging, biting beasts under all those weeds that I just might happen to step on. I spend an enjoyable afternoon alternately rowing and pulling. My fear of getting stuck at low tide dissipates as we approach low tide and the shallows mostly remain with a good nine inches of water or more, with no sandbars.

I spent the night at a friendly, shoreline campground. Next day, same conditions: a gentle following breeze, hot sun, but not brutal Carolina hot the way it can get. I rowed into the afternoon. My whole body ached, worst of all was my hands and wrists. The hardest part was starting up again after a 3-minute break for hydration—watered down Gatorade—and some salty mixed nuts. During those few minutes, everything tightened up in wrists and fingers making any motion, especially motion combined with muscle effort, downright painful. I gingerly pushed the oars outboard, then placed a hand on each one, barely grasping it, letting my fingers fall into a natural curl around the rubber handle. I slid forward, the oar blades pivoted back, I twisted the handles—a Ping! of pain—I dropped the blades into the water and pulled. The correct approach for pulling on the oar is not to grasp it firmly but to hold it loosely in the curl of your fingers. The pulling motion holds it so there is no need to grasp. Good thing because grasping was not a strong point today. Pulling felt okay, no strained muscles there, which is strange because that's where 90% of the muscle work happens. At the end of 10 hours of continuous full-on effort, the muscles in my back, arms, legs, and abdomen felt not so bad. It was my wrists and my fingers that fell apart. Here's why: at the end of a long pull, the oar handles are right up against your solar plexus and your upper body is leaning way back. In that position, you need to flick your wrists to turn the oar blades parallel to the water just before the return slide that readies you for the next stroke. It's that flick of the wrist executed in a highly unnatural orientation of wrist to hand to fingers, alternating with the intense muscle work of the pull, repeated thousands of times in the course of a day of hard rowing that did me in. Ten thousand strokes in 10 hours. Way too much unnatural wrist flicking and maybe a touch of arthritis.

So, there I was, three days in, with the weather blowing perfectly in the direction I needed to go and I could barely hold the oars. How do some people row across an entire ocean? I managed to lose the use of two limbs in just three days on a protected body of water. Just then, the wind picked up, there was a bit of a swell, maybe one foot, which meant I needed to mind the oars to keep stern to the weather. This distracted me from my pathetic little aches and pains. After a few more tentative strokes, the pinging in my wrists dulled, or maybe I got used to it, and the boat began moving at a good clip. My left wrist was swollen. I'd wrapped it in white medical tape (Laurie: "Take this. You might need it.") on Day 2. Conveniently, the wind on Day 2 was oriented so I had to pull harder with my right arm, which meant that by day's end, it was sore and swollen, too. Day 3, with both forearms and wrists taped and swollen and very tender, I'd headed out and rowed a following sea for 4 hours, 16.5 miles to Avon. The conditions couldn't have been more perfect. For 90 percent of the journey, sea and wind were exactly astern. Especially notable because my compass heading changed several times. Due south, then south by southwest, then southwest, then south again. Like that, wind and compass-heading shifting in tandem, all the way to Avon.

Later, walking from the Avon marina, where I stashed the boat, every third house had a "Thank you Jesus" sign, with no comma, perched in the front yard. Shortly I arrived at my campground. "Thank you Jesus" stood in front of the building that said, "Office." It hurt to carry the reusable grocery bag that held my essentials for the night. Later that evening, my hands and wrists had the dexterity of a claw. Using both hands, I was able to hold my toothbrush well enough to run it lightly across my teeth. No way would I be able to row a boat tomorrow. The heck with it. I'd walk the last six miles, straight down highway 12 to the Swell Motel, where I had a reservation. Then, on Saturday, with Laurie, as planned, we'd walk across the narrow barrier island to the Cape Hatteras Lighthouse, with its barber pole paint job of black and white stripes. Could I row it? A bare maybe. And most likely I'd do long term damage to my 62-year-old body. Not worth it. So, like a penitent, I'd walk. Maybe on my knees. But I'd get there, under muscle power alone.

Dear Friends, Colleagues and Family Members,

We did it! And I mean we! On Friday, a homemade rowboat carrying one passenger and the unspoken hopes of future students who will benefit from the Mary, Joan, and Nancy Scholarship came ashore on a beach near Cape Hatteras, North Carolina, concluding a journey that began with the boat's construction in 2016, and continued over four summers and 500 miles of travel from Conference House Park on Staten Island. Together, our team, 378 strong, have raised $70,000 so far, which boosts the annual scholarship to nearly $3,000, a sum that will be available every year, in perpetuity.

Thank you! Whether you donated money or sent your well wishes, whispered a prayer, or gave a thought to the challenges faced by many first-generation college students, felt gratitude for a care giver in your family, or, perhaps, remembered a teacher who made a difference in your life, you have contributed!

The final stretch was arduous. I rowed into a gale for 10 hours on Day 1. Nearly lost my oars on Day 2, and grappled with painful swelling in my wrists and fingers (How do some people row an entire ocean?). By the end of Day 3, my fingers were stiff, and I could no longer hold the oars. I beached the boat and walked the last six miles. My brief physical challenge is a small reminder of the major life-challenges so many of our first-generation students endure, and surmount, in getting themselves to college and seeing themselves through to graduation.

This fundraising campaign will continue through the end of July, as we share the news of the successful rowing journey. Please tell a friend about this opportunity to support first-generation students, honor caregivers, or remember a favorite teacher who made a difference. Remember, all contributions are doubled through an anonymous matching gift. With oars at rest and a heart full of gratitude.

Sincerely,

Jim

Chapter 19
Deeper Meaning

Adventure is a powerful source of learning. Repelling off a cliff or kayaking a giant ocean swell are, for most people, so outside their ordinary routines that, having once done them, they serve as emotional touchstones that can last for years. Couple the experience with instruction about overcoming your fears and taking on new challenges and you get personal transformation with long term impact. The fact research bears this out is no real surprise. Meanwhile, however, our schools mostly fail to tap into this powerful source of learning. At school, we increasingly turn our back to the outdoors, imaginative play, unstructured time, and reflective thought. Society as a whole is becoming more sedentary. We are systematically robbing ourselves of the physical, mental, and emotional benefit of the kinds of experiences for which a million years of evolution has designed us.

So, here I've been in the Great Outdoors, risking life and limb, refusing to succumb to a world narrowed to the dimensions of my laptop's Zoom screen, my email inbox, and short drives from air-conditioned home to box store shopping mall. Have I accrued any of these benefits? Having taken the progressive ideas that define my career—real world problem solving, expeditionary learning, follow your passion—and turned them on myself, have I learned anything?

I can attest that fear of injury or death in a small boat definitely takes the stress out of workplace problems. All the time I was worrying about tidal currents on the Navesink that might drown me, or riptides in the Oregon Inlet carrying my boat out to sea, was time spent <u>not</u> worrying whether there'd be an instructor for every course the School of Education was required to offer in the upcoming fall semester. Same was true about the possibility of a lightning strike during a five-mile crossing, capsize by a monster wave, or meeting up suddenly, mid-channel, with the towering hull of a container ship in a thick fog. All those dangerous prospects made the ornery personality of that colleague I'd have to confront so much less of an issue, as well as the four student complaints against a junior instructor I was managing, or the relentlessly bureaucratic administrator one level above me, blocking every good idea that came their way.

And I was discovering that, even in my seventh decade. I could still learn new stuff. I knew nothing about fiberglass or boatbuilding until a panel truck dropped off four boxes and I learned how, from a pile of boards, a thick instruction manual, a bunch of random Youtube videos, and 200 hours in my garage. Also, I learned I can set, work toward, and accomplish a long-term goal of considerable scale. From the time I looked out my office window at rowboats on the Merrimack and wondered about a water-borne adventure, to my arrival at Cape Hatteras, was a total of six years. In between, I learned to row, built a boat, planned a voyage, figured out a million details, revised a half a million details, raised a bunch of money, and rowed 500 miles. I was learning I could solve problems, too. My garage was too cold to build a boat. So, I built an insulated shop space with a steady temperature, through the winter months, of 65 degrees.

Also, I was learning something about personal preferences. In the future, if I want to get somewhere under my own steam, I think I'll bike or walk. Rowing is a lot more work to cover the same distance. I was learning, also, how to define a goal and manage progress toward it. My goal, really, was never to row to Miami. My goal was to complete a multi-leg rowing trip that felt to me like an awful lot and sounded to other people like something big enough that they would donate money for a scholarship fundraiser. When plans for Miami turned out to be unrealistic, I scaled it back, ultimately, to Cape Hatteras, which it turned out, still felt like an awful lot to me and was impressive sounding enough to my donors. I was learning something about priorities, too. I could have made the longer trip, but it would have entailed greater risk. I could have made this a 10-year project, but I have other things I want to do with my life. I could have pushed myself to row the final 6 miles closer to the Cape Hatteras Lighthouse, but I might have done real, permanent damage to my hands and wrists. As it was, both arms spent a month in braces after I returned home. I wish to live, as best as I am able, a long, fulfilling life with functioning limbs, and varied experiences. Keeping my body from needless damage and devoting my time and energy to things other than any particular adventure, are ingredients in achieving that goal. Elite athletes and world class adventurers have different priorities. They will devote ALL to the singular pursuit of X. And when they achieve it, they win a place in the record book. I, on the other hand, will conclude my life with no world records. I could say that's my choice, except, even if I really and truly tried, it's unlikely I'd actually achieve anything world record-worthy.

I did not plan on writing a screed against contemporary education. But, as I said in the opening pages, the studying I did during my sabbatical, after I'd completed the three adventures chronicled here, constituted the fourth adventure of the book's title. Like all true adventures, the outcome would be uncertain.

Maybe it was the open-ended aspect of my sabbatical questions—What is the nature of adventure? What is the relationship between adventure and learning—coupled with the psychic distance from work routines that a sabbatical provides, and which a slightly dangerous rowing trip down the east coast offers, that unearthed some deeper reflections on what, really, we are doing in our schools. I have deep roots in a progressive vision of schooling that is sharply at odds with what passes for education these days. All of that came bubbling to the surface. My fresh experience with adventure and the research I read on the nature of adventure confirmed my deeper convictions, and I'm newly persuaded that what we're doing in schools is by and large the opposite of what we ought to be doing. Sir Ken Robinson, a British educator, now deceased, was an ardent advocate for the arts and the central role that creativity *should* play in education. In a memorable lecture captured in a YouTube video that is both entertaining and devastating, he demonstrates that the longer children spend in school, the less creative they become. [80]

I have a brother who lives largely off the grid. He and his wife home-schooled all their children with brilliant results. While I do not embrace their separatist lifestyle, I find my visits to their farm and conversations with them always refreshing. I'll call my brother Tom because he doesn't like it when I use his real name in stuff I write. Tom has a lot to say about food and where it comes from. What most people, not his family, eat is "industrial" food. He regularly points out the environmental and health problems associated with the way American society, in general, produces "industrial" crops: mono-cultural farming, petroleum-based fertilizer, poison-laced insecticides, highly processed products. These are features of large-scale production systems. Our schools are no different. They are part of a system of mass production. We batch-process our children by grade levels that are poor proxies for developmental stages. Instead of teaching individuals, we teach types. We teach "ELs" (English Learners) and "SPED" (special education) students with "strategies" that are "targeted" for demographic groups. Against the better judgement of our teachers who wish to connect with their students and nurture growth through relationship-building, the system insists on treating children like widgets. I've written elsewhere about how to change all this.[81] And, approaching the traditional age of retirement as I write this book, I increasingly find myself thinking it is time to hand off the work to a younger generation of rebels to go out there and make good trouble.

Feeling reflective as I write this, and, seeing as this part of the book is a reflective-style chapter, and seeing as adventure writers are expected to explore the "deeper meaning" of their adventures, I feel compelled, somewhat against my wishes, to move into the "deeper-meaning" part of this chapter.

I have a writer friend who asks, "What are you afraid to write about?" It's a question he regularly asks himself, and which, clearly, he takes seriously. His books are filled with stunning personal revelations. His books are also critically acclaimed, in part, because he asks that question and answers it so well in the pages he writes.

On several occasions, he's asked me, "What are you afraid to write about?" True answer: a lot! Frankly, though, some things I'm afraid to write about, I won't ever write about because they have to do with people I love and care for, and writing about them would be devastating to them, to me, to us. It would be a betrayal. Maybe that's why some writers write novels. They get to share stuff, transposed by fiction, that they would never share with true names, identifying details, and accurate descriptions.

But there are other things I'm afraid to write about that have nothing to do with protecting people I love.

Adventure writers, at some point in their writing, are generally expected to explore the "deeper meaning" of their quest. I've pondered this aspect of my chosen genre and am dreading writing about it because, from the department of deeper meanings, I actually have very little to report. I know that, as an adventurer, I am supposed to return from my hazardous journey with a "boon," something that will save humanity, or, at least, maybe, constitute an original insight. Here's the thing I'm afraid to write about: I don't have anything original to say, except, maybe that the whole idea of deeper meanings is over-rated. Why do we need deeper meanings anyway? Isn't living meaningful enough without having to slide something deeper under it? If I have a nice breakfast of blueberry pancakes, do I really need to find a deeper meaning?

We have a quarter board that hangs on the wall above the stove. It's eye catching when you sit at the kitchen table, which is where most social activity in our house happens. It says, "Live well. Laugh often. Love much." One of my daughters has said on more than one occasion that it's dumb. I'm guessing others who see it might think the same thing. It looks like something you'd buy in a resort town gift "shoppe". That's where I got it, actually, but I like it. I think it pretty much covers all the bases. When I was growing up, there was a pewter serving platter in our house that surfaced now and then and it had a Spanish saying that went, "Salud, Amor, y Pesetas, y tiempo para disfrutarlas." The translation is, "Health, love, and money, and time to enjoy them." Same kind of message. I like it, too. So, I've been trying to think about life's deeper meaning and what my adventuring has taught me about it. I'm not sure there is a deeper meaning. Maybe the living is all there is. And that's plenty good.

Except when it's not, which I sometimes think about as I enjoy my adventuring surrounded by that force-field of privilege. It's something I became even more aware of during my readings on my sabbatical journey and since then. Civil rights leader Fannie Lou Hamer said, "Nobody's free until everybody's free." There is a great deal of work to be done to make the world of adventuring more inclusive, more accessible to everyone, not to mention society in general. In my kitchen quarter board, the "Love much" is more than just squooshy sentiment. It's an imperative to heal the world. That can feel daunting, overwhelming, which is why I also remind myself no one heals the whole world. You do what you can in your corner of the universe. I have a favorite passage from the Talmud, which says, roughly, *you are not responsible to complete the work of creation, but neither are you free to abandon it.*[82] So, there's my take on deeper meaning. Not so deep. Seems like it's all right there, all right on the surface, if you just pay attention.

On the other hand.

There are moments, episodes, when, even if I'm not seeking a deeper meaning, something like it surfaces and finds me. In Japan, people talk about ikigai, the pursuit of purpose, which brings deep joy. It's been popularized as the idea that we can all find meaning by locating the intersection of what we love and are good at, with what the world needs. And when we find that connection, sometimes, the moment expands beyond the sum of its parts. Martin Buber, the Jewish mystic philosopher drew a distinction between the world of *experience* and the world of *relation*. In the world of experience, he wrote, we observe merely. In the world of relation, we enter in, with living presence. *Experience*, he said is the world of "I-it", and *relation* is the world of "I-Thou." *I and Thou* was the title of his most famous book.⁸³ *Thou* may be a friend or an intimate partner or a room full of people, or, in a transcendent moment, something like the universe. So, I guess I'm of two minds about this deeper meaning business. Maybe what's true is that if you spend your days trying to find it, you're chasing a chimera, but if you strive to live well and generously, in relationship, and not just by accumulating experiences, it finds you.

There's another side to the deeper meaning question, that's not quite visible if you're looking just at the "living well" aspect or spirituality *per se*. It's the meditative state I was learning to achieve from repetitive physical motion. I'd encountered it cycling and rowing. It was distinct and apart from anything I'd previously experienced. Little did I know, all these ideas would move front and center on the road to Santiago.

Part III
Walk to Santiago de Compostela

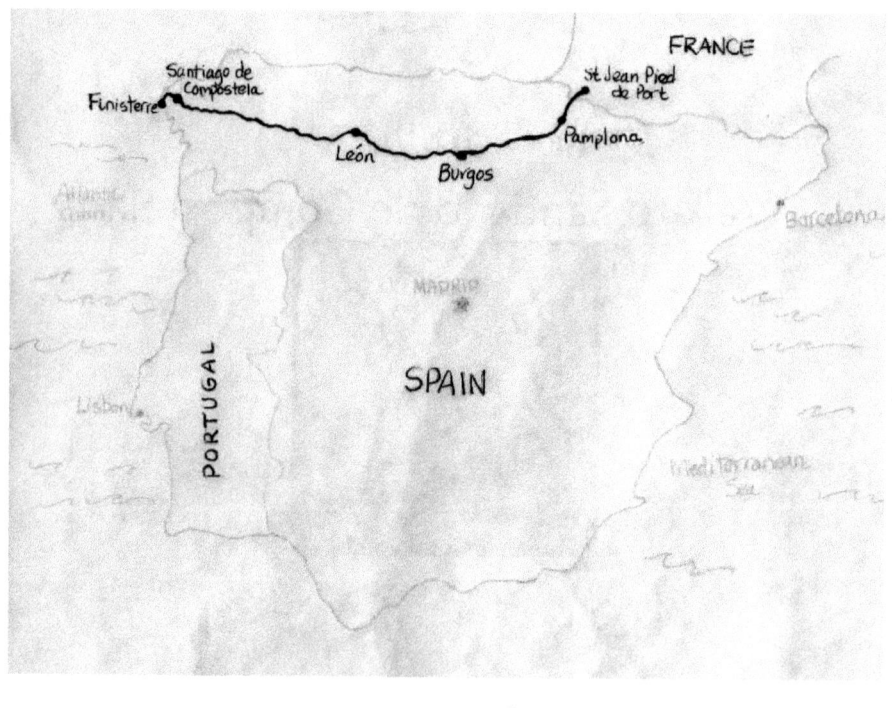

Chapter 20
Soy Pellegrino

I push back the chair at the little desk in my hotel room where I've been sitting for an hour, journaling. It's day 19 of my walk. My plan is to reach Santiago in 29 days, tag the Cathedral, then go three more days to the Atlantic Coast, to a place called Cape Finisterre, literally the "end of the Earth." That's what early pilgrims on the Camino believed. Most modern pilgrims finish in Santiago at the broad plaza of flat, fitted stones worn smooth by a thousand years of tired feet. There, weary souls gaze up at the towering, ornate façade of the Romanesque church that holds the bones of St. James. They stand in awe as much at the majestic sight before them as the 500-mile trek across northern Spain they have just completed. For me, Finisterre will be the icing on the cake, the extra mile, so to speak, that will put me a notch above the average pilgrim.

YAACK! A shooting pain spreads around my left hip. I drop back in my seat. I wait a beat and try again. Slow and easy. Easy does it. I get half-way up and … WHAM! The same sharp pain radiating in all directions from my left hip forces me to drop back to my seat, sending a second jolt—YEOW—on the way down.

Okay, this pain is serious. But where did it come from? So far, I've felt the usual little aches and pains for most of the Camino, nothing major. What's been worrying me, if anything, is the cold I caught a week ago and can't shake. During the last two days I've picked up a phlegmy cough. Like the cold-that-won't-go-away is turning into something worse, bronchitis maybe. Other pilgrims have been experiencing the same. "Camino cough" they say and dismiss it like it's something everybody gets at some point. No big deal.

Seated, I lean my torso over the desk and try again, rising in a semi-crouch. Halfway up, WHAM! The pain hits me like a hammer blow in my left hip. I ease back into my seat. Feeling a little panicky, I re-group and try again, in the same crouch but, this time, with my back arched — pelvis rolled forward. I slowly rise. No pain. I keep going, straightening my torso to the vertical as I go, still rolling my pelvis forward. I'm standing, straight and tall. No pain. I head toward the bathroom and quickly discover that certain ordinary moves, like shifting all my weight to my left side, produce pain, but other ordinary moves, like taking small steps straightforward, I can perform without a problem. I spend the rest of the evening figuring out how to move around my hotel room as a thought cloud of gloom starts to form. Is this injury serious? Am I done? No. Can't be. This is temporary. Something got a little twisted and soon there will be a popping sound deep in my hip joint and instantly everything will return to normal. I sleep poorly that night. No position is comfortable for more than 10 minutes and moving to a new sleep position involves navigating around the still opaque logic of which muscles or joints or ligaments seem to be the problem. At midnight, after my third trip to the bathroom, mainly for something to do other than lie uncomfortably in bed, I pull out my tablet and google, "Back pain remedies Camino." A quick scan of several reliable-looking websites leads me to the hunch that this is a muscle spasm, as opposed to a joint, skeletal, or tendon issue. Okay, "spasm," I think. A spasm is just a temporary, quirky kind of malady. I read some more. There are suggested stretches and simple massages for the affected area. I experiment with both. They provide some relief. Digging my fist aggressively into the muscle tissue at the back of the pelvis seems to work best. I start to feel hopeful, like this may be a condition I can manage. The show will go on.

And it does. Maybe. By morning, the severity of the condition has diminished — enough that I can move (slowly) through my morning routines. But I worry that when it comes time to heave my backpack onto a shoulder and wiggle it into position, it will prove just too much for my spasm-ing muscle and all hell will break loose. Departure time arrives and, very gingerly, I get the backpack up on my back. It feels fine, like my body is saying, *this is what I'm used to. Let's go.* I take the elevator — which I almost never do-- down three floors, head slowly across the marble floor of the lobby and out the front door into the bright, warm Spanish day. I move deliberately. I can feel my hip is right on the edge of another spasming, and what would that be like with a 20-pound pack on my back? Would I drop my load, and would the contortions required to do that cause the spasm to spread, sending shockwaves up and down my left side? Would I fall to the ground and writhe like I was having a seizure? I cough, an unsatisfying cough that fails to pull up the phlegm I can feel has pooled somewhere in my bronchia. I'm tired, and the day has only begun. I ache. I've been averaging 30 kilometers, almost 19 miles a day, sometimes as much as 40 (25 miles), which is nearly a marathon, but there's no way I'll cover that distance today. Forget about Finisterre. I'll be lucky if I make it to Leon, let alone the great cathedral of Santiago. No icing on this cake. Maybe no cake. Maybe I'll have to quit two-thirds done, defeated by a not particularly demanding trek across the most civilized backpacking route you're likely to find, one that reliably produces a café with espresso and croissants every four kilometers, a bed and a shower at the end of the day, and abundant red wine, cheap and good. I head out into the morning, unsure what it will bring.

How did it come to be that on an early morning in June, I found myself alone, struggling to keep it together in a dusty little town in Northern Spain?

Laurie said, "Hey, ALFA has something on walking the Camino." We were in the kitchen. It was February. I was grating cheese. Laurie was at the counter going through mail. Sunlight was streaming at a low angle through the windows by the table. ALFA stands for Adult Learning in the Fitchburg Area. Run by the state college, it offers inexpensive courses in needlepoint, ballroom dancing, bowling, mystery novels, memoir writing, dog breeding, you name it. Among its offerings for the fall was a series of eight sessions on how to prepare to walk the Camino de Santiago, taught by a person who'd done it twelve times. I wondered why anyone would walk it twelve times.

Before I finished my rowing trip, I knew I wanted to do something that involved a long walk. I also knew I did not want to hike the Appalachian Trail or anything like it, i.e., remote woodlands, sleeping in a tent on the ground, humping a sixty-pound pack eight to ten hours a day, bugs, no shower, no toilet, interminable damp, and general grunge. No thanks. Not for me. More power to everyone who loves that kind of thing. I'd been vaguely aware of the Camino de Santiago for years. My niece walked it after she finished college in 2000. Then I saw the movie with Martin Sheen, *The Way*. If the Hollywood version was anywhere near the real thing, then the Camino offered physical and mental challenge plus camaraderie, in a traveling community of seekers. Plus, showers, toilets, beds, and cold beer. After watching the movie, I googled around the web and was excited to see that the Martin Sheen Camino seemed, actually, pretty close to reality. In the realm of epic quests, what was not to like about this experience? But could I walk long distances every day for many days?

Laurie's sister lives on beautiful Seneca Lake in upstate New York. We visit most summers. A week ahead of our summer trip, I undertook an experiment. I boarded a train in Boston, headed to Utica, New York, and walked west along the Erie Canal bike trail. It was flat, straight, and hot, with day-time temperatures in the 90s. It took me four-and-one-half days to go 120 miles to Geneva, a town in the heart of the Finger Lakes. On arrival, I was sore all over and run down. I had no interest in going any farther. I'd averaged 26 miles a day and realized this was not a sustainable pace. I figured maybe 18 to 20 would work. Since Camino guidebooks have everything in kilometers, I started planning for 30K a day.

Summer turned to fall. I bought a Camino guidebook and started thinking I could do this trek. I signed up for the fall semester course with the twelve-timer. It turns out that, unlike the Appalachian Trail or the Pacific Crest Trail, the Camino is not a single route. It is a web of footpaths that crisscross the Spanish countryside converging on Santiago de Compostela in the hilly Northwest. My teacher was not crazy. Walking it twelve times can take you on a different route each time. Santiago is the Spanish name for James, one of the original twelve disciples of Jesus, who, according to legend, traveled to the Iberian peninsula and preached in Galicia where the city bearing his name is located. The main origin story for the Camino centers on the supposed interment of the disciple in what is now the city. A grand cathedral was erected in the 12th century, and it has served as the destination for pilgrims for nearly 1000 years. As recently as the 1980s, only a few thousand people completed the Camino each year, but the popularity of the Camino has exploded in recent decades. In 2022, almost a half million pilgrims from around the world completed the Camino de Santiago.

My teacher for the Camino course was Karen. A former nurse, who became a therapist, she's found a calling, ministering informally to pilgrims along the Camino. Many people walk the Camino to seek healing. Karen helps them by providing first aid, comfort, and a listening ear. All through the Fall, I came home on Friday afternoons revved up from my class with Camino Karen, eager to tell Laurie everything I learned. Here is some of it:

- Most people walk 10 to 15 miles a day.
- Your backpack should have good padding on hips and shoulders; nothing bigger than 40 liters. If you pack only what you need, it should weigh 10% of your body weight.
- A wide range of accommodations are available along the Camino from public albergues with dormitory style sleeping to fancy hotels. "Albergue" is equivalent to "hostel" in English-speaking countries. (Because it is the pilgrim tradition, I decided I would stay in the albergues, with maybe an occasional private hotel room thrown in for sanity.)
- Albergues are very social places. You meet people from all over the world and eat together in a shared kitchen and dining room.
- For bedding, get a silk sleep sack that has a pillow slot and opens on one side so you can get out of it. Silk repels bugs.
- Make all reservations for your accommodations before starting the trip. The Camino has become that popular. If you use an app like Booking.com, you can usually cancel reservations later if your plans change. (The wisdom of this advice later became clear from my first day on the Camino as I observed pilgrims who had not booked accommodations frantically calling ahead.)
- Luggage transport is regularly available from point to point along the Camino. Arrange it the night before. It costs about 10 euros. Good to keep in mind if you injure yourself and can walk but can't carry a load.

- Ear plugs are a must for the crowded dormitories, and some people wear eye masks.
- Bring your own toilet paper and soap—don't expect the low price albergues to have any.
- Bring your own towel.
- Handwash your laundry every day—bring some line to make a private clothesline to hang in your bunk if it's raining or there's no shared line available.
- In May - June, when I was planning to go, the average low temperature along the Camino is 48 degrees; the average high is 73.
- Beware of bed bugs. In general, it is okay to trust bed sheets, which get washed fresh for each customer, but maybe not a comforter or blanket.
- Many Spaniards eat dinner as late as 10 p.m., but most pilgrims are in bed by then. Many restaurants have an inexpensive "pilgrim dinner" or *menu del dia* (menu of the day) available earlier, which includes a three course meal with wine, up to 7 p.m., just before the regular dinner crowd starts to show up.
- In bigger towns, restaurants are open during siesta; but in many towns, everything is closed from about 2 p.m. to about 5 p.m.
- Use ATMs that are attached to a bank, not free-standing, when the bank is open so that help is available if the machine eats your card or there is some other difficulty.
- Travel with two different credit cards and two different debit cards.

In a letter that Karen wrote me after we got to know each other, she added the following:

- "Shoes should have a good tread for shale in some spots and mountain passes and for when it is wet; a high boot is not needed; low cuts are okay. Waterproof is not recommended—

feet sweat. Feet just get wet sometimes; you just walk with it; you want shoes that will dry fairly quickly.

- "Do not bring any type of heavyweight water bottles or hydration systems. The weight makes no sense and systems are generally difficult to fill in some places and hard to clean properly. I simply buy larger bottled water with sip tops and refill them a few times until they look compromised. Those bottles are the lightest I've found and serve the purpose. I tote drink powders (Gatorade, Propel) to restore electrolytes and use one bottle specifically for that.
- "I bring a lightweight poncho. I have a heavier one for fall/late fall walking but make do with a travel one in warmer weather. My thought is you don't want your pack, especially the padded pack straps, to get wet. In driving rain, no raincoat/umbrella/rainfly/dry sack combo will keep your stuff dry. You don't want to spend your evening trying to dry out your pack (and if it's still raining, there will not be an outside line)."

The final three bits of advice Karen gave were a little cryptic, but became clear later when I walked the Camino:

- "Everyone you meet along the way is a lesson or a blessing."
- "It's your Camino."
- "The Camino provides."

Part way through the Camino course, I drew up a list of stuff for my bag, using Karen's highly evolved packing list. I bought myself a new backpack for Christmas and spent the winter months gathering and fussing over gear. Around February, I started walking nearly every day, at least three miles, sometimes six or seven. I bought my airline ticket and, come April, I was ready to go.

They say a journey of 1,000 miles begins with a single step. Actually, it starts way before that, especially if the starting line is a remote town in the French Pyrenees, called Saint Jean Pied de Port. Here's what I had to do just to get to the famous *single step*. Leave house in Central Massachusetts and walk to train station. Take train to Porter Square in Cambridge. Transfer to subway Red Line and ride seven stops to South Station. Transfer to Sliver Line, ride to airport, Terminal B, American Airlines. Walk upstairs and check in at American Airlines Kiosk, proceed through TSA screening—always fraught and rushed. Head to gate to make sure it's the right gate and the time posted is what I think it should be, then wait. American Airlines agent shows up at gate. Ask her if the seats I'm assigned—Boston to New York; New York to Madrid—are aisle seats.

She says, "Yes.

I say, "Hooray!" My bladder says Hooray!

Buy a tea at Starbucks, find a seat where it's not too crowded and read my Pilgrim Guide. Feel slightly bored, slightly nervous, and slightly celebratory. I'm super-early for my flight. Put away Pilgrim guide and cross the hall to a bar and order a martini. Chat with guy on barstool next to me who is headed to Fort Worth, Texas, where he goes twice a month and, otherwise, works remotely at home in Plymouth, MA. Ponder how the world has changed since Covid. Go to gate. Sit there. Watch people. Stylish-looking woman next to me is headed to Mexico with awkward teenager. Daughter? My flight starts to board.

Shortly, the desk agent announces, "No more rollaboards."

My section is called. I wear my pack like a duffle bag and make it look small, over one shoulder, mostly hidden, pretending it doesn't weigh much—anything to avoid having to check it. I make it past the baggage police, but because the plane is full, I have to stow my pack in the overhead bin 10 rows behind my assigned seat, the closest empty spot. This will make getting off the plane harder, and slower, and I'll have just an hour to catch my New York to Madrid flight, and the American Airlines agent at the Gate told me, when I asked, that my departure gate for Madrid is 38 gates away. It's in the same terminal, and there's no further security check, and it's a short flight to New York, 45 minutes. I picture myself running through the terminal leaping over rows of plastic lounge chairs like a track and field star. Read several New York Times articles I downloaded prior to boarding because I can't or don't know how to access the wifi on board. Before take-off, I go to the back of the cabin to ask for a Diet Coke and something salty to snack on. I get scolded for leaving my seat, but two minutes later am served my Diet Coke and a bag of pretzels. A college-aged girl sitting next to me is on her phone toggling among multiple social media platforms. She spends most of the trip scrolling. I notice she takes a break twice to look out the window. Then I feel old and judgy for noticing this. We land. As soon as the you-can-get-out-of-your-seat bell dings, I jump up and race back 10 rows, open the overhead bin, pull out my bag and walk it back five of the 10 rows before having to stop, not wanting to appear ruder than I already am as other people fill up the aisle. I de-plane and walk briskly 38 gates. I do not leap over the plastic chairs. When I arrive at my gate, passengers have mostly boarded. Again, I have to walk my bag 10 rows behind my assigned seat to find a bin with space. I take my seat. We take off. I read my pilgrim guide, chat briefly with the guy next to me. He's from Galicia, one of the provinces I'll walk through. He says his people are more laid back than the people in Castile. I ask him in bad Spanish, left over from high school and several previous trips to Spanish speaking lands, what advice he has for someone walking the Camino. He looks confused and we sort out the wrong vocabulary words I used in my question. I said *aviso* and I should have said *consejo*. He clarifies I'm a *peregrino* not a "Pellegrino." I laugh at myself and thank him for helping me with my Spanish. I watch a movie with Anthony Hopkins and Anne Hathaway, while eating my special-order ovo-lactose vegetarian meal. Not bad—dinner and a movie. I try to sleep and find it impossible to scrunch myself into any resting position at which I truly feel at rest. I doze. I give up trying to sleep at 5 a.m. Madrid time, figuring, well, its morning, time to get up, which will get me in sync with Spanish time. There's nothing to do. I try two movies before finding one that's good. I fast forward through the last 45 minutes to get it all in before we land. We land. I repeat my race-back-10-rows bit with roughly the same outcome. I deplane and must find my way to the C1 or C10 train that will take me from the airport to the train station in Madrid. This involves asking several official looking people and several others who just look friendly or knowledgeable or whose eye I catch. I work my way to the train platform and miraculously the QR code on the train ticket for Pamplona that I printed back home opens the electronic gate so I can board. Apparently, I bought a combo ticket which includes a train from airport to central train station, train from there to Pamplona. I ride six stops to *Estacion Atocha*. It's a huge hybrid train station and shopping mall. I see multiple levels, retail concourses, elevators, escalators, and enormous hallways leading in different directions. I spend more time asking several people questions in Spanish and English. I make it to my train and take a seat. I ride three hours to Pamplona. I arrive well after the once-a-day bus to St. Jean Pied de Port has departed. I planned for this. I make my way on foot to the albergue I reserved a month ago. I get settled and go in search of a sim card, which I find at a downtown Vodafone store. Next morning, I walk around Pamplona and head to the bus station for a noon departure. Another three-hour ride, this one goes up, up, up into the Pyrenees. I arrive at St. Jean Pied de Port in the middle of the afternoon. I get off the bus and am now ready to begin my journey of 500 miles, except I have to spend the night so I can get a fresh start in the morning. That's when I'll take my *single step*.

The bus I took from Pamplona to Saint Jean was full, sixty people. It took us through little villages with chalet style homes—timber frames with stucco walls, and big eaves that shield you from the snow. Through lush green alpine meadows and forested mountain passes, up we went. When you hike from Saint Jean Pied de Port west, at the start of your Camino, you go up steeply for twelve miles, which means the last bit of the bus ride into St. Jean was a steep descent with hairpin turns so tight they forced the bus not just into the other lane, but all the way across it, onto a pull-over gravel area. I'm guessing, hoping, unwritten rules exist about how opposing traffic does this dance. I snapped a selfie as we pulled out of Pamplona. It was a stealth selfie. I was seated at the front of the bus. I aimed the camera down the rows behind me to the back of the bus. Row upon row of expectant pilgrims, full of stories, aspirations, reasons they've chosen to begin this epic walk. It wasn't until we were pulling into Saint Jean, it occurred to me, the people on this bus will be my community during the coming weeks. The individual scheduling and planning of these sixty strangers over the last few months, randomly assigned them to a group, including me, that will walk west starting on the same day and likely intersect, join, re-join in small sub-groups all the way to Santiago. Stories will be shared, casual friendships formed. Bonds that go deeper than most casual friendships will be knit from the mud and dust and the albergue dorms full of snoring and body odor and communal meals. A very few of these friendships may endure beyond the Camino. Most, I suspect will fade away once we all depart. It will be an important, ephemeral community.

At several moments along my way to the start of the Camino, emotions I didn't know I was feeling bubbled to the surface. For example, going through customs on arrival in Madrid. The passport control guy looked semi-friendly. From the back of the line, I could see he wasn't wearing that hard, I-don't-care-about-you, bureaucrat look. Soon it was my turn. I stepped up, said

Buenos Dias in my best Spanish accent, and placed my passport on the counter, open to the main page.

He asked me, in Spanish, "How long will you be in Spain?"

"Treinte y quatro dias" (i.e., 34 days).

"Where are you going?" again in Spanish.

"Pamplona, entonces Saint Jean Pied de Port, entonces El Camino, hasta Finisterre. " He nodded with what looked maybe like admiration. I added, "Soy peregrino". I am a pilgrim. Thanks to the coaching from my seatmate on the plane I did not declare myself a bottle of Italian mineral water.

He closed my book, pushed it across to me and said, *"Buen Camino"*, the traditional salutation for a pilgrim.

Unexpectedly, I began to tear up. I choked out, "Gracias", turned and moved to the Nothing-to-Declare line.

It happened again at the Pilgrim registration office in Saint Jean Pied de Port. The friendly agent, about my age, from Atlanta, Georgia, stamped my new Pilgrim booklet with a firm forearm, handed me the booklet, said, "Buen Camino" and shook my hand. I got misty-eyed.

Ax, the albergue owner for my first night's stay, is from Australia. He walked the Camino twice, fell in love with Saint Jean Pied de Port and moved here. He renovated an old building into a way cool albergue, complete with spiral staircase that takes you from the cozy reception—couches, wood stove, magazines scattered around, worn paperbacks on bookcases—up two floors of dorm style sleeping. At each level, your first step off the winding staircase, with sculpted metal rail, lands your foot on a floor panel made of glass, (i.e., you see through it to the floor below). Dramatic, yes. Strategic placement on winding stairs maybe not so smart. Each time I start down the stairs, I do a stutter-step when I see the hole in the floor—oh yeah, not a hole. Here's the thing, a few days from now, I'm going to come across a hole on the Camino and in the back of my mind I'll think, oh it's just a decorative feature.

He makes a chopping gesture with his arm when he tells you his name. Ax. All this makes him sound scary. He's not. He speaks softly, gently, wears an earring, plays Gordon Lightfoot on the Samsung speaker resting on a doily on the buffet table, and hosts yoga retreats. He says the Camino is a community, which is what everyone tells you, but then he says there are two things that make it special, one is a simple shared purpose—walk so many miles each day—and the other is anonymity, which, he adds, gives you freedom. No one knows anything about you.

At dinner, Ax said that for the early risers, there would be "some words of encouragement for the Camino" at 6:30 a.m. before we leave. I was with the first group, and we were ready to hit the road at 6:20 a.m. We were more than ready. Eager. I could see it in everyone's darting eyes, tapping feet, quick jerky moves, as we all busied ourselves with last minute tasks in the reception area—securing water bottles, setting backpack straps just right, double knotting shoes, getting walking sticks at the ready, checking to see that the outlet adapter got packed and not left in the socket upstairs, the phone is charged up, and sunglasses are in pocket, etc. Ax was standing in the reception area with us. I could tell he was looking for his moment to invite us for the word-of-encouragement. I'd be willing to do it if it was quick. This morning wasn't like last night when we luxuriated in long conversation about why we're doing the Camino. *Then*, we had the time. *Right now*, everyone just wanted to get underway. It felt like the moments before a marathon. All the runners are clumped behind the starting line, bouncing, stretching, looking anxiously here and there, spitting short bursts of conversation with others nearby, or just spitting. The Camino is not a race, of course. Like everyone says. But it sure feels like a race. At 6:20 a.m., I didn't want words of encouragement. I wanted to get my butt moving down the Camino. Every muscle was twitching, and every brain cell had one focus.

"Okay," Ax jumped in. "If you can all wait just a moment, Yu went upstairs to use the toilet. As soon as he returns, we'll begin. Our eyes met. He could see I was impatient. He said to the group. "Is that okay? I think you'll find this worthwhile." I nodded to indicate okay. It would be an insult to not let Ax have this moment with us. I took a breath, reminded myself that moments like this one on the Camino are important. Yu returned, after an interminable 60 seconds. Ax asked us to stand in a circle, asked us to be in the moment. Right, I thought. My mind was climbing those green meadows. The sooner I got there, the better. He asked us to take deep cleansing breaths. I did it. It felt good. He asked us to close our eyes. I did it. He asked us to let go of our sorrows, our anger. Okay, got it. Sounds good. He asked us to let go of our ambitions and goals and thoughts for the future. Um. Actually, this walk has a lot to do with ambition and thoughts for the future. I was thinking, how can I make that request work and actually NOT let go of my ambitions and thoughts for the future, like my ambition to finish the Camino and go home? Maybe like *just for now* is what he meant. Okay, that I could do. He said all we have is this moment. True enough. Focus only on this moment, he said. Okay, for this moment I'll do that, but as soon as we're done meditating, I'll return to planning and strategizing and anticipating the moment when I arrive at Santiago and when I arrive at the Ocean in Finisterre. Then he hit the audio remote for the Samsung speaker on the doily. John Denver started singing *Sweet Surrender*, which is all about being present in the moment because that's all we have. We listened in silence to the first couple verses. I opened my eyes and discovered I was one of the few who'd had them closed. Others were looking partly anxious and eager to go and partly grooving to Ax's new-age mini sermon. It was cool, and I was hoping it would end soon. It did. I have my doubts about "being present" and "in the moment" and "letting go." I like the richness of being in the present, the past, and the future all at once. Planning, recollecting, acting, engaging with other people, thinking for myself, moving into and through time with plans, hopes, memories, ambitions, recognizing it is all contingent, which is what gives it the edge that makes life exciting. As for letting go, there are reasons I don't trust certain people about certain things. If I let go of that, forgive-and-forget, I rob myself of wisdom, which is the learning that comes from living with less than perfect people, including me. I have no interest in letting go of that.

Ax finished. I was ready to bolt. I looked around. Everyone else was fussing with their stuff or running upstairs for something or other. I turned to Ax, thanked him for everything.

Then I asked him. "So how does this work? Do I wait for everyone, or do I just go."

Ax replied, "It's your Camino. If you are ready, you should go." I thanked him. This was the permission I needed. He walked me to the door, shook my hand and said, "Buen Camino." I thanked him and, with *a single step*, was out the door padding down the cobblestone street into the half-light of a chilly, spring morning.

Chapter 21
Buen Camino

We stumble-step out the front doors of albergues throughout the town at widely different times. A few, no doubt, get underway before six, the rest of us somewhere between 6 a.m. and 8:30; little trickles of pilgrim feet moving down a score of alley ways, joining and gathering in small lanes, coming together on the Rue d'Espagne like a brook and then a steady stream, flowing across the bridge at the Porte Notre-Dame, then out of the old town onto the Route de Saint-Michel and, defying gravity, up. Up and up and up. Into the green meadows dotted with sheep and cattle, all clinking with the hollow sound of the big bells hanging from their necks. They could be racing fans lining a mountainous stage of the Tour de France or the giant slalom at the Winter Olympics. Only our crowd was walking the Camino de Santiago, and we were all starting in Saint Jean Pied de Port with 500 miles to go. Against my better judgment, I found myself slipping into the mind-set of a race. Stepping briskly along the 28 kilometers to Burguette that first day, there were times when the sound of someone's walking sticks or the scrape of their shoes on the path's rocky surface, behind me, made me, instinctually, start walking faster. I would not be passed. I also felt that familiar little adrenaline burst when I realized I was gaining on someone ahead, and, as the meters between us closed, the thrill of moving one person closer to the front of the pack. Then good sense kicked in. I'd relent, let the friendly peregrino to my left meet and overtake me with a shared little "Buen Camino." Or I'd realize I was pushing myself to catch up in a way that was not sustainable if every person ahead of me were to become the target for moving up. What would moving up mean? We didn't all toe a line on Main Street in Saint Jean Pied de Port and jump to a sprint at the smoke from a starting gun. There was no front of the pack, just a continuous stream of pilgrims from here to Santiago.

Everybody was walking at their own pace. *Es su Camino.* "It's your Camino." It turns out Karen's advice is a motto invoked regularly by pilgrims along the way. It's meant as an affirmation, a recognition that anyone walking 500 miles has taken on a monumental challenge and any way that helps you accomplish it is fine, as long as it's on your own two feet. It's what you say to a fellow pilgrim when they tell you how they're getting it done.

"I have back problems. I can only walk 15 kilometers a day."

"Es su Camino."

"I'm walking 30."

"Es su Camino."

"I'm staying in hotels and having my luggage sent ahead."

"Es su Camino."

"I'm staying in the cheapest albergues I can find."

"Es su Camino."

"I'm walking one week every year for five years."

"Es su Camino."

It was starting to sink in: this journey is not a race. Oh, but I love a race. I like beating people. I like winning. *The Camino is not a race.* Okay, because we were not competing, maybe I could get to know some of my fellow travelers. It couldn't hurt. We were all pilgrims after all. We had a shared purpose, a natural bond, like Ax said. Maybe we could have a chat while walking together. I tried it. It worked. Days went by and I found meeting new people along the way was fun.

"*Hola! Buen Camino!*" I chirp as I come abreast of a couple clicking their walking sticks along the hard packed dirt road, studded with stones worn flat by centuries of pilgrim footwear. I'm several days into my walk. There's bright sun at 10 a.m. and I can see the wind trails as the breezes run across enormous fields of early wheat, bending the stalks this way and that, making patches shaded lighter and darker. I've been wondering what people wore on their feet 500 years ago. They did not have Hokas with synthetic uppers precisely stitched to conform to left and right foot and synthetic soles produced by intensive research-and-development to provide just the right balance of comfort and bounce. Did they wear sandals? Did some people walk barefoot? And how did they get home? I'll take a bus, a plane, and a train to get home. They must have walked, which means the pilgrimage was X hundred miles walking to Santiago, and the same again walking home. For them, the pilgrimage began when they walked out the front door of their home somewhere in Spain or France or Italy or wherever else they lived, not at Saint Jean Pied de Port after a bus ride from Pamplona. I've read that your pilgrimage begins when you leave your home. That way of thinking is true to history. I'd thought about it as I turned out of my driveway and walked down the hill to the Ayer train station just a week before.

"*Hola,*" they both say turning toward me with smiles. They are an older couple. "*Buen Camino!*" they both add.

"I'm impressed with how small your packs are," I offer in English. I'm guessing they're German. I could have tried speaking German, but if I was wrong and they're something like Dutch, then it would be hard to untangle my attempt and land on whatever language works. They look at me confused. I try Spanish. "*Muy impresivo que sus mochilas son tan pequenas.*" Very impressive that your backpacks are so small. I gesture toward their backpacks. I add, gesturing to mine, "*Lo mio es bastante grande!*" Mine is awful big! I make like I'm straining under a superheavy load.

The man suddenly brightens. He gets it. He says in English, "Oh. Well. We are not carrying our luggages. They are with the taxi now. We just walk."

"Yes," the woman chimes in, also getting it now, "We are such old now which we cannot carry all the luggages together." She pretends to be an old person, bent over, taking little steps, which is kind of funny because she is old, kind of bent over, and taking little steps.

We talk. I learn they are Norwegian, staying in pensiones each night because they want a private room and they've arranged to have their "luggages" transferred every day. They started in Roncesvalles, just past the big climb you get if you start in Saint Jean Pied de Port. She says she has back issues and can't do steep climbing. They mention they are meditating on a single word each day. This practice seems a little random when they say it, but they explain that they belong to a "pilgrim society" — maybe a church? Not sure. And their "priest," they definitely said priest, suggested they meditate on a single word each day. Today's word is spirituality. Yesterday was silence.

At some point in the conversation I say, "Don't worry."

And she says, "That's our word from three days!" Somehow, I guess, *Don't worry*, is a single word in Norwegian. They are impressed that I'm carrying all my luggages and that I'm walking 30 kilometers each day. They say they have done two Caminos, each time getting a little closer to Santiago. She adds that if they are alive next year, they might make it to Santiago. I say we each do our own Camino. Like they say, I remind us, it's "Su Camino." They know this phrase and nod and smile. I add, acknowledging their comments about their age, back issues and more, "you're doing what you can."

She says, "Yes, we are doing what we can. That's all everyone has doing!" We all smile.

I say, "It was a pleasure to meet you, I'm going to walk on ahead."

We all say, "Buen Camino."

So, it goes. You strike up a conversation. It runs its course, maybe 10 minutes, maybe 3 hours, and then you part, as one of you chooses to stop and rest, or take a picture, or you announce that you will fall behind or walk on ahead. *Es su camino!* It's so different from riding a bike solo across the country or rowing a boat down the east coast. On either of my first two adventures, I could go a day or more with almost no interaction. Miles of lonely highway, miles of lonely shoreline. One day rolling across Montana, the only words I uttered the entire day were "Thank you" to the store clerk who sold me a bag of Cheetos. There was something beautiful about all that solitude. But there was something new and magical about all these people with all their stories, willing to share them as we walked the Camino. Maybe that deeper meaning can find you in solitude as well as in good company.

Here's a sample of people I met in a single day. Catherine from Ireland works as a therapist, and has two children in their late 20s. She's 46. She got pregnant at 16 years old, was shamed by the doctor she saw for guidance, and was told she'd be reported to officials. She explains it happened right before things changed in Ireland and birth control became available, and women could divorce their husbands, rape in marriage was recognized, etc. She has a partner of 20 years, who works as a special needs assistant in a school. He's Italian and has been trying for years to get a regular teaching credential, which he holds in Italy. Catherine and I walked together for over an hour talking lots about Ireland, Northern Ireland—where I've lived and studied the schooling system—and the progressive changes the Republic of Ireland went through in the early 90s.

Lucas is also from Ireland. He designs interiors for cruise ships and background architecture for theme parks (i.e., not the rides). He's 26 and just quit his job of five years to spend some time traveling. He says his company already wants him back as a manager when he's done. He'll be headed to India after completing the Camino. We walked together for possibly 3 hours and kept up a lively banter. Then we ran into Michelle.

Michelle is German, I'm guessing in her late 20s. She was at my first albergue in Saint Jean, the one with Ax, and we ran into each other again today. Lucas and I were walking together when we caught up to her. We greeted each other like we were old friends—we had walked together the first day for a good hour discussing how we trained for the Camino. She walked 20-25 miles a day with hills, rode a stationary bike an hour a day. She's very fit and kept a good pace, but when we ran into each other on this particular day, she was not well. She said she had a bad cold which she guessed she caught on the plane, but she was walking, nonetheless. Going all the way to Pamplona today, a good 35 kilometers. We three walk together and I encourage Lucas to take the lead in talking with Michelle since they would be continuing on to Pamplona today while I would be stopping in Villava. They're age mates, and, I learned, Michelle recently broke up with her boyfriend. I had shared this intel with Lucas previously. Presumptuous of me, but you never know.

Arkady is from Ukraine. His parents live in Kiev, his daughter and grandson have been in Poland for over two years to take advantage of Poland's health care for the granddaughter who has a rare heart condition, which requires costly medicine. It's all paid for by the government health program. Arkady finished his term of service in the army and headed to Qatar where he worked in insurance, having previously run his own agency in Ukraine before the war. He is sure the Ukrainians will win because they are fighting for their families, their land, and their country. Arkady and I walk together for a couple hours.

Shortly after my arrival at my albergue that day, I meet three French people: a couple in their 30s and a man who looks to be in his 50s. They speak only French. Two live in Avignon and the older guy is from Dijon. Mustard, I note, drawing from my shallow well of cultural references. We're out on the rooftop sitting area, three floors up with lovely views of the surrounding neighborhood. It's four o'clock in the afternoon, there's a breeze, and the day is just starting to cool. They're stretched out in lounge chairs. I'm at a table on my tablet. I hear them on their phone trying to make a dinner reservation. It's a complete mess. The person on the other end is speaking Spanish and a little English. On this end, it's the younger of the two men with the phone. His companions are commenting and gesturing. It's pretty chaotic, but they manage to make it through *reservation-for-three*, only now he needs a what's app number to confirm the reservation. First, they have trouble finding the number, then they can't translate the numbers into anything understandable at the other end. I offer to help. He hands me his phone. I explain to the restaurant guy in my simple Spanish what's going on. We're all laughing. Then the older Frenchman hands me his phone and punches in a number. I read it to the restaurant guy in Spanish.

It's looking good, but then the older Frenchman gestures urgently to say, I think, "No, wrong number." He tries to give me a different number, but it doesn't have enough digits. Finally, he gives me a passing number and I read it to the extremely patient restaurant guy. He reads it back to me to confirm, but I can't hear what he's saying because the older Frenchman is saying something to me the whole time. I tell the restaurant guy it sounds good. He says he'll send a message to the number to confirm. We hang up. Then, using the internet translator on one of their phones, I tell them if they don't get a message soon, they should call the restaurant again. Then, I ask to use their translator again to say something else. I speak into the phone. It does only one sentence at a time:

"We are organizing a simple dinner here at the albergue for anyone who wants it." It translates. They crowd around the little phone screen, read it and nod.

"Oui!"

I add another sentence. "It will be very simple—spaghetti and salad."

"Oui!"

"And wine!"

"Oui. Oui!"

This leads me to the next person I met earlier in the day. Elena is a taxi driver from Madrid. She and her husband, also a taxi driver, have four children, all of whom have gone to university or are currently attending. She mentions her father died recently, which is one reason she's walking the Camino. Elena and her husband can't afford to take vacations together, so they are taking turns walking portions of the Camino. In three or four years when they retire, they hope to complete it together. We met while walking, earlier in the day. We talked about how much we like the sociability of the albergues, and in the course of talking, we discovered we were headed to the same albergue and decided we'd organize a communal dinner for anyone who wished to join us. Later, the Frenchies on the rooftop are my first recruits, and they've chosen us over a real restaurant.

I also meet Denise, a florist from Dresden, Germany. Her son is 24. Her husband is riding his bike from Germany to Santiago. She is walking from Saint Jean to Santiago where they'll meet. She says she's walking because she's tired of working as a florist. She loves the flowers, but the customers are ... she doesn't use any word. She just shakes her head and clucks in disgust.

You can get as much or as little socializing as you want on the Camino. You can go quietly about your business in the albergue and no one will bother you, or you can engage people in conversation, plan a meal together, drink coffee and get to know each other. On the Camino itself, you can walk alone the whole day if you want, or, when someone catches up to you or you, them, and you say *Buen Camino*, you can offer a simple comment about the weather or ask where they're headed for the day or ask them about their—boots, walking sticks, cool backpack, whatever—and strike up a conversation. They'll bite or they won't. English is the *lingua franca* of the Camino. But I find I use plenty of Spanish and German, which, if I'm not careful, results in a weird mix of confusing grammar and vocabulary.

One night, early on, I stayed in a pension because, when I booked my accommodations three months before the trip, Booking.com said there was nothing else available. I no longer trust Booking.com's scary assessments. Anyway, the pension felt very luxurious, private room, but lonely. Everybody went quietly to their quarters in the upstairs hall and offered no more than a cordial greeting. So different from the albergue culture, which I was falling in love with. I could continually adjust how much socializing I want depending on how extroverted or introverted I was feeling.

Elena and I did, indeed, organize dinner: the three Frenchies, another French woman who, thank goodness, spoke some English, and a young guy from Taiwan, who was working in Malaga as a software engineer. We had a riotously good time shopping with very limited communication ability, then we all prepped the meal, and all ate together. Kind of magical.

I was trudging up a steep *calle* (road) on the way out of Najera. It's amazing how these medieval alleyways designed for foot traffic and the occasional donkey cart have been repurposed for Citroens, Kias, and Toyota pickup trucks, despite the irregular angles and slopes, varying widths and occasional arches, overhanging roofs and cantilevered upper floors. Where the road narrows, scars adorn the walls of the adjacent buildings where a sideview mirror met its end or the entire side of a car got scraped. I was busy avoiding the small service truck that was coming downhill too fast for current conditions when a man maybe about my age, stocky, carrying a small day pack, came up from behind and was suddenly walking beside me. I'm not used to people my age catching up, especially when they're not a wiry build like me. I was impressed and definitely a little challenged. He was not huffing and puffing, just going along at his natural pace. So, of course, after saying Hola and Buen Camino, I added that I liked how small his pack was. Subtext: you're going faster than me only because you are carrying less. He explained he has his luggage sent on ahead each day, which I already knew. We fell into talking. He was from Madrid, 66 years old, and just retired. In the course of talking, he said he'd been having some problems with his family, his job, and his health. He made a promise—to God apparently—that if everything turned out okay, he would walk the Camino. Everything turned out okay. He said his Camino was a simple act of gratitude. He said many people do the Camino for religious reasons. Many people have many different reasons, he said. Some people, he added, do it for sport. That's not right. The Camino is not for sport, he said, wagging his finger in the air. This comment prompted me, when he asked later, to change my answer a bit to the why-are-you-doing-the-Camino question, and I emphasized how I was turning 65 this year and about to retire and it seemed like a good time to do the Camino. He accepted this explanation. I find I tend to customize my answer based on who's asking. Because I actually have a bunch of reasons, I'm not actually telling a lie. It's like the politician who says something different to each group—sharing *different aspects of the vision* for different audiences. Okay, maybe slightly sketchy. But the truth is I don't really know which of my reasons is the main reason: I like adventure, I like walking, I like long boring multi-day endurance challenges, I like physical activity, I like eating lots of food, I like beer and wine, I like chocolate, I like butter and olive oil and pasta and cheese, I don't like getting chubby, I like being outdoors, I like looking at cool scenery going by, I like meeting new interesting people, I like being alone, I like stepping away from the new interesting people once I lose interest without appearing rude (like taking a bite from each of the assorted chocolates in the box without anyone caring or even knowing — I really like that), I like time to think, I like thinking about nothing much at all, I like having happy thoughts, I like that my thoughts tend to become happy when I exercise, I like having rare deep or potentially interesting new thoughts, I like supporting a cause I believe in, I like reaching a fund-raising goal, I like the bragging rights that come with a successful adventure, I like mentally replaying memorable moments, I like writing about my adventures, I like having simple expectations for a given day (i.e., walk from point A to point B, do laundry, eat, sleep, repeat), I like staying in touch with loved ones and friends back home, I like looking forward to it all being over and returning to normal life, I like getting away from normal life, I like the feeling of accomplishment at the finish, I like celebrating at the finish, I like celebrating as many times as possible after the finish, I like sharing my adventures once they're over, I like going home. Meanwhile, the guy who was walking fast because he had the small backpack was raring to move past me. I could tell. So, I said I was going to stop for a minute to put away my coat and he should continue on. *It was nice chatting. Buen Camino.* What stands out from this episode is that the whole conversation took place in Spanish! My Camino-ing friend was just chatting away, maybe talking slower than usual, maybe making his talk a little simpler, but other than that, the two of us were chattering away almost like normal. Yay! Not only was my Spanish coming back, I think it was improving from whatever time in my life it was at its peak.

One day I was walking along the Camino, which is what I spend about half my waking hours doing, when I noticed a feeling. I felt like I wasn't doing any work at all to keep moving along. It was my legs, not me, that were working. I, in contrast, was relaxing and enjoying the scenery move slowly past. I appreciated what my legs were doing and was thinking I need to take good care of them, but *I* was just along for the ride. In the days following, I built on this idea by imagining that I'm actually riding a bus and not walking at all. The bus picks me up most mornings between 6:30 a.m. and 7:00 a.m., right after breakfast. It motors along, reliably, at 4 kilometers per hour and makes stops for snacks along the way. I started planning my days to have a meal stop around 3 to 4 hours in—think warm Spanish omelette with bread, juice, and tea—and another stop about two hours after that for a sandwich, made the night before. Two hours after that, I'd arrive at my destination. The bus ride was a little bumpy and slow, but it sure beat walking.

Back at Saint Jean Pied de Port, Ax had said the dinner does not include wine, but I could bring wine. An hour later found me browsing the wine aisle at the Carrefour Supermarket just outside the old city. It was a supermarket worthy of the name, unlike some of the little holes in the wall where the banner sign "Supermercado" is actually wider than the store. But I didn't know that yet, because I had just landed in Saint Jean Pied de Port, starting line for the Camino, and assumed, wrongly, that a place bearing the name would be something like the Stop and Shop back home, the size of a warehouse with 20 aisles of every food imaginable plus hardware and housewares and more. This market *was* super, unlike most of the others I would shortly encounter. The wine aisle was ample, even by American standards. I thought about getting a "nice" bottle of wine, which I decided in the moment would mean something costing around

10 euros. But then I saw a price sticker on the shelf that said 2 euros and above it stood a rank of corked bottles, red, of French origin. Was this price a mistake? A bottle of French wine for $2.50? I studied the shelf. It looked legit. I bought one. Partly, I was curious to see how a two-buck-chuck here in the global wine capital would compare with back home. And partly, I was conjuring mischief. Fast forward three hours. It's 6:50 p.m. at the albergue as I come down the spiral stairs from the dorm area to the reception, bottle in one hand, and a brand new 3 euro multi-function knife with corkscrew in the other—also purchased at the Carrefour. Dinner is at seven, and Berta, from Belgium, is already there. We'd met earlier in the afternoon and hit it off. She's a 70-something widow out to live life fully and well. She rode her bike from home to here, where she will stash the bike and walk to Santiago. I take a seat and prepare to open the bottle. A minute later, I'm struggling to get the cork out. I ask Berta if she's strong. She takes the bottle and, a few grunts later, her strong arms wriggle it out. Pop! I ask her if she'd like a glass. Domenic in the kitchen provides two glasses. I pour. Berta inspects, tilting the glass, holding it up to the light, swills the wine, sticks her nose in, takes a sip, rolls it around a bit, swallows, and nods approvingly. I try some. It's good. Not brilliant. I tell her the truth—2 euros. We laugh. At dinner, I offer wine to whomever of the eight people around the table would like some, but nobody else takes any. Berta and I polish it off together and become good friends over the course of a very lively meal.

Note to self: a bottle of wine, which need not cost an arm and a leg, is a great way to invite sociability in an albergue. I can buy a bottle for less than four euros, carry it into the kitchen or dining area, pour myself a glass and then offer it to others. Usually there are one or two takers and conversation ensues. One night, in Belorado, I put together a simple dinner for myself of a Spanish omelette and sliced tomato with oil and salt. I had a bottle of

Rioja, which I purchased for 2.65 euros. At the next table was a woman I'd met earlier when we were checking in. She was bent over her phone doing email or paying bills or checking bookings or something that was making her look grim. Would you like a small glass of Rioja, I called to her? She waved me off, but, 10 minutes later, joined me at my table. Her name was Ingrid. I cut her some bread and poured a little dish of olive oil and added salt for dipping. She was about my age, from Holland, married with a daughter. The husband and daughter were fishing somewhere else in Spain and apparently were having a good time because, Ingrid reported, her daughter said in a recent phone call not to walk too fast. The plan was they'd all meet up in Santiago the day after Ingrid arrived. She had a second glass and I poured off the bottom third of the bottle into an empty plastic bottle I'd been saving and screwed down the top for tomorrow. Very Camino-ish, I decided. I'd be walking with a bottle of water in the pocket on one side of my backpack and, in the other, I'd have my Rioja for the evening.

Sometimes people are nicer than they appear at first. I was second in line at the Hostel B in the medieval city of Belorado for check-in. Ahead of me was a woman who spoke no Spanish. It was Ingrid, with whom I would later share the Rioja. The man at the desk was gruff and not making a lot of sense, even in Spanish. There was a bunch of paperwork, which also made no sense because at all the other albergues, check-in took about one minute with a look at your passport, credit card handoff, and some quick instructions about bunk assignments and the wifi password. Mr. Gruff was form and stamp crazy. Three forms, one of which he pasted onto another form. Then he required three signatures and then, with grand bureaucratic flourish he wielded his stamp, bringing it down firmly in three places, then initialing each stamped spot. The stamp read "Carpe diem", part of the whole not-making-any-sense theme. Later, I was looking to boil water for tea. I saw a sign at the entrance to the kitchen area. It said, in three languages. "This is my kitchen, not yours. Stay out." Okay then. This prompted me to check the sign out in front of the albergue, which advertised, "Kitchen". The implication being that the kitchen was an amenity, as with many albergues, a place where pilgrims may prepare food. Not here apparently. I started practicing for the big confrontation about kitchen use with this puny tyrant. He was shorter than me and acted generally sarcastic and dismissive, making him a handy target for my ire. Against my natural inclination though, the next few hours involved several encounters in which I ended up saying something nice to him. For example, I noticed that despite his bad temper, he was working very hard, and the place was clean and orderly, and he was processing the steady stream of weary peregrinos, getting them settled. I commented that he's working so hard and that I hope he manages to get some breaks. Then I said to him, what if I want to make some spaghetti? He said that would be fine, he just has to be careful with the kitchen because he needs it to make the *menu del dia* for people that sign up each day. Later in the evening, I noticed him chatting merrily with diners after the meal had been served and eaten and people were lingering with their last glass of wine. His name was Emiliano. When I left the following morning—he was working at 6 a.m. after working the previous evening until at least 9 p.m.—I thanked him for his hospitality.

He warmly put his hand on my shoulder and wished me, "Buen Camino."

The next day landed me at Burgos where I collapsed, after 35K, in a private room I'd arranged, feeling oh so pleased that tomorrow was a scheduled rest day. Hooray! And the next day, rest is what I did. I woke at 7:30 a.m. with no real plan. I puttered around my 10x10 foot room, went to the bathroom down the hall, enjoyed a breakfast of bread, cheese and marmalade, scanned the New York Times headlines, responded to two emails, wrote a page in my journal, and was ready for a nap at 10 a.m. So, I lay down, fell asleep fast and woke up at 11:30 a.m. This time I rose with purpose, and made a plan: laundry, walk to cathedral, then lunch back at my room. I did all that and at 1:45 p.m. sensed I was ready for an afternoon nap. Feeling slightly lost after 10 straight days of a singular, all-consuming purpose—walk, walk, walk—and now, facing a day of rest, not clearly defined, I chose, instead of a nap, to watch the 24-hour NBC News on my tablet, which was featuring long format true crime investigations. I watched, just for something to do. It didn't seem right to be napping again. A woman was shot to death in her garage, no apparent motive, turns out it was her son. I don't know exactly what psychic lift I was seeking, but this show did not produce it. I napped and woke up at 3 p.m., feeling achy. I took two ibuprofen, one vitamin, and chewed on an aspirin. I decided to gather up my tablet and poncho (chance of rain 80% on my weather app), put them in my drawstring bag, which can be worn handily as a backpack, and headed out into the big city in search of caffeine and a proper café in which to occupy a table with my tablet. This plan, I hoped, would produce a feeling of normalcy. Twenty minutes later found me at a window seat at the Café Bertiz with a double espresso and a chocolate croissant, pecking happily at my tablet keyboard, paying partial attention to the three young women at the next table talking really fast, the two good-spirited baristas frothing drinks and making change with lots of smiles, and the older woman (okay, my age) slowly sipping a coffee alone at the facing table.

I hadn't really thought, in advance, about what my "rest" day should look like. If it's really a rest day, I suppose that means it's okay to not know what it will look like, but because I relentlessly plan everything, I felt like I should be planning how to rest, which is why I spent so much of the day feeling liked a swamped vessel on a mist shrouded sea. An hour in the cafe and a good caffeine jolt later, the automatic bailers had kicked in and my little boat was rising to its proper draft. My aches seemed to be diminishing and the general fog of the day was lifting. I was indeed resting, mission accomplished, but I was also getting a few things done and not just feeling useless and disconnected. I think, as much as anything, it was the caffeine. Recently, I'd found myself lagging around noon time, which is the point in a day of Camino-ing when I've walked two-thirds or more of the day's route, am no longer amped-up for my forced march, but still have a ways to go, and just don't have a whole lot of energy. So, I decided to experiment. I'd never ventured into the world of energy drinks. They always seemed slightly scary, something my mother would deeply frown upon. But people drink them. One person I know who works the night shift at a Mobil gas station downs two or three in an evening, partly so he can stay up for the morning afterwards to get his son off to school, and then he crashes. Another person I know recently said how he downed several on a driving trip back from Florida when his wife, with whom he usually swaps off driving, was not able to drive, and they had to get home because the cat sitter left. Stoked by these two valuable anecdotes, I decided to go for it. My Red Bull beverage in the slim can tasted like cough syrup going down, but it did the trick. I powered through the last two hours of walking. I did this three days in a row. Each time, while downing the magic elixir, I read the label, offered in Spanish, Italian, and German. I understood it only partially, but what was clear was the fact it had a lot — I mean a lot — of ingredients you do not find in your kitchen. Then I had another idea. What about an espresso and a banana instead? The espresso would give me a solid caffeine energy-burst from a much less processed, far more natural source, and the banana would replenish my electrolytes and provide a good dose of potassium, both of which I am vaguely aware are in bananas and are good for you when you're exercising and sweating a lot. My next thought was,

I am not a coffee drinker. I gave up coffee 15 years before because it made me jittery. It made me jittery because I drank too much. So, I'd switched to Black tea as my daily beverage, which I could drink too much of, and not get jittery, because it has half the caffeine. Should I really experiment with espresso? Would that first espresso be my downfall? Would my years of recovery from supposed coffee addiction be instantly erased and I'd find myself, once again, craving as much coffee as I could get my hands on? I was pondering this dilemma the next day as noon approached. Shortly, I found myself in a little shop. I noticed a refrigerated case with energy drinks against a darkened wall in the back, and at the front of the cramped little store, a bright, cheerful counter with a friendly barista and happy people sipping the alternative elixir from tiny cups. Those cups looked so cute. So, I ceased my nascent chemical-laden energy drink habit and, for the next two days had an espresso (*café solo*, in Spain) and a banana. I found it did not make me crave coffee first thing in the morning, nor did I crave it through the day. I was very happy with my Black tea, but when noon rolled around, a double espresso felt just right.

Chapter 22
Traffic

In all of 1986, only a few thousand people completed the Camino de Santiago. In 2003, the number stood at 74,000. In 2022, nearly a half-million people made the famous trek, according to the Pilgrim Reception Office of Santiago de Compostela.[84] Traffic on the Camino has exploded over the last 40 years. Why the sudden interest? Why do hundreds of thousands of people, every year, from around the world, lace up their sneakers and hiking boots to walk weeks-on-end across Spain's rugged northern mountains and arid plains to visit a Catholic shrine at a time when few people place any stock in religious relics? Why did I? Part of the answer is, if you want a well-marked walking adventure, and you don't want to do it in a wilderness, because you like the idea of sleeping in a bed under a roof every night, there aren't many options, and the Camino has fantastic infrastructure. But there's something else about it. It's a pilgrimage. What it's a pilgrimage *for*, depends, but, regardless, the label gives it an aura. It's adventure-plus. It's adventure with some kind of deeper meaning. Maybe that's what attracted me. What it has meant to people over the centuries is complicated.

People have been walking the Camino for a thousand years, and interest has risen and fallen with shifts in politics, religion, and popular culture. The Camino, as we know it today, walking paths that crisscross Spain to the tomb of St. James, has been trekked by pilgrims since the ninth century. Tradition says a shepherd miraculously discovered the remains of the apostle James buried in a hillside near the northern Spanish town of Compostela. Supposedly, James had traveled to Spain to preach the Gospel and, after he got martyred by King Herod, his body was carried to the Iberian peninsula for burial. The find was verified at the time by none other than the archbishop for the area and, shortly, the King made a pilgrimage, and it became a shrine, then a church, and, finally, in the 13th century, a cathedral that stands today in the city that took the apostle's name, Santiago de Compostela.

What is sometimes overlooked in this story is the fact that long before Christians walked the Camino, and well before Christianity made its way to Spain, ancient Celts were trekking to the Atlantic coastline not far from Compostela to revere the sun as it sank into the western sea. They, too, were after some kind of deeper meaning, just a different kind. Centuries before the Roman Empire conquered most of Europe, a loosely bound Celtic culture ranged from the British Isles to the Black Sea and south through most of what is now Spain and Portugal. When the Roman empire expanded, it took over Celtic lands and sucked the formerly Celtic people into Roman culture. The fringes of Europe, however, remained beyond Roman rule. In places like Ireland and Western Spain, Celtic culture survived. Celts were closely attuned to nature and its cycles. Whether they actually worshipped the sun is not clear, but evidence suggests that a shrine to the sun was located on a hillside near the coast, 90 kilometers west of Compostela. It may have been a pilgrimage destination for the Celtic people long before Jesus was preaching at the other end of the Mediterranean Sea. The modern Spanish Province of Galicia takes its name from the Celts and shows, today, strong ties to its Celtic roots. It's only fitting that some modern Camino pilgrims, who are not focused on Catholic relics, choose to continue past Santiago, on a lesser traveled path, to the Galician coast and the presumed location of the ancient shrine to the Sun in a place called Finisterra, from Latin for *end of the Earth*. Ancient people believed the rocky coastline at the western extreme of Europe was truly where the flat Earth came to an end. Today, at the very end of that trail, near the lighthouse of Cape Finisterra is a bronze boot set on a rock overlooking the Atlantic Ocean, marking where pagan and Christian traditions come together as the sea crashes ashore at the bottom of Finisterra's craggy cliffs.

How much the Christian Camino owes to its Celtic predecessor is a mystery, but something in the popular imagination of Galicia was fired up by the idea of a pilgrimage during the middle ages and grew more intense from the politics of the day and a Catholic Church hungry for control of Europe. Pilgrimage is embedded in Christian myth and history. The first Christian pilgrims were the Wise Men who followed the star to Bethlehem, etc... Early Christians went on pilgrimages to Palestine to visit locations from the life of Jesus: Jerusalem, Bethlehem, Cana, the Mount of Olives. After the Church got set up in Rome, the Pope's patch of real estate became another pilgrim destination. But what is a pilgrimage without souvenirs, proof that you came close to God? So it was that relics became a thing. In the fourth century, an early, famous pilgrim to Jerusalem, Helena, mother of Emperor Constantine, supposedly found the wooden cross on which Jesus was crucified and brought it home. She handed off the nails to her son who had them soldered to his helmet. The cross itself was delivered to the local bishop. Over the centuries, bits were, apparently, chipped off and dispersed, making their way to churches across Eastern and Western Europe. Today, splinters of the holy cross are claimed by churches in France, Switzerland, Serbia, Istanbul, and elsewhere. Other supposedly ancient relics held in contemporary churches include the head of Saint John the

Baptist (San Sylvestro in Capite, Rome), the shroud in which the dead body of Jesus was wrapped for burial (Turin), and Jesus' original crown of thorns (Cathedral of Notre Dame, Paris). Hundreds, if not thousands, of relics have been claimed by churches around the world.

    The church's devotion to relics was driven largely by the cult-like worship of saints. Early Christians venerated defenders of the faith who died for their beliefs. As time went by, such individuals were seen to have special power to positively influence the lives of individuals who earnestly petitioned them. According to the Church, saints are not to be the object of worship because that would be idolatry, but Catholicism teaches that the faithful may pray to a saint to intervene on their behalf. (Not sure what the difference is.) There are more than 10,000 saints officially recognized by the Church today. Many are seen as the patron of a cause, vocation, or place. Some of the more famous are St. Jude, patron saint of impossible causes; St. Franics of Assisi, patron saint of animals; St. Patrick, patron saint of Ireland; St. Michael for soldiers and police, and St. Christopher for travelers. There are also plenty of lesser-known saints with special jobs. Polycarp is the patron saint for earaches. Matthew is patron saint of accountants. Apollonia watches over dentists, and even the Internet has its own saint, Isidore of Brazil.[85] Because of the supposed preaching of the Apostle James in Iberia, and his later martyrdom, he became the patron saint of Spain. Then, because of the Camino, he became the patron saint of pilgrims.

    Fueled by the cult of sainthood and the quasi-magical draw of religious relics, pilgrimages grew in popularity during the Middle Ages. Interest in the Camino, which was widely seen as the third most important pilgrimage after Jerusalem and Rome, owes much to the politics of the times. After the fall of the Roman Empire, Spain was ruled by Germanic tribes which carved up the Iberian peninsula into smaller kingdoms. Aside: I wonder sometimes why the only European tribes are "Germanic". Were there no French tribes? Dutch tribes? Polish? Meanwhile, Islam was becoming a potent force in the Middle East and North Africa. Like Christianity, Islam began as a religious faith that moved from the edges of society to the center and was adopted by rulers. Also, like Christianity, Islam was driven by an evangelical mission to spread the faith to all people. Missionary zeal is like gasoline to the fire of empire building. It gives power-hungry rulers a justification for their quest to expand their territory. Soldiers marching in the name of God is the fearsome story behind much of world history. So it was that soon after its beginning in Mecca in the early 600s, Islam became the driving force behind an empire that extended west across North Africa. In the early 700s, a Muslim army crossed the Strait of Gibraltar, poured into southern Spain and defeated the Germanic kingdom centered in the city of Toledo. From there, Muslim armies continued north and quickly took control of most of the Iberian peninsula. The next seven centuries in Spain became a seesawing of control between Christian and Muslim kingdoms, with Christian armies at times pushing the Muslim forces south and Muslim armies then repelling the Christians and moving the boundary line once again north. Seen from this vantage point, the discovery of the bones of an apostle in northwestern Spain in the 800s was an opportune event for the cause of Christian empire-building. The establishment of an important shrine at the far western edge of Christendom provided a foothold and a magnet to draw Christian common folk to the region. The church poured money into the building of the Camino infrastructure, which by the 13th century included a network of roads with hostels, bridges, and inns all leading to Santiago de Compostela with its magnificent cathedral. The cult of St. James that grew up around the Shrine and its famous relic became a powerful motivator for pilgrims. One scholar conjectures there may have been between a half million and two million pilgrims per year trekking to Santiago at the height of the Medieval period.[86]

Accounts of the Camino pilgrimage from the Middle Ages make for a fascinating read. The most famous is the Codex Calixtinus, named for Pope Calixtinus II, the attributed author, though someone else wrote it.[87] One portion of the Codex is a travel guide for pilgrims, identifying towns and sites to visit along the way. The descriptions can be quite colorful. For example, the author describes the people of Navarra:

> In some places, like Vizcaya and Alava, when they get warmed up, the men and women show off their private parts to each other. The Navarrese also have sex with their farm animals. And it's said that they put a lock on the backsides of their mules and horses so that nobody except themselves can have at them. Moreover, they kiss lasciviously the vaginas of women and of mules.

Somehow this all fits with the warring-Germanic-tribe thing. The author also warns of dangers along the way. Of the ferry service at one river crossing, we read:

> These boatmen have been known to collect the fares and pile the boat full of pilgrims, so that the boat capsizes and the pilgrims are drowned. Then the evil scoundrels delight in stealing the possessions of the dead.

But it's not all nasty folk and deadly scams. Arriving in Santiago, the author offers an awe-inspiring description of the cathedral:

> The church has no cracks or defects. It is an extraordinary work, with great space, bright, of fitting size, proportioned in its width, length and height, of extraordinary craft, with two levels like a royal palace. He who goes up to the upper galleries, if sad going up, will see the perfect beauty and will rejoice and be happy.

If an amazing cathedral, the venerated bones of a famous saint, and an official tourist guide were not enough to get a medieval commoner on the road to Santiago, then possibly the promise of remission of sins could seal the deal. The church taught that most sinners stood a good chance of having to spend some part of eternity in Purgatory before proceeding on to the bliss of heaven. Purgatory was where you went after death if you were penitent but had not quite made up for all your many sins with sufficient attendance at church or almsgiving. Monetary contributions and other demonstrations of piety were essential. Purgatory, though on the path to heaven, was a place of continuous punishment and something to be avoided if possible. The church of the Middle Ages took advantage of this fear of purgatory by selling official documents granting anyone who would pay, pardon, in part or full, from the chastening fires of purgatory. These documents were known as indulgences, and the church was made rich selling them. Not so different from the scammers you might encounter along the Camino. Walking the pilgrim route to Santiago was also generally seen as a significant step toward reducing your time in Purgatory, sometimes in combination with the purchase of an indulgence, and, therefore, millions of medieval pilgrims made the trek.

By the end of the 13th century, a stream of pilgrims was flowing across northern Spain. Keep in mind that, unlike today, where the return journey is by train or plane, medieval pilgrims had to walk both ways, coming to Santiago and returning home, which meant a doubly arduous journey and double the traffic along the route. But a series of events, starting in the early 1500s began a gradual decline in the Camino. Most notable of these events was the penning and posting of Luther's *Ninety-Five Theses*.

Martin Luther was a German monk and a professor of theology in the early 1500s. His reading of the Bible and his observations of Church activity led him to conclude that the sale of indulgences was corrupt and only God could forgive sins. He became increasingly outspoken against the Pope and the Church on this and related matters.

In 1517, he issued a tract challenging the Catholic Church. It is believed that his anger led him to nail the manuscript, called the *Ninety-Five Theses,* to the front door of All Saints Church in Wittenburg. This commenced a life-long dispute with the Church that led to his ex-communication by papal decree and the expansion of a social movement, already underway, that questioned the Church's authority. In the end, followers of Luther and others who challenged the Church of Rome, separated from the Church and organized what they believed to be the true Christian church. Over time the movement spread beyond Germany and became known as the Protestant reformation.

At the heart of Luther's grievance against the church was the sale of indulgences. Three of his 95 Theses make the point:

27. They preach only human doctrines who say that as soon as the money clinks into the money chest, the soul flies out of purgatory.

28. It is certain that when money clinks in the money chest, greed and avarice can be increased; but when the church intercedes, the result is in the hands of God alone.

32. Those who believe that they can be certain of their salvation because they have indulgence letters will be eternally damned, together with their teachers.[88]

Luther also took aim at pilgrimages. In a tract from 1520, "To the Christian Nobility of the German Nation" he took a particularly harsh tone:

All pilgrimages should be stopped. There is no good in them: no commandment enjoins them, no obedience attaches to them. Rather do these pilgrimages give countless occasions to commit sin and to despise God's commandments.[89]

Other protestant reformers held similar views. Since the veneration of Saints was seen, by them, as idolatrous and since saintly relics were often the prize of a pilgrim's long trek, pilgrimages fell out of favor in the growing protestant world. A stunning blow was dealt, in 1534, when King Henry VIII of England left the Catholic Church. Because the Pope refused to annul his marriage to the Queen and make legitimate Henry's marriage to the woman he really liked, Henry severed England's ties with the Roman Church and declared himself head of the new Church of England to get a proper divorce. Though not a protestant *per se*, his break from the Pope gave fuel to the English Protestants, and pilgrimages, for the English, gradually fell out of favor. All of this did not bode well for the popularity of the Camino. Unfortunately, at about this time, another completely unrelated occurrence dimmed any hope of restoring the Camino to its Medieval glory days. To understand this occurrence we have to first note two important historical facts: the defeat of the Spanish navy, and the Spanish king's obsession with holy relics.

1588 was not the best year for Spain with the defeat of its seemingly invincible naval fleet, known as the Armada. King Felipe II of Spain began the year with high hopes for a plan to sail the Armada up the English Channel, attack, remove Queen Elizabeth I from the throne, and restore Catholicism to England. The plan failed miserably because the large Spanish galleons were outmaneuvered by the smaller English vessels and unfavorable winds blew the Armada first toward the Dutch coast and then out to the North Sea where they were further pursued. The following year, the English launched a naval counter-offensive, attacking the northwest coast of Spain. It is the fierce counter-offensive that interests us because it no doubt created a climate of fear in Northern Spain, in 1589, that the English would advance inland, plundering cities along the way, with Santiago de Compostela likely a prime target.

Meanwhile, the same king that launched the Armada against England was busy building a palace, the Escorial, to his own glory near Madrid. One of his side hobbies was collecting holy relics. As the Escorial rose and as his collection grew, relics became an obsession. By the time of his death in 1598, he had amassed nearly 7500 of them from all over Europe.[90] Acquiring relics from the likes of France was cheered by Spaniards, but Felipe coveted many of the holy relics held in churches around Spain. This caused quite a stir with the regional clerics and rulers for whom having some relics of their own, bolstered their prestige. Was the King going to take them for himself? It was clear he was zeroing in on Santiago de Compostela when, in 1572, he sent his royal chronicler to Northern Spain to catalog all the relics and antiquities located there. Would he seek to remove the bones of Saint James interred in the great Cathedral? Such an act would deal a devastating blow to the city's high status in the Catholic world. Concern must have risen further when it turned out that a cloister of nuns in Santiago de Compostela held the head of St. Lawrence, and Felipe wanted it. After lengthy negotiations and a fair amount of arm twisting, he got it. Then, in an undated letter by the King to his chief minister, he unequivocally stated that he wanted all of the remains of St. James held in the Cathedral. In the letter, he makes his case, arguing that the Camino pilgrimage would continue in the absence of St. James' remains because many lesser relics were in the area and, besides, it was inappropriate that the bones of the great, martyred saint should be allowed to languish so far from the center of Spain in a place named Finisterre.[91]

This brings us to the unfortunate occurrence. In 1589, the Archbishop of Santiago had plenty to worry about. Fearing English pirates to the north and an avaricious King to the South, he decided to secretly move the remains of St. James to a safe location where neither the marauding English nor the covetous King could find them. He hid them very well. Too well, as it turns out. When he died in 1602, nobody knew where the famous bones lay. In fact, the remains of the Saint were so well protected from discovery that their location was a mystery for nearly 300 years. Then, in 1878, the Church began an archeological excavation inside the Cathedral. An ossuary, the official name for a kind of box, containing bones was found, and the Church, no doubt eager to restore the famous reliquary, declared them authentic and the Camino was back in business after a centuries-long period of decline.

The 20th century saw renewed interest in the Camino, particularly beginning in the 1940s under the regime of Francisco Franco. Central to Franco's vision for Spain was an embrace of traditional Spanish institutions, including the Catholic Church. Pilgrimages were suddenly popular again, as evidenced by the "Great Youth Pilgrimage" of 1948 which drew an estimated 80,000 young Spanish pilgrims.[92] Franco also declared James the Patron Saint of Spain, further stimulating interest in Santiago de Compostela and the Camino. When Franco died in 1975, government support for the church declined sharply. Surprisingly, though, traffic on the Camino continued to grow. The post-Franco years saw a period of secularization for Spain and a resurgence of regional identities, which had been harshly repressed during the Franco era of centralization of power and nationalist fervor. Regions along the Camino route saw the economic possibilities of a resurgent Camino and infrastructure grew to accommodate the interest that had been established in recent decades. Further attention and prestige came in 1993 when the United Nations Educational, Scientific, and Cultural Organization (UNESCO) declared the major routes of the Camino a World Heritage Site.[93]

In recent decades, secular interest in the Camino has more than compensated for the general decline of traditional Catholic spirituality among Europeans. The UNESCO award provided global cachet while the tourism industries in the Northern

Spanish provinces built up infrastructure and promoted the ancient walking path as a modern tourist destination. Books and movies have followed. Famous memoirs of the Camino include Paul Coelho's *The Pilgrimage* published in 1987 and Shirley Maclaine's *The Camino: A Journey of the Spirit*, which came out in 2001. The most popular movie by far is *The Way*, a Hollywood feature released in 2010, starring Martin Sheen.

In the last decade, interest in the Camino has exploded. Pilgrims now complain of crowds, especially during July and August. Lodgers compete daily for accommodations, racing to the next town to get the last available bed. Those seeking spiritual renewal lament the touristic vibe of the new Camino lined with souvenir shops. In our era, will the ancient path become a victim of its own success? Is tourism the enemy of authentic spirituality? Is the Camino headed toward some lesser, secularized version of itself? Will it no longer be possible to experience the Camino as an adventure of the spirit as it morphs into a Disney-like parody? Taking a step back, considering the history, is the meaning of the Camino defined for people by powerful forces over which they have no control, or do individuals make their own meaning in their own ways despite the powers that be? And what was my place in all this drama? We will return to these questions, but, at the moment, the Spanish Meseta beckons.

Chapter 23
The Meseta

Ron Clements, director of the live action *Little Mermaid* movie, said that, for a song to work in film, the timing has to be just right, otherwise it feels forced. The action has to reach a point at which words will no longer serve, and the moment naturally rises to song because there's nothing else that will do. I was listening to the *New Yorker Radio Hour* on the internet in my miniature hotel room in Burgos on that rest day, and this interview with Clements made me want to go watch the movie just to see if the song entrances met his standard. I had a feeling they would.

Next day I was a kilometer out of Tardajos at about 8:30 a.m., right at the point in the day when the long cool shadows of early morning are dissolving into the full sun of a warm, late spring day. I was passing what appeared to be the last few buildings on the outskirts of this last little town on the fringe of the city, and I was catching glimpses of the expansive plains of Spain's central mesa rising gently ahead of me. The road took a turn and, suddenly, right in front of me was a colorful mural, spread across the entire wall of a barn. It showed an adult and a small child walking a long road into a sunset, perhaps like the road ahead of me. A Bible verse was written, like a banner, across the top of the mural, "Dejad que los niños vengan a mi ..." which in

English means, "Let the little children come to me …" The rest of the verse, which didn't appear, I recalled roughly. The exact wording, which I looked up later, continues, "and do not hinder them, for the kingdom of God belongs to such as these." The road took another turn, and, along the wall of the last building, another barn, was a famous verse from Genesis, "Vio Dios todo lo que habia hecho, y era muy bueno." Or "God saw all that he had created, and it was very good." And then there were no more buildings. The town gave way to an enormous blue sky accented with the occasional puffy cloud and, beneath it, the Meseta, as the Spanish word 'mesa' suggests, a big flat table, actually, several big flat tables joined at slightly different angles reaching to the horizon, covered with early wheat. I walked up the road, into the scene. Wind gusts were surfing across the planted fields creating swatches of different hues. Everywhere I looked, in front of me, up the road, and to either side was the same endless landscape. I was overwhelmed. The moment was rising to song, and in an instant I knew just the right music.

Now, unlike a movie, where the music needs to appeal to a broad audience, my music, for this moment, only had to appeal to me. I'll tell you what it was, and you may cringe, or smile, or smirk. For me, it was the only thing possible because the moment was beyond words. Like Clements said, nothing else would do. It occurred to me, I could actually listen to the music that was now in my head. I had an iPhone, and, with its Spanish sim card, I could access YouTube. I checked: three bars. I called up the album. I plugged in my earbuds, which I'd been carrying in my waist pouch for the last 13 days and had not used because I think of myself as *not* one of those people who's plugged into their phone and ignoring the surroundings. Okay, I was going to be one of those people. I pressed the play arrow on the YouTube album cover. The shofar sounded its familiar call, and then the confident tenor, singing unaccompanied, began, "Prepare ye the way of the Lord." It was the album to *Godspell*, a play I've loved since I saw it in New York in the 1970s as a teenager. Other voices join in and eventually the entire cast is singing "Prepare ye the way of the Lord," the only line in the song. Instruments join one by one, and the ensemble moves into an ecstatic frenzy, ending abruptly. This piece is followed by "Save the People" then the iconic, "Day by Day." With each song, I walked deeper and deeper into the enormous landscape accompanied by a soundtrack I'd listened to for 50 years. What I love about the play is the innocence of the characters. They are like children, in love with the idea of peace and kindness, following their teacher. This is how I imagine the earliest Christians, before the rag-tag following got organized, and then coopted by the Roman Empire and distorted into a patriarchal religion with rules and rituals and ideology. What I love about the music is its respect for Biblical stories, its playful lyrics, and range of musical idioms. There was no one on the Camino visible ahead or behind as I dwelt a good half hour in a state that simply had to have a song or six. Nothing else would do.

You can think of the Camino divided into three parts. First is St. Jean to Burgos, which is hilly. Next is Burgos to Leon, which is flat, the Meseta. Last comes Leon to Santiago, which is hilly again. The three parts are not equal in length. It took me 11 days to get from St. Jean to Burgos, then just six days to cross the Meseta, and then, the final stretch consumed over two weeks, at 15 days of walking. The Meseta is Spain's central plateau. In the north, it is covered with wheat and in the south, vineyards and olive trees. Sheep roam everywhere. Outside of the major cities, like Madrid, the Meseta is rural and getting more so as young people have been moving to the big cities since the 1970s, sometimes leaving whole towns abandoned. Rural depopulation is a problem in Spain, and, in recent years the national government has been trying to incentivize people remaining in the countryside. It is this rural, wheat-carpeted land, dotted with small villages, through which I was now walking, with my traveling community of pilgrims, all marching toward Santiago. Several days into the Meseta, I noticed people were chattier. Because we weren't all huffing and puffing uphill or minding our steps downhill, it was easier to talk. And that flat, straight road was—breathtaking scenery notwithstanding—sometimes boring. All the new chattiness carried over to the albergues in the evenings.

"I'm 40, and if I'm going to have a kid, the time is now. I'm calling my partner tonight. We're discussing it," Kathleen emphatically states. She occupies the bunk bed next to mine. She's *arriba* (upper bunk) and I'm *abajo* (lower bunk). We're each making up our bed for the night. She's English, looks like a fashion magazine model, says she works as an organizational consultant. She is educated, confident, and friendly. We've known each other for about 5 minutes.

She continues, "When we got together four years ago, he already had a kid, and we thought one is good, then we split up, then we got back together, and he wanted another and I didn't. Now I want to have a child and he doesn't. We have to talk. It's hard. When I divorced, I wasn't planning on getting into a relationship right away, but then he came along quite quickly." I'm trying to not look astonished as she pours out all this personal detail. I wiggle my pillow into the fresh pillowcase I was handed with my bedsheets just minutes before by our friendly Korean host.

Kathleen continues, "I could just make it happen while I'm on the Camino." Naively, I think she's suggesting some sort of artificial insemination technique with her partner, involving the postal service.

So, I say, "That would be challenging."

She says, "It would be immoral."

Ah, I get it. Not the postal service. I make a joke. "You could say, 'Gosh, he was handsome, smart, and all four of his grandparents are in their 90s and in good health.'" She laughs.

The Camino might be the only place in the world where it is common for someone who was a perfect stranger just moments ago, to suddenly reveal intimate details of their life. There's an assumed trust in the traveling community, which, I've noticed, has been growing, the longer we spend walking, eating, and sleeping all in close proximity. It results sometimes in remarkably candid conversation. And it extends beyond talk. We walk around the dorm rooms, in dim light, sometimes in our underwear, padding to and from the shower, getting dressed for dinner. The assumption is, if you're a peregrino, you're honorable. I have not seen this trust betrayed at all in any way in two weeks on the Camino in close quarters with hundreds of strangers in dormitories, restrooms, dining halls, kitchens, laundry rooms, etc. The presence of wine, sometime lots, doesn't seem to compromise any of it. I've asked several women, and they report the same. Though my limited experience, as a man, suggests the Camino is safe for women, there are reports to the contrary, and, like other environments, sexual aggression toward women on the Camino is likely under-reported.[94]

With Kathleen and me in our six person dorm are Ricardo, a physician from Italy, Vincenzo, also from Italy; Suzanna, a young law professor from Texas; and Huston, a retiree from Florida. Suzanna was a public defender in New York for six years, lost faith in the law, and moved to Texas to "try to change the system." She's a smart, passionate idealist. Huston was among the first people I met in Spain, in the albergue in Pamplona where I stayed on my way to St. Jean before I started the walk. A young retiree, he is footloose and traveling the world. Later that evening, with lights out, there's a free-flowing conversation among the six of us as we lay in our bunks in the dark. I can't recall the words or topics, only the feel of it. Easy.

Light-hearted, but intimate. Some laughter. What I imagine summer camp might be like, if I'd ever gone. Or maybe siblings sharing a bedroom. You could almost hear someone's parent at the door, "No more talking. Go to sleep."

Two days later, more Meseta, more flatness, and a new friend, Andres. He shared:

> When my daughter, Mariela, turned 15, I sat her down, and I said, "Mariela, you are like a kite and you are flying, and I am guiding you holding the strings. As you get older, I cut some of these strings and you begin to fly on your own. Now you are 15 and so there will be a new rule. On Friday, Saturday, and Sunday you do not need to ask permission for going out with friends. You only need to make sure you are home before 1 a.m."

Andres is from Ecuador. We've been walking together for a couple hours from the outskirts of Castro de Jeriz, beside a highway with very few cars, a long flat stretch, with fields of alfalfa reaching to the horizon on both sides. The sun is strong today. I'm using sunblock for only the second time. Because almost all my body is covered with clothing or in shadow as I walk west in the early morning, I tend to not use any, but Andres was rubbing it on his arms and ears at the stop we made a while back. He offered me his squeeze bottle. He said his daughters keep telling him to use it. So, I did too.

We lift our packs from where they've been resting against a rock and shrug them onto our backs. As we pick up walking, our shoes kick dust from the dry earth of the trail. Andres has more to say about Mariela, like he's told this story before. It's okay. It's a good story so far. He continues:

> When Mariela was 18, I sat her down again. I said, "Mariela, you are now 18 and there are only two strings still attached. Love and economics. I will support you financially through university until you get your first job, and, of course, I will always love you."

Andres pauses here, puts his hand on my shoulder and turns toward me while we walk. He says:

Then, when she finished University, before I talked with her again, *she* came to *me*. She said, "Papa, we are cutting the string, I am finished with university and I have my first job. You no longer need to support me." I was very touched that she came to me and said this, and I replied the only string remaining, the one that will never be cut, is love.

We walk in silence for a few beats. Then I tell him it's a beautiful story.

As Andres shares this and other tales — he walked the Camino with Paula, his younger daughter seven years ago — It makes me think about my own parenting. Do I have any wise and earnest tales like his? Hmm. Nothing comes to mind. I think, lucky me, my kids turned out strong and kind. We walk together through the morning, as the day heats up, and a blazing afternoon, the strong Spanish sun arcing slowly across the southern sky, to Carrion de los Condes, within spitting distance now of the Camino's halfway point, just before Leon. We are the same age. Andres was in banking, retired the previous year. He worked for the International Monetary Fund for many years and then Chase Manhattan. He's friends, apparently, with the finance ministers of several Latin American countries. I ask him what his plans are. He says he's been learning German because Mariela lives in Germany and Paula, though she lives in Madrid, works for a German company and will likely end up in Germany, too. He also wants to learn to play guitar, and he wants to learn to cook because he can't cook at all, and he wants to keep consulting informally in banking. I thought *I* was a planner. He says he separated from his wife eight years ago. Amicable, he adds. Suddenly, he's talking about Outlook, the computer app everybody uses for email. He says he used it to organize his workday. Really? I think. I'm finding I like Andres and I'm also feeling like I can't possibly compete with this guy. He describes a system he figured out for managing his workflow and the people who work for him. I didn't know you could manage people with an app. I don't think my work has ever flowed, like some kind of a river, at least not on a regular basis; more like choppy seas, fast moving rapids, occasional duldrums, once in a while a tsunami. Maybe it's the difference between banking and public schools. We walk on, through the afternoon, keeping up a friendly banter. He speaks slowly in Spanish, all day, for my sake, and invites me to ask whenever I don't understand so he can teach me new vocabulary. He says he likes being a teacher. He is patient.

Andres is olive-skinned. I wonder if he has some indigenous ancestry. I observe many peregrinos from Latin America and many are darker skinned. There's also a substantial East Asian presence on the Camino, and, of course, plenty of White people—the majority. Though I am unaware of any official or other credible statistics for race on the Pilgrimage route, it looks like the Camino suffers from the same absence of Black people as other outdoor spaces. Camino Forums, individual Facebook posts, Reddit posts, and similar casual spaces where Black people have reported on their Camino experience suggest as much, and for the same reasons. Work to be done.

Walking and chattering through the day with friends, stopping at cafes and other rest areas, its easy to get distracted, which also means its easy to leave important stuff behind. Flashback: It was my third day on the Camino. I was approaching my destination for the day of Puente La Reina, about 25K past Pamplona. It had been a long day. It was a little chilly and my clothes were sweaty, an unpleasant combo—cold and wet. I sat for a moment's rest, checked my guidebook for the name of that evening's albergue, then got up and kept walking. Wait! I stopped 10 steps later, looked back and saw my wide brimmed hat sitting on the bench. I'd been wearing my gaiter like a hood for warmth, so it was easy to overlook my hat which rested on top, where I didn't feel it directly. I walked back, grabbed it and carried on. It was a good lesson and timely. I needed a system to make sure I had all my important stuff every time I got up to leave somewhere. I'd done this type of routine for my bike trip and found it comforting and effective. Over the course of the next couple days, a little ritual evolved. In its final form, I would name each important item and touch it. Once I'd gone successfully through the list, I knew I was good to go. These were both the most important items and items most likely to be left behind. My alliterative verse included 11 things and went:

Pouch, pack, phone.

Purse, passport.

Glasses, glasses, glasses (meaning, eyeglasses, case, and sunglasses)

Guide, gaiter, hat.

Once I brushed the rim of my hat, I was cleared for take-off. Sixteen days in, it was the ritual I'd stuck with and, so far, nothing was missing—at least that I noticed.

It's June 1. Turning a page on the calendar, even if it doesn't line up with any special event, feels like a milestone. I've been at this Camino-walking for 15 days now. My feet look horrible, toenails discolored and misshapen, at least two of them are dead and will come loose at some point. I've got a sizable blister on the second toe on my left foot. Amazingly, though, my very ugly, scary looking feet are fully functional. They carry me 30 to 40 kilometers every day without complaint and are pain free. The rest of me is a different story. Minor aches whine from every joint and muscle in my body at the end of each day. Nothing like a hot shower and a comfortable bed! Side note: Just another plug for how much better this journey is than wilderness hiking. Set up a tent? No shower for all the grime and stink? No sink for daily laundry? Freeze-dried mac and cheese? Sleep on the cold, hard ground? No thanks! I'm getting old and soft. So be it.

Actually, it's starting to look like there's more going on than minor aches and pains, and I'm worried. Four days ago, I caught a cold. First, I ignored it, thinking it would go away if I did not acknowledge it. It got worse each day. Last night was bad. I slept poorly, hacking up phlegm, mild sore throat, and fever. Not even my trusty blue Advils tamed it. I gargled with salt water before I went to bed and drank a lot of water, and, therefore had to get up and pee five times during the night. Hydration vs sleep. This morning, when the motorcycles started up (my new, favorite iPhone alarm sound), instead of rolling right out of bed, eager to rev into the day with the Harleys, I wanted only to pull the covers higher, up over my head. But the Camino was calling. So I said to myself, okay, I'm not "getting up", I'm just going through the motions that people go through when they get up: silence the motorcycles, pull on pants, pack away charger cords, pee, brush teeth, drink water, then, because I'm feeling worse, gargle, take two Advil, stand distractedly for an unknown amount of time and suddenly remember I'm supposed to be doing my get-ready-for-the-day routine. Then drink more water. I notice the eczema on my right hand is getting worse. Scaly skin that flakes off when I scratch it. I'm turning into a lizard, I decide, starting with my hands. If I treated it more than once a day, it would do better, but besides looking funny and giving me an itch to scratch, what difference really does it make? My hand works fine and treating it takes time. Then there's my right thumb, which has been pinging vigorously at night, a weird nerve issue I've had for years. Only, during the last few days it's getting worse. Nothing makes it stop. I try squeezing it, stretching it, letting it just be, and in all cases it pings away. The sudden sting of pain wakes me at random moments during the night and keeps me awake while I try, without success, to make it go away. Eventually, it subsides, and I fall back asleep. Until it randomly picks up again an hour or two later. The x-ray I got a few months ago shows nothing wrong. I wonder if a surgeon could just cauterize a few nerves. I'd much rather have no feeling in that thumb and risk the occasional kitchen burn than continue to sleep poorly every night.

I didn't realize until later that I never seriously entertained the possibility of Covid for all my flu-like symptoms. The May and June I walked the Camino, 2023, was a bare 18 months past the worst of the global plague, but it seemed all precautions were gone. Very few pilgrims were masked, even in the crowded albergues with strangers from all points of the global compass. It is possible the Camino cough was actually Covid and the mass of pilgrims humping the Camino that month was a traveling super-spreader event. But I don't think so. Perhaps the good physical shape of pilgrims generally warded off the virus. Maybe the fact that so much of the Camino experience is outdoors lessened the risk. But still, all those crowded dorm rooms, shared bathrooms, and kitchens were an inviting opportunity for any random bug to take hold. Maybe we were all foolish and lucky, or maybe, the fact that people were not getting seriously sick in any noticeable numbers persuaded us, we were over this thing that had stilled sociability around the world for two years, and we were ready to take whatever risk was required to re-connect with people. We are a herding species after all. Maybe, bottom line, that's why people walk the Camino, we like being together, in shared purpose, even if we're not entirely sure what the shared purpose is. Oh, yeah, make it all the way to Santiago.

Despite my reluctant start, I got out of my pension private room (luxury night) early and decided to get a proper breakfast in the café downstairs: omelette with cheese, fresh orange juice, black tea, and NO bread. They eat too much damn bread in this country. Every meal, there's a half a loaf on the table. I guess they have to do something with all those endless fields of wheat.

At 6:22 a.m., half-light, full tummy, bad night of sleep, I wanted to crawl back into bed, but I hit the Camino. I put one foot in front of the other. Half a kilometer in, moving like a slug, it occurred to me if I walk faster, I'll cover ground faster, and get to a proper bed sooner. I picked up my pace and started feeling better under the warming sun. With the help of two café solos (espresso), strategically swallowed at 11 a.m. and 12:30 p.m., plus very deliberate consumption of about four times as much water as I usually drink, I made it to the Albergue Castillo de Moratinos at 2 p.m. And, thanks to the four liters of water I downed throughout the day, I also improved my skill at stealth peeing by the side of the Camino. Facilities are sometimes few and far between. Easier for men. Shortly, I was in bed, comfy with my winter coat, cap, and an extra blanket. My window, facing the courtyard was open to let some warm afternoon air into the room. The ancient stones of the building retained the cool night-time temperature. My plan for the rest of the day: sleep, get dinner, take Advil, gargle, chew an aspirin, sleep. My laundry was below, in the courtyard, getting dry in the sun and the breeze. I heard distant thunder, so I'd have to keep an eye out, I thought, as I drifted off to sleep.

Next day, I woke up slightly better. My cold was at that point where, if I took care not to stress myself, it might finish its course in one more day. Except, today's plan was a 39K epic march across the last bit of Meseta to the great city of Leon. At least it would be flat, but that also meant it could be very boring. I needed a plan. Towns on the way to Leon were spaced at 14K, 6K, 6K, 5K, and 8K. Okay, I thought, I'll break it into three chunks. That way it won't feel as massive. I'll rest lots and hydrate. If I got started promptly and walked with diligence and purpose to Reliegos (14K), where, according to my guidebook, there was at least one food stop, I'd have a proper breakfast there. That would motivate me to make tracks and fuel me for the road beyond. Stop two would be at Puente Villarente, two towns further and the next 12K chunk. There I'd get a café solo and, if I was lucky, a banana, my preferred energy snack—naturally-sourced caffeine, potassium and electrolytes. From there would be a challenging 13K finish, more than a just coda on the day's walk, a full third of the total distance. I started as planned, but, with limited energy, I ended up stopping at each of the towns, where I sat down, pulled off my sneakers and socks, let my feet breathe and drank at least a half-liter of water. Probably a good practice in general if I don't want my brain to shrink and my skin to get leathery. Or lizardy. Too late for both, I guess. I feel flabby and old. I had a look at my naked self in the mirror this morning. I *used to have* well defined pecs.

I got a little boost, mid-morning, when I ran into Andres. It had been a few days since our memorable walk. In the interim, he'd made the acquaintance of an attractive 50-ish blond-haired woman from Amsterdam. We all sat together for a rest stop. She said she's a little lost in her life, no longer believes in herself, hoping to get her head straight on the Camino. At that moment I looked over at Andres, man of planning and purpose, who was regarding her with interest. Maybe he'd be good for her. Maybe she'd be good for him.

On the last 13K, I felt my energy sinking. Despite some healthy fruit, a second café solo, and an excellent Snicker's ice cream cone, my little engine was running out of steam. Thankfully, the last 4K was all downhill to the Leon Cathedral and my albergue, on a nearby street. Two hours later, showered and sipping tea with my feet up, I was relieved to finally be at rest for the day. But tomorrow morning would come too soon and, because Leon marks the western edge of the Meseta, the terrain would start to rise again. In just a few days, I'd be climbing the steepest bit of the Camino to the Cruz de Ferro at 1500 meters, and my cold was getting worse.

Chapter 24
Finding God, or Not

As a walking pilgrim in the years 2000 and 2001, I was taken aback by the commercialization and crowding of the summertime pilgrimage. Westward of the city of Leon, we walked in a crowded line from morning to night, a sort of slow-motion race in groups, the goal of which was to reserve a clean bed and a shower before the others arrived. Though not a religious pilgrim myself, it occurred to me that we modern pilgrims were perhaps desecrating something holy, because I felt the pilgrimage lacked the austerity and sacrifice of "authentic" pilgrimage. In fact, I became so disgusted with the crowds that in the first year I stopped short of Santiago and finished the journey later only after having reflected for a year. —Elizabeth Kissling[95]

Reports from the Camino increasingly lament its commercialization. The ancient path, they point out, once offered a unique opportunity for meditation, reflection, solitude, and spiritual renewal. Through a self-imposed hardship of walking long distances every day and attending minimally to the needs of the physical self, the spiritual self would be liberated. But, these days, cafes, souvenir shops, bars, and boutique hotels line the streets of every town. Mercedes cargo vans shuttle luggage ahead on a daily basis. Adventure travel companies operate eight-day package trips featuring "authentic experiences" with "local encounters." And pilgrims pose for selfies and text their friends back home while hustling to the next famous site. It's getting hard to find authenticity, let alone God.

Or so we are told. But what's true is the Camino has always served multiple purposes. The people who walk it have always brought a range of motivations, and the larger social and economic forces that try to shape the experience have always been there, shifting and evolving from century to century. Whatever those forces are in any given era, individuals still bring to the Camino what *they* want, and they take from the Camino what *they* need. Most of the time, that's not just one thing. The motivations of a person walking the Camino are typically complex and varied: part spiritual seeker, part tourist, part adventurer, etc. These categories are not mutually exclusive. And whatever cultural forces hold sway, we pilgrims are part pawns in a larger drama and part personal power brokers for our own aspirations.

Lluis Oviedo, Scarlett de Courcier, and Miguel Farias are academics interested in the intersection between psychology, science, and religion. In 2009, they were curious about why people walk the Camino, in light of the fact that pilgrim numbers were exploding at a time when organized religion was declining. The Catholic Church, especially, was in steep descent following world-wide revelations of widespread sexual abuse of children by trusted clergy. Why was the Camino so popular? Had the Camino suddenly transformed itself into a tourist attraction? Were people seeking a more eclectic, less defined spiritual experience? Were traditional Catholics seeking renewal for themselves and their Church through the cleansing power of pilgrimage? Scholars of religion were debating these very questions, so Oviedo, de Courcier, and Farias decided to find out for themselves. They drew up a questionnaire and, during the summers of 2009 and 2010, they handed it out to pilgrims along the Camino Frances, usually at the end of the day as trekkers arrived at their albergue or inn. They collected a total of 470 completed questionnaires, and they also conducted interviews with pilgrims, hospitality workers, and priests serving pilgrims along the Camino.[96]

The first thing they found was that people who walk the Camino are, in general, no more or less religious than most Europeans. In other words, pilgrims are a representative sample of the general population, not an especially religious bunch. Mainly, the questionnaire focused on reasons why people walk the Camino. It asked questions about 48 possible motivations. Six got the most hits: spiritual growth, sensation seeking, seeking life direction, religious growth, community, and religious devotion. The difference between "spiritual" and "religious" growth is interesting. Spiritual growth questions, like "expand my consciousness" and "find my deeper self" got more hits than questions that were more specifically religious, like "grow in faith" and "be closer to God." This suggests that while strictly Catholic religiosity does not explain the popularity of the Camino, a less defined spirituality is still, for many pilgrims, right at the center of their Camino experience. The lowest scoring factor among the six was religious devotion, with questions focused on "repentance" or "fulfilling a promise." This suggests that the most traditional reasons for pilgrimage, in the eyes of the Church, do not register for most contemporary pilgrims, though are still of interest to some.

The second most popular motivation after spiritual growth was "sensation seeking" based on questions that named "proving myself," "testing my limits," and "search of adventure." People who checked the questions for sensation seeking tended to also check the questions for spiritual growth but not religious growth. This suggests that an undefined spiritual experience coupled with aspects of personal development are core motivators for many contemporary pilgrims. The authors concluded that pilgrims, in general, are seeking some form of renewal by stepping outside of the normal experiences of daily life. While some pursue it through the framework and symbols of traditional religion, more find it through an eclectic and less defined path. As much as the church would like for pilgrims to embrace the Camino's very specific Catholic features, the study demonstrates that people who walk the ancient route exercise their own agency. And this is not just a modern phenomenon. Though Catholicism is currently in decline in many places in the world, even when it was a ubiquitous force during the Middle Ages, people were people and brought all their very human qualities to pilgrimages. Pilgrimage has never been only or even mainly about religious devotion.

If Geoffrey Chaucer's account of the English pilgrimage to Canterbury during the Middle Ages is any indication, and if medieval life on that famous trek was anything like life on the medieval Camino, then it's pretty clear that the pilgrim experience was quite varied and not always in line with what the Church would approve. Chaucer was writing fiction, of course, and a kind of social satire at that, but it is still reasonable to infer that his exaggerations were meant to capture a contemporary truth of the pilgrim experience.

Consider for a minute just a few of Chaucer's pilgrims. There's the Wife of Bath who is anything but submissive to the five husbands she has wed. She flaunts her sexual prowess. The Miller, who is drunk for the telling of his tale, shares the story of a boarder who lusts after his host's wife and schemes to sleep with her. It is pure medieval-style vaudeville with fart jokes and sight gags. The Nun's Priest tells a story of romance set among the chickens in a barnyard. It features a playboy rooster who copulates vigorously with the prettiest hen and who, in the end, escapes the jaws of a fox through clever deception. My point here is that, at ground level, where real pilgrims walked the dusty roads, the experience was a lot more complicated than the image of pious rectitude the Church would have projected. There was laughter and mischief, romance and sex, drinking and the telling of bawdy tales, fights and merry making. Though powerful cultural and economic forces aimed to channel the pilgrim experience, people exercised agency. They made the experience their own. Try as the church may to impose fear of purgatory, veneration of saints, and spiritual cleansing through corporeal suffering, people found a way to make the Camino experience a fuller expression of their humanity. It is no different today. And part of that experience is the sheer adventure of it.

If we look at the Camino as an adventure experience, which is just one of its many aspects, we pretty quickly realize that, as an adventure, it has a very distinctive quality that sometimes appears in other adventures, but which is essential to the Camino. Spirituality is at the core of the Camino experience, both in terms of its history and how it is experienced by the majority of modern pilgrims. It might make you wonder how important is spirituality to adventuring overall? What is the place of spirituality in adventure, in general?

We tend to locate spirituality in places of worship. That's where people officially get spiritual, but we also know that, for many of us, our greatest moments of deep, spiritual renewal occur when we step out of our daily routines, stop being busy, move into natural surroundings, engage in some form of physical exertion, and enter a space, physical and mental, in which certainties about ourselves and the world we inhabit are challenged. A service of religious worship may possess some of those elements, but adventurous journeying encompasses them all.

Donna Little, whose work we've discussed in connection with the ways in which women define adventure, has also written about adventure's spiritual aspects. Little's research on adventure is situated within the broader field of leisure, or leisure studies. Though a hard-core adventurer will bristle at the suggestion that their death-defying ascent of the vertical rock face of El Capitan is considered "leisure," the fact is, that's where the academic world locates it. If you want to find out what research is saying about adventurous pursuits, you often end up scanning the contents of leisure journals. In 2007, Donna Little and her colleague Christopher Schmidt, both at the University of Waikato in New Zealand published a study about the spiritual experiences of adventurers. It came out in the spring issue of the *Journal of Leisure Research*.[97]

Schmidt and Little had a hunch that spiritual growth was a bigger part of adventuring than was generally acknowledged. In their study, they began by recognizing that there is no one definition of spirituality that everyone agrees on, yet there is a near universal agreement that, somehow, it is central to the human experience. They pulled together words and phrases that others have used like *transcendent, greater reality, subjective experience of the sacred, whatever one considers to be the ultimate, consciousness of the infinite, oneness and strength, awareness and attunement to the world and one's place in it, a deep connection with the divine.* For purposes of their study, they settled on a broad definition: "the ways in which people seek, make, celebrate, and apply meaning in their lives" which usually involves "a frame of reference wider than the immediate, the material, and the everyday." Armed with their definition, Schmidt and Little interviewed 24 people who said they experienced spirituality during their leisure activities. Some were religious, some were not. For a few of the participants, leisure meant sedentary activities like reading and meditation. These are not directly helpful to us. But for most, leisure activities meant different forms of vigorous outdoor adventuring, like rock-climbing, wilderness hiking, surfing, horse-riding, SCUBA diving, and even firewalking. During the interviews, the authors took care not to suggest any established ideas they had in mind (e.g., God, nature, risk) that they wanted their participants to discuss.

Instead, they wanted to capture whatever categories or patterns emerged from the "lived experiences" of the people they interviewed. In the research world, this approach is called phenomenology and it can be a powerful way to discover how people truly experience the world, rather than simply confirming what you think you're going to find. That said, what Schmidt and Little found could have been predicted, yet, because they went in with a truly blank slate, we can feel assured that the results are authentic, and not just confirmation of the researchers' own biases.

The interview findings for this study suggest adventure has four aspects that can trigger a spiritual experience. They are nature, newness & difference, challenge, and ritual & tradition. People said they were deeply moved by the majesty of nature or that, in nature, they felt a powerful connection to something universal and essential. Nature, the authors summarize, offered people, "a reprieve from the everyday, an awe-inspiring vista, and a grounding option where the respondents felt, were aware, were freed, or gained a notion of connection with self, the living world, and/or God" (p. 237). Similarly, *newness and difference* prompted a spiritual awakening for many. Whether it was a wooded path that a person was traveling for the first time, or a country very different from home, newness and difference caused people to look at the world differently, it heightened their awareness of their own actions and beliefs. Familiar thoughts and well-worn habits taken for granted suddenly stood out and announced themselves and became subject to inspection. This often led to a kind of renewal, so deep and hard to describe, people felt it was spiritual. A third trigger was *challenge*. Some people spoke of a physical challenge, like hiking a mountain. Others talked about a combination of physical and skill-based challenges, learning to surf bigger waves or mastering the moves of body combat. Some talked about the element of risk, which produced fear (hiking a cliff edge, paragliding) and how fear heightened awareness and the overcoming of fear deepened religious faith or produced greater self-efficacy. In general, people spoke of the role of challenge in "altering their perception of self, enhancing their awareness, pushing their boundaries of knowledge and perception" (p. 238). Finally, there was *ritual and tradition*. These included daily walks, attendance at annual outdoor events, ritualized physical exercise such as yoga and tai chi. People commented that the repetitive nature and structure of rituals is freeing, conducive to reflection. Overall, many people experienced a combination of triggers—nature and ritual, newness and challenge—that heightened their spiritual experience.

Now this study selected only people who stated up front that they had a spiritual experience in connection with their adventuring. So, we can't conclude that everyone encounters God or some form of the ultimate whenever they venture forth. But we can say that adventure opens up huge possibilities to explore the spiritual side of life and achieve deep, personal renewal. The Camino, in particular, offers such opportunities, and not just because of its association with traditional religion. Extended walking, and, in particular, walking through mostly natural surroundings along an established path can promote a meditative state.

Kip Redick is a veteran hiker of the Appalachian Trail. He is also a professor of philosophy. He has devoted years to a study of the connection between wilderness hiking and spirituality and has coined the term *spiritual rambling*. He describes it in a bit of philosophy-speak as "a walking exegesis of one's life story and scripting a new story in the quest for meaning" (Redick, 2016). In simpler terms you might say that the repetitive nature of walking produces a semi-hypnotic state in which your thoughts flow freely, you put together new ideas about yourself and what your personal story is, and you come away with a clearer, more satisfying sense of who you are. Redick has found that wilderness is better than cityscapes or parks for producing this effect because the more the landscape differs from the day-to-day, the better. Unfortunately, he singles out the Camino as second rate due to its comfy hostels, restaurants, and quaint villages. Not enough hardship and difference for him. Maybe he'll come around.

Redick is not the only person who has studied the relationship between walking and spirituality. Thich Nhat Hanh was a Buddhist monk who first came to the attention of the World during the U.S. war in Vietnam. He spoke out for peace and became controversial. He founded monasteries in Vietnam, studied and taught in the United States and France, and wrote widely on Buddhism. He is credited with introducing the west to mindfulness with a book published in 1975 called *The Miracle of Mindfulness*. He also developed a practice of walking meditation. He wrote:

> Many of us walk for the sole purpose of getting from one place to another. Now suppose we are walking to a sacred place. We would walk quietly and take each gentle step with reverence. I propose that we walk this way every time we walk on the earth. The earth is sacred and we touch her with each step. We should be very respectful, because we are walking on our mother. If we walk like that, then every step will be grounding, every step will be nourishing. [98]

For many years, Nhat Hanh went for a daily walk around the retreat center in France that he founded and where he lived. His followers would walk with him. He even wrote a book about it with the disarming title, *How to Walk*.[99] Walking, for Nhat Hanh, was clearly a spiritual practice, but because it is slow, meditative, and mindful, it might not actually be very practical for a pilgrim trying to cross the Meseta on that long flat road to Leon, which is why a third, slightly different take on walking as spiritual practice is in order.

Mihaly Csikszentmihalyi grew up in Hungary during World War II (Side note: his name is pronounced muh ·hay ·lee chik ·sent ·mee ·hai ·ee). As a result of the terror and tragedy that surrounded him during and after the war, he observed that many of the adults in his personal circles were never able to regain a sense of purpose and meaning to their lives. He became curious about how people find purpose and meaning. This led him to the study of psychology, and it was through interviewing people who claimed to experience intense satisfaction in their work that he began to develop a theory.[100] He noticed that when very skilled people were immersed in their work and the work was at just the right level of challenge, which was pretty high, they began to lose themselves in their activity. They stopped being aware of anything, including themselves, as the work completely took over their consciousness. Interviewed about this experience, his subjects reported it was intensely satisfying. For example, he interviewed an Olympic figure skater about one of her skating routines that went really well and she said:

> It was just one of those programs that clicked. I mean everything went right, everything felt good ... it's just such a rush like you feel it could go on and on, like you don't want it to stop because it's going so well. It's almost as though you don't have to think, it's like everything goes automatically without thinking. It's like you're on automatic pilot, so you don't have any thoughts. You hear the music, but you're not aware that you're hearing it because it's a part of it all. (From TED talk)

Csikszentmihalyi heard similar reports from people in many different fields of work. He saw patterns in their descriptions:

complete involvement, sense of ecstasy, inner clarity, knowing the task is doable, sense of serenity, timelessness, and the task is its own reward. He called this experience *flow*. He wrote about it in a book published in 1990, and the idea took off.[101] Flow is now a widely accepted idea in the world of psychology. It has also influenced Kip Redick. Redick writes that when he is hiking a challenging path with a full backpack filled with just the things he knows he needs to survive, surrounded by a beautiful wilderness landscape, breathing hard as he scrabbles over rocks, he experiences flow. He talks about Csikszentmihalyi's theory and makes a case that his kind of hiking produces the same sort of effect as that expert figure skater.

Whether you're drawn to Reddick's idea of spiritual rambling, Thich Nhat Hanh's walking meditation, or Csikszentmihalyi's idea of flow, all three speak to the spiritual possibilities of walking. An adventure that is based on walking can include a spiritual experience as one of its many aspects. I would extend these benefits to rowing, cycling, and probably any other physical activity that is repetitive and continuous, especially when there are long periods with minimal distraction. Practiced with intentionality, it rises to a form of meditation, one characterized not by mindfulness, but the opposite. When I'm rowing a three mile crossing, or pedaling a straight Indiana county road for twenty miles, or traversing the meseta under a hot summer sun, I enter into a very agreeable *absence* of thought. *Mindlessness*. What a pleasure and restorative to be free from rational thought! To the larger question, though, of spirituality and adventure in general, it's clear to see that some kind of encounter with the ultimate or deep renewal that can't be adequately put into words is a big part of adventuring for many people. And even for those who don't like the word *spiritual*, it can't be denied that often something about a great adventure experience simply transcends language. And, despite the souvenir shops and the crowds, despite the commerce and tourism industry that produce the shops and crowds, pilgrims continue to make of the Camino what they choose, as they always have. As did I. Meaning and renewal were growing from the fertile mix of meditative walking, a traveling community of pilgrims, a slow reckoning with my physical limitations, and the majestic landscape that presented itself mostly sun-washed and undulating across the final third of my 500 mile trek.

Chapter 25
You Gotta Like Walking

I was in Palestine maybe. Someplace known for conflict. There was a troublesome White kid, a teenager, maybe 16, with a boyish face and a pocketknife, discretely stabbing strangers in a crowded place. I knew what he was doing. He knew I knew. Scene change: I'm skippering a small motorboat with several passengers, people I know, but I don't remember who, except the kid with the knife—he's on the boat. It's a perfectly nice day and the water is calm, but I crash the boat. I go to call the Harbor master, but I don't know the number. Then I can't remember who all the passengers are. The three people on board tell me the kid—they don't know he has a knife—didn't get on the boat. He stayed behind on the dock. I feel incompetent and cowardly.

I wake up, open my eyes. It's dark. My clothes are sweaty, my sheets damp. I check my phone, 3:20 a.m. My mouth is dry. I get up to pee and get a drink of water. It's been a day since the horrifying back spasms hit just past Leon. Earlier this evening, I was still feeling wobbly, and I'd gone to bed early thinking that in the morning, I'd look into finishing my walk at Santiago instead of pushing on to Finisterre and use the three extra days to slow down the pace a bit. As I shuffle in the direction of the bathroom, I give a phlegmy cough. My cold is not getting better, and, I think to myself, colds that linger sometimes turn into bronchitis, and if bronchitis hangs around, it can turn into pneumonia. That could mean a hospital stay and an intravenous bag and days in a place I don't want to be, risking infection from hospital-friendly bugs.

Job done, I pad back to bed and crawl in. I grab my phone, turning toward the wall to shield my neighbors from the screen light. I check to see how many of my bookings can still be cancelled for free. I look at each one. Almost all can still be cancelled, no charge. I put down the phone and think, maybe that's what I'll do. Later that morning — it's the second of my two planned rest days, thank goodness — I've re-booked everything. The trip will now end at Santiago, the official destination of the Camino de Santiago. I won't get the extra points for the Finisterre add-on. I won't get to stand in the wash of the Atlantic Ocean. But now my 30K average can drop to 22K. The thought of walking only 22K each day produces a wave of euphoria each time I think about it. I know now what back-to-back 30K, with the occasional 35 or 40 thrown in, does to my body. It occurs to me, I'm not 25 years old. I'll be 65 in October.

Half-way through the next day, with the new plan to cut my daily trek by nearly one third for the rest of the trip, I started to feel better. Incrementally, over the next few days, heading toward the Cruz de Ferro, despite the rising terrain, my body began to bounce back. I started to remember that I like walking.

One morning, I'm talking with Debbie from Seattle. The day is breezy as we walk together, at some elevation now with a view of soft hills ahead of us that disappear into a haze. We pass through uncultivated meadows with long grass. Debbie works for Microsoft. She negotiated six weeks away to walk the Camino. When she returns, she is getting a promotion. Well done. She can't be older than 30. We chat amiably, working our way through the usual questions about jobs, family, blisters, where else have you traveled, and then, when we're talking about why the Camino, she says something remarkable: "It will be an important experience for my future self." And then she says something else, and then a couple peregrinos pass us and we exchange greetings, and then Debbie starts chatting about something different. I really want to follow up on the future-self comment, but it gets lost. Later, we part at a rest stop where I choose to keep walking. I hope I run into Debbie again, I think, as I step away. I'll be on the lookout for the next 11 days. Her comment lingers like a mysterious answer to something, just out of reach. So, in the absence of an explanation from her, I consider its possibilities. I may not have a lot of future selves left. On the other hand, from day to day, moment to moment, situation to situation, I slide into different selves. I'm the hearty adventurer, the fit almost-retiree, the sensitive listener, the chatty storyteller, the planner, the bumbler, the fraud, the failure, professor, father, husband, and son, the introvert, the extrovert. My Camino experience could be important for any of them. Her comment feels like a really good answer to all the related questions about why Camino, but I can't sort out anything concrete. Now that I'm traveling with the threat of real pain (Are there more, crippling back spasms in my future?) and fresh knowledge about my physical limits, this walk feels like it is taking on higher stakes, maybe a deeper meaning for some future self, but I'm not sure what future self, or what meaning. I read graffiti, written with a sharpie, on a Camino sign I pass just before the end of the day's walk. It reads, "By accepting your vulnerability you will reveal your true essence." Not sure what that means, but it seemed relevant. Two days later, I'm inside a portico where everybody leaves their packs before stepping into the crowded pastry shop at one end. I've enjoyed an excellent chocolate croissant and am wiggling my pack onto my back to leave, when I look up and see a person nearby take their pack off and lean it against the wall. It's Debbie! I call her name. She looks my way in surprise, then she recognizes me and smiles. We say hi, and then I say I've been thinking about something she told me. She looks pleased at that. I ask her what she meant when she said the Camino was an experience for her future self. She says, after a short pause, that the memories, the people she's met, the landscapes, etc., are all important to be able to look back on because you never know what will happen in the future. It seems an inadequate answer, but I thank her. Walking away, I think, maybe it's just the right answer. You have all these exceptional experiences that the Camino provides, and you store them away. Later, depending on what happens in your life, you can pull them out selectively to assemble whatever narrative you need, whatever story you need to tell yourself about your life to help you continue to move forward. Meaning is not something you find. It is something you construct. The more varied and exceptional the experiences you pursue, the deeper and more wide ranging the reserve from which to draw. And long solitary periods that accompany many adventures provide the opportunity for those accumulated experiences to find a shape. Maybe that's one reason we pursue adventure.

While walking the Camino, what feels amazing but shouldn't is when you meet someone whom you previously got to know a bit by walking together, or sharing a bunk room, or having a meal, or all of the above. Sometimes it will be just the next day. Sometimes it will be a whole week later. The longer the lag, the more miraculous it feels. Now here's why it really shouldn't feel all that amazing. Every single peregrino you meet is walking that exact same route to the exact same destination. The route is very narrowly defined by one particular road at any given point and there are only so many cafes and albergues along the way. Why *wouldn't* you constantly keep re-meeting people? Still, it feels amazing because, when you meet someone initially on the Camino, it's fairly random, and they could be anyone from anywhere in the world, and to think—single narrow route aside—that you would ever meet that person again, given there are something like 8 billion people in the world, *feels* against all the odds. A full week after I'd said goodbye to my three French friends with whom I'd made and shared a spaghetti dinner, and who spoke no English at all, and with whom I'd had a great time, I "randomly" ran into them sitting at a café by the Cathedral in Burgos. They shouted my name as I walked across the plaza. Our re-meeting felt like something worthy of a celebration, but we all had other plans. Nonetheless, there were lots of smiles, laughter, handshakes, and goodbyes, as they said it was their last day on the Camino. Then there was Christian from Hungary. For five days running, I ran into him spontaneously, when I arrived at whatever albergue I'd chosen for the day. There he was as I stepped into the bunkroom or entered the kitchen looking for the fridge. After separately walking all those miles and having independently chosen which town to stop at for the day, and which albergue, there we'd be, together again. Christian spoke no English, so we didn't talk, but he'd shoot me a big smile when he saw me and was always friendly enough. And then, one day, he wasn't there, and I never saw him again. Lukas from Ireland turned up three or four times. Same with Kathleen from England, and Ingrid from the Netherlands, and Andres. Sometimes, along the Camino, I'd see someone who looked familiar, but I wouldn't be sure. We'd look at each other just a bit longer than you normally look at a stranger and then, we'd both smile, I think, because we sensed we were both wondering, *Do I know you?*

Three days into my new, relaxed pace, things were looking up. The spasms were gone, the aches and pains were back to normal end-of-day weariness, and the cold had retreated from a raging, pneumonia-inducing storm inside my body to an occasional sputter, a breezy, almost friendly camino-cough. One day, walking by myself, I started to think about my recent reckoning with my body and, for some unknown reason, I began to see it as a labor negotiation. As I climbed upward through a woodland of evergreens—we were that high again—I amused myself by working out the details.

"Our members are unanimous. You're pushin' us way too hard." This is Big Leftie, a tough old toe and President of United Body Parts (U.B.P.), local 1958. I've been summoned to the negotiating table via certified mail. I had no idea the union was having a problem.

Big Leftie continues, "We're hearin' from the shop stewards for muscles, ligaments, joints, and organs. They're all sayin' the same thing." Leftie pushes up the big dead nail that hangs low over his forehead. His cheeks are red and scarred. He's got a huge blister that looks like a goiter on the side of his neck.

Lung, seated next to Big Lefitie, chimes in, "You gotta slow things down, Mister. You want these workers to keep workin', ya gotta treat 'em with some respect!" He exhales sharply, sending a stiff breeze across the table.

I'm feeling a little defensive. "I've been providing massive quantities of food. Bread, cheese, eggs, fresh fruit, juices, wine, and some really good desserts. Do you all want more?" I offer.

Big Leftie speaks, "It ain't the food." Then he adds, "Actually, I shouldn't be tellin' you this but Stomach says stop sending down the cheap two-euro Rioja. That stuff tastes like used rinse water. "

Throat, seated next to Lung, gives a significant cough. I look over at him. He starts, "It ain't about compensation. It's about working condi-" He stops abruptly and coughs, then coughs again, a phlegmy hack that trips a series of coughs and sputters like you get with a head cold. He winds it up, takes a drink of water, and says, "con-ditions."

Big Leftie jumps in, "You hear Throat coughin' like that? It affects all of us—joints, muscles—you name it. The temperature in all the shops goes up and everyone's sweatin' and can't get no work done."

Lung, who's been listening closely, speaks up. "You know, if Throat gets really sick, pretty soon, all that shit he can't handle is gonna come my way, and my shop's not set up for fluid, ya know. My shop floor gets wet, it's all over. You'll be sending yourself and the whole Union membership to the hospital. Is that what you want?"

Big Leftie again. "Yeah. Then you won't have no Camino to brag about, and maybe you gotta re-book your flight home and everything just turns to shit."

The table goes quiet. I speak up. "Okay. Let me think about it. I'll come back tomorrow with a plan."

That's when lean and leathery Spaz, silent until now, jumps in. "Hang on a minute. Not so quick." Everyone looks at Spaz. "I been workin' the lower back division. Interdisciplinary team down there includes muscles, ligaments, you name it, and the scene is not pretty. I walk the shop floor, and every fifth striation, I see some poor guy doubled over with cramps. No sooner we replace him, and the next guy is down. Everyone's workin' double shifts. Pretty soon we're just gonna have to shut everything down."

There's a pause. I say, "Okay. I get it. Thank you. I'll have a plan for you tonight."

And I did. I told the Union leaders I'd forego the walk to Finisterre and use the extra three days to slow down the pace to Santiago. I also promised no more two-euro Rioja. They said okay, they'd do their best. We shook on it, which caused Big Leftie's nail to fall off. I think he was relieved. "Not a problem." He said, "I'll grow anotha'."

That afternoon landed me in a tiny village consisting of four streets and two albergues. Mine opened to a lovely interior courtyard with tables, and a stone staircase to a balcony with a bar and more tables. I spent the late afternoon sipping Estrella Galicia, the regional beer of choice, up on the balcony where I could look down on my fellow peregrinos as they did laundry and chatted at the tables. I could also look up, over the rooftop to the pine covered mountains. Yes, mountains. We were in Alpine country. Several times today, I'd had a sudden feeling like I was hiking in Vermont or Switzerland.

"I was in the fashion industry for many years," This is Kemal, host of the albergue. He is Turkish from Istanbul, 50-ish, wiry build, with a head of curly hair, a few nicely placed tattoos, an olive complexion, and a ready smile. He's chatting at our table of albergue guests. It's later in the evening. He's finished serving dinner and he's sipping a glass of red wine. He moves comfortably from Spanish to French to English to accommodate everyone at the table. He continues, "I had risen high up. I worked for X (he said the name of a company) and was the manager for Southeast Asia. Fast Fashion. Factories all over Vietnam, Malaysia, Thailand. But I couldn't do it anymore. It was all work, work, work, and… the ethics." He stops for a sip of wine. Everyone at the table is leaning in as his story unfolds. He makes a side comment to the Frenchman at the end of the table that he'll translate in a minute. He continues. He says how the working conditions in the factories were horrible, how producing one pair of denim jeans took 10,000 liters of water. Then he says how the production of a particular tee shirt required a chemical that stayed in the fibers and, if left on the shelf too long, leached out, exposing a potential customer to a known carcinogen. He learned this fact at an executive meeting and submitted his resignation the next day. His wife had left him sometime earlier because he worked too much. He was alone and jobless. So, he packed his rucksack and headed to Spain to walk the Camino. It was, he said, an intensely emotional experience. Afterward, he worked as a volunteer at an albergue for three years. He loved it: cooking, cleaning, sleeping. Simple. He felt restored. So, he bought an albergue and started running it himself. He said he loves it. He has found his place in the world, away from the madness.

I was warned. For days, peregrinos at the dinner table, in the dorm, at the sinks in the bathroom, had been murmuring to one another.
"Massive descent."
"Very slippery."
"Extremely steep."
"Many accidents."
"Difficult terrain."
"It's a fucking cliff."
They were talking about the 25 kilometer stretch from the Cruz de Ferro to the city of Ponferrada. Cruz de Ferro is the highest point on the Camino at 1500 meters. By the time you get to Ponferrada, you're at 500 meters. The profile map of this section in my guidebook is like no other. It's a steep diagonal line from left to right across the whole page.

"You don't want to do it in the rain," said one of the volunteers at the albergue last night. Not what I wanted to hear. After 22 straight days of almost no rain, the forecast was showing rainclouds through the morning and afternoon. I woke up at 4:15 a.m. because the garbage truck right outside our dorm window was banging large metal containers. Shortly, the truck pulled away, but as the truck sounds faded, I could hear the beating of a million raindrops on the metal roof and the road, and the rush of a torrent through the gutters and the downspouts. It had the sound of serious steady rain, not your momentary squall. I feared it was defining the day ahead. I braced myself.

Fast forward to 11 a.m. I arrive at the Cruz de Ferro. It's not raining, but all morning, climbing higher and higher through woodlands and alpine meadows, the very big sky has been acting finicky. A patch of blue here, one layer of dark clouds there, two layers of darker clouds over there, puffy white clouds over here, and fog rolling up the mountains over there. Wait five minutes and everything has moved around. If I tell myself to quit worrying about the rain, it's really beautiful. It's dramatic the way the cloud patterns shift as you watch them and the big splashes of sunshine that appear on a far ridge, then disappear, and reappear somewhere up ahead. We're high enough that when we look down into some of the valleys, we see clouds below us. After a couple hours, I'm walking along and all of a sudden, there's a cross up ahead standing in the middle of the Camino on a big pile of little rocks. Cruz de Ferro. The Iron Cross. It just appears without any fanfare, the thing everyone has been talking about, the great spiritual turning point of the ancient Camino. The mound of rocks holding up the cross is several hundred years' worth of small stones peregrinos have carried from places near and very far to leave as a token of *many* things. It's apparently elective symbolism. Your stone can mean gratitude, or contrition, forgiveness, a wish for good luck, etc. I pause. None of the dozen or so people standing by is speaking. I gather that's the mode we're supposed to adopt—reverent. I think for a minute, then I pull out of my waist pouch the round white stone that Ax gave me way back in St. Jean Pied de Port to deploy at this moment. I've thought off and on about what it will mean for me. I decide it represents an acknowledgment of errors and omissions I've made in my life. It's not a leave-them-all-here conviction, because I think it's important to remember them. Carrying the stone for 22 days and occasionally reflecting on stupid things I've said or done has, on more than one occasion during this walk, led me to feel like a true idiot. Like the opposite of what a therapist does when they use cognitive behavior therapy—trying to get you to think good thoughts about yourself. My Cruz de Ferro stone has reminded me of so much stupid stuff I've said and done, I'm getting into a habit in recent days of thinking mostly bad thoughts about myself. Is that how this is supposed to work? Not sure I'm on board. I straighten my pack and start walking. As I pass the rock pile, I gently toss mine on. It bounces and falls into a gap between a couple larger stones. I keep going. Check that off the list. My mind turns to this supposedly epic descent beginning, according to my guidebook, in four kilometers.

Chapter 26
Going Solo

Some adventurers prefer to go alone. Consider Felicity Aston and Mike Libecki. If you fly due south from Auckland, New Zealand, over the vast and empty Southern Ocean, you come, eventually, to the Leverett Glacier at the edge of the great landmass known as Antarctica. In November of 2011, Felicity Aston, a British meteorologist, started there for a planned solo expedition that was supposed to take her all the way across the enormous southern continent. She was determined to make the trek without the aid of dogs, motorized devices, wind power, or other human beings. Just her. Muscle power alone. She endured extreme isolation with days of total white outs, commenting:

> A real, proper Antarctic whiteout is almost blinding. You have no sense of up or down. You have no sense of scale. No contrast, shape, or form of any kind. When you're staring into that nothingness—and this is not over a matter of hours, but over a matter of days, or occasionally it would be a week or more—your brain isn't getting any data.[102]

She also endured dangerously crippling self-doubt. "Every moment of every day, there'd be a voice saying, 'You can pitch your tent now. You can call it a day now. Just get in the warmth for a few hours. It was always tempting me to take the easy option and do things that I knew weren't good ideas.'"[103] Fifty-nine days and 1084 miles after setting out, despite the extreme conditions and mental challenges, she emerged at the coastline of the Ronne Ice Shelf on the other side of the continent, roughly below South America, making her the first woman to cross Antarctica alone and unaided.[104]

Mike Libecki seeks out those remaining, extreme places in the world that have not yet been the feature of any adventurer's "first", and he tags them at an astonishing pace. In 2012 alone, he conquered a 2000-foot sheer face in Borneo, made the first ascent of several towers of flaking rock in a little-known range west of Kabul, Afghanistan. Then he headed north, way north, to Franz Josef Land in Arctic Russia, where he traveled on a sailboat amidst the ice flows to the base of a never-summitted mass of crumbling stone and made the 400 meter solo trip to the top. The year continued with explorations of Greenland and Antarctica where he picked up several more firsts.[105] He said:

> For me, solo expeditions are about going to climb the biggest, steepest walls in the world that no one even knows about and doing first ascents. When you're up there, you're constantly living between the line of dangerous and *too* dangerous. You have the choice to make things 100 percent mathematically safe and if you get out of that zone, you'll die very quickly.[106]

Aston and Libecki are not alone in going alone. There's a breed of adventurer that prefers solo exploration despite the enormous downsides. Why do they do it? Why do they choose to suffer physical and emotional isolation and assume extreme risk that the presence of just one other person would greatly reduce? Are they a weird species of misanthropes, abused as children? Are they victimized by some genetic anomaly that turns them away from society? Are they angry at how the world has treated them? Do they have a death wish that keeps going unfulfilled, until it isn't? Are they all, maybe, just fundamentally hermits?

Aston and Libecki are definitely not hermits. Libecki climbs often with his daughter Lilly, leads tours for National Geographic Expeditions, and makes frequent media appearances. Aston, in addition to her solo exploits, has led all-female team expeditions to the North and South Poles, more than once. She also works as a motivational speaker, and, with her husband Gizli and son Thrainn, farms duck down. True, they've chosen to live on a remote, private island off the coast of Iceland, but their house has 10 bedrooms, and they have frequent visitors.

Some solo adventurers *do* have hermit tendencies. They seem to thrive on long periods of boundless solitude. In 1968, solo sailor Bernard Moitessier was on track to win the *Sunday Times* Golden Globe Yacht Race, having nearly circumnavigated the world, single-handed, without putting into port. He was about to set a world record. After rounding the Cape of Good Hope, in first place on the home stretch to England, he had a sudden change of heart. Inexplicably, he turned his boat around and headed, in the opposite direction, back to the Cape and then the Indian Ocean, abandoning the race and remaining at sea for another three months. He sent a folded paper message via slingshot to a passing ship, the heart of which read simply, "I am happy at sea."[107] In the end, he circled the globe nearly twice before pulling in at Tahiti with 37,000 miles of non-stop sailing under his belt.

Moitessier named his boat *Joshua* for another solitude-loving solo sailor, Joshua Slocum, from a century ago. After a life as a successful seaman and commercial captain, Slocum yearned for a solo adventure at sea. In April of 1895, at the age of 51, he took off from Boston Harbor on a 36-foot vessel he'd recently rebuilt and named *Spray*. He spent three years at sea. Though he had many land-bound adventures along the way with colorful characters, he was mainly alone with his boat, the wind, and the ocean swells. Forty-six thousand miles after setting out, he pulled into the harbor at Newport, Rhode Island, the first person to circumnavigate solo. After that, he lived comfortably off the royalties from a hugely successful book he wrote about his round-the-world adventure.[108] He bought a farm on Martha's Vineyard. But he longed to be at sea, alone. He regularly left the Vineyard for extended solo voyages south during the winter months. It was on one such voyage, in 1909, that he vanished at sea. Maybe what drives Moitessier and Slocum and others is best captured by contemporary wilderness trekker, Jack Turner, who wrote, of a simple week-long trek into the Escalante River basin in Utah, "No one knows where I am, for the simple reason that I don't know exactly where I'm going. Not knowing is a key ingredient in this game."[109]

Not all solo adventures turn out well. Chris McCandless has been held up as an example of how not to approach a solo trek into wilderness. His story, captured in Jon Krakauer's 1996 bestseller, *Into the Wild*, starts in suburban, New Jersey, where McCandless was raised in a comfortable, middle-class family.[110] On graduating from college, he gives away his savings account to Oxfam and heads west in his Datsun 210. He eventually abandons the car and takes up hitchhiking and riding the rails. He becomes more and more disillusioned with society as he works his way further into wilderness. He winds up, at last, by himself, in an abandoned school bus at the end of road near Denali National Park in Alaska, as winter settles in. That's where the story takes a dangerous turn. Lacking backwoods survival skills, he is unable to provide for himself, and ends up scrounging for berries that turn out to be poisonous. He gets sick and crawls into his sleeping bag. His body is found later by hunters. The story is told as a cautionary tale that underscores the foolishness of adventuring when you're unprepared, or don't know what you're doing. But I wonder if his quest, except for how it turned out, is any different from so many high risk, poorly informed youthful escapades that are almost a rite of passage for adventurous types. Later, we joke casually about how foolish and lucky we were. McCandless was not so fortunate. Had he survived that first winter in his school bus at the end of the road, might he have written a memoir celebrating his escape from the materialism of modern society? Would he now be living off the royalties in a remote cabin in Montana with wifi, giving occasional interviews about the simple life, a modern-day Thoreau?

If you read nothing but books about solo adventures, you'd come away thinking humans are very solitary creatures, but the fact is we are herd animals. We have evolved to survive in highly coordinated groups. Which is why a great deal of adventuring, probably most adventuring, takes place with others, in teams. Maybe the reason we find a solo adventure so thrilling is because it violates the rule of our herding breed and piques our interest. Ryan Zwart knows something about this. He has worked as an expeditionary tour leader for cycling, climbing, sea-kayaking, and backpacking. He is a professor of Outdoor Recreation Studies at Montreat College in Black Mountain, North Carolina. He and his research partner Ryan Hines, noticed that certain outdoor locations served not only as the jumping off spot for particular sports, but as a hub for related social activity. They were curious about that socializing aspect of adventurous sporting activity and decided the best way to learn more was to talk to people there. Red River Gorge in Kentucky and Linville Gorge in North Carolina are popular rock-climbing locations. The Gauley River in West Virginia and the Nantahala River in North Carolina draw white water kayakers, while mountain bikers congregate in certain locations in Asheville, North Carolina. Associated with these locations are parking lots at trailheads or put-ins, nearby gear shops and popular restaurants and breweries, all of which serve as natural gathering places.

Zwart and Hines printed up some cards describing their study with a phone number and an invitation to participate in a 15-minute interview. They headed off to all these various locations and handed out hundreds of cards. Then they spent a lot of time on the phone. What they found is that people in all of the outdoor adventure sports were after three things: promoting their physical health, being in nature, and building social connectedness.[111] When asked to pick one, people in the study had a hard time. They tended to say that all three reasons mattered. The magic, for most people, came from a combination of hard physical exercise, the freedom and beauty of the outdoor world, and the company of like-minded individuals whom they turned to for safety and social connection.

For the solo adventurer, the element that's missing, obviously, is social connection. For 59 days, crossing Antarctica, in frequent total white-outs, Felicity Aston did not encounter another soul. For 303 days, Bernard Moitessier was alone in his boat, in the middle of the ocean, with no radio. For some solo adventurers, going alone is a retreat from social connection, a test of their ability to prevail without it for a finite period of time. Eventually, however, they return to society, which is their natural, default mode of living. A few, like Moitessier, acclimate to solitude and discover it is their preferred state.

For those of us who like the idea of eventually returning to society, the solo adventure is a test of courage and strength, plus, perhaps, a quest for wisdom that grows from the soil of solitude, which brings us right back where this book began: Joseph Campbell. Remember him? The college professor who made it big by cracking the code of adventuring. He said all adventures are fundamentally the same: you leave your normal life as the result of a calling. You enter a world that is different and mysterious, possibly dangerous. You face challenges, but, along the way, you get help from others. You either save people or learn something. Then you return, a changed person. Think about it. Felicity Aston felt a calling to cross antarctica, she endured hardship in the form of white-outs and extreme cold. She was assisted in persevering through the intervention of her satellite phone. She returned and now makes a living as a motivational speaker, bringing the wisdom she found in her ordeal to others. Even Moitessier eventually returned from the sea spending his later years in Tahiti, the United States, and finally retiring in Paris. He, too, wrote books about his adventuring, focusing on the spiritual aspect. Campbell's template fits. For all the legitimate criticism Campbell's theory has endured, there is still something to it. The solo adventure excites us because it breaks the rule of our normal social state, and, in so doing, offers the adventurer the boon of wisdom.

The Camino is a paradox when it comes to solo adventuring. While many people undertake the 500 mile pilgrimage as a solo experience, it is almost impossible not to join in the sociability of the traveling community that forms around you. My final week on the road to Santiago would prove to be no exception. Maybe part of the appeal of the Camino is that solitude and community are available options nearly every day.

Chapter 27
Santiago de Compostela

Three hours later, I decide this trail is the worst I've ever walked. I'll note first, however, that it did not rain. It was mostly overcast. There was some occasional spitting, and I saw one couple stop to wiggle into their yellow rain pants and jacket. It was quite a production. They'd dropped their packs, and what looked like half their gear was scattered around their feet.

As I passed, the woman huffed to her partner, "You *know*, once we get this on, the sun will appear." Occasional splashes of sun did appear and lifted the day.

The trail is mostly loose rock on hardened soil, or just lots of loose rock, or lots of very uneven fixed rock. And it is all downhill, sometimes steep. In all cases, it is tricky to navigate. I find myself wondering who is in charge of trail maintenance. In places, it is so bad, some peregrinos choose to walk on the highway which goes roughly the same direction, winding like a vine around the Camino and intersecting conveniently at all the towns along the way. After a couple hours of picking my way among the rubble, taking care not to trip or slip, and beginning to feel the difficult descent in my quads and my knees, I join the renegades on the highway. Since there's only one car about every five minutes, it's not especially dangerous, but you have to keep an eye out. The "highway" is two narrow lanes. Two tiny

Fiats might do fine passing each other. Anything larger (i.e., almost all of what you find on the roads today) will mean a tight squeeze or a side scrape or a really nasty crash. There are guardrails about half the time on both sides, and, more or less, no shoulder. You need to look sharp as you walk. Though the cars are only occasional, you'd better be ready to press yourself against the guardrails at any moment.

A couple hours later, I've moved back to the trail, hoping it is better. It's not. I pass one party who've stopped along the trailside, four or five people, and one of them is sitting on a rock with his left shoe and sock removed, gripping his ankle. He has a pained look on his face. As I pass, one of his friends hands him a chemical ice pack. At the next intersection, I take the highway again, but I quickly learn the stakes are higher. We're descending more steeply into a narrow, ravine-like valley. The highway hugs the side of the ravine, and on the other side of the highway is a drop of several hundred feet at least. The turns grow tighter the further down I go, and, pretty soon, it's all switchbacks with blind turns, guardrails, zero shoulders, and steep drop-offs. I proceed very cautiously, vigilantly, especially at every turn, pressing myself against the guardrail whenever a car passes on either side because, at any moment a car could appear around a turn going the other way. I do this dance for an hour and notice it's put some spring in my step. Nothing like life-threatening hazards to liven up the day. As long as I keep a good lookout, it's safe enough. Just as I'm having that thought, a tour bus appears, well up the road, maybe three or four switchbacks above me. The thing is simply outsized for this road—think 60 passenger, massive, American style tour behemoth. It lumbers down toward me. The driver has enough sense to proceed cautiously. Whenever it takes a turn, it covers the entire road, plus a few inches extra on either side. When it eventually appears just above me, I press myself tight into the guardrail where I'll stay until it is well past, regardless of whether I see anything coming the other way. It goes by me without incident. After making the hairpin turn just below, it comes to a full stop and appears to be stuck. I see other cars coming down. I signal to them to slow down because just around the blind turn that I can see but they can't is the gigantic rear end of the stopped tour bus, a steel wall in the middle of the road, just out of view. Finally, by some means I can't see, the bus wiggles through.

Two hours later, I'm settled in my albergue. Showered, laundry washed, an Estrella Galicia accompanies me at my table with my tablet. I decide I deserve two tonight. I head to the bar for number two and while the bartender is pouring, I ask him in Spanish, "On what day of Creation, did God create beer?" It's a question with its own punch line. He laughs and so do the other peregrinos in line. I'm smiling because I pulled off a joke in Spanish. He pours me one extra tall.

A little while later, I'm enjoying dinner upstairs with about 30 others, at several banquet style tables set in rows. The lentil soup is a meal by itself. It is thick, well-seasoned, hot, and abundant. Our albergue host scoops two generous ladlefuls for each of us from a tureen he holds in the crook of his arm and brings to each diner. Fresh, sliced, artisanal bread is piled up in baskets every fourth person, and a carafe of red wine, looking more like a gigantic martini pitcher, stands in the middle of the table, also about every fourth diner. If everyone in the dining room drank all of the wine, it would be about a bottle per person. Just as I'm finishing the soup and thinking I'm full, our host and his helpers appear from the kitchen with platters of mixed greens salad which they place every several diners for service family style. After salad, here comes the spaghetti Bolognese. Large mixing bowls full of it are placed next to the salad platters. Then, as everyone is winding down from the spaghetti, he and his team appear one last time with individual containers of Greek yogurt for our dessert. Had I purchased this meal at a restaurant in the same town a la carte, it might have cost 30 euros, without the wine. But at my friendly albergue, this sumptuous feast set me back a grand total of 10 euros! No charge for the good company of strangers who become friends over a shared meal.

Later that evening, I'm all tucked into my bunk. Others, like me, are settled in. Some still bustle about quietly in the softly lit dorm room. In the bathrooms next door, water runs, toilets flush. I hear people earnestly brushing their teeth. I am now about one week from the finish. I'd walked the first three weeks of the Camino like a multi-day marathon, pushing continually to make my quota for the day. That's not to say it was bad. I enjoyed the challenge, and there *was* time at the end of the day to settle in, do laundry, plan out the next day's walk, relax a bit, journal, socialize, and enjoy a good meal. Covering more ground than most, I felt myself pulling ahead of the crowd each day, which satisfied my competitive itch. But then my body protested, I was forced to revise the big plan and significantly reduce my distance each day. Since then, the Camino has felt different. There's no pressure and no competition—well, less. Most days, I sleep in an extra hour, get started as late as 8:30 a.m., instead of 6:00 a.m.. I'm still covering distance, I still feel that good feeling for each day's progress, but I make more stops, linger at the cafes, chat with old friends or people I've just met, and I arrive at my destination an hour or two earlier, which means more time for all those end of the day activities. Maybe this is a metaphor, I think, as I lie in my bunk, eyes closed, waiting for sleep. Most of my work life has been a multi-year marathon. I've pushed myself, covering ground, striving to pull ahead of the crowd to satisfy my competitive itch, with, maybe, enough time for my children, my marriage. In a year, I'll retire. I can already feel the tight spring of my inner competitor loosening with no more career milestones ahead—no promotions, no salary bumps, no more carrots, no more sticks. Maybe I'll cover less distance and linger in the cafes.

Sometimes you don't know who a person is unless you ask. She introduced herself as Sue when I offered her tea at the albergue. She said yes and, apparently confused by my offer, asked if I worked there.

"No," I said. "Tea is cheap, and I have lots of it and I'm happy to share."

She thanked me slightly more than the situation warranted when I brought it to her. "You're so kind! Gosh, thank you so much! This is really lovely!"

I placed the steaming mug on the coffee table in front of the couch where she sat. And then she didn't say much as several of us seated around the room exchanged bits of conversation about weather, blisters, where to eat, the usual. There was talk about the Cruz de Ferro, different opinions on the leave-a-rock thing, the killer descent, and the fact that we were already climbing again, headed for a peak almost as high as the Cruz. Several of us agreed to meet for a beer at the bar next door at five. Sue did not jump in to ask or say she'd like to join. Sensing she was maybe shy, I asked, and she said yes.

So, then, it's later, and we're all gathered at the bar where we've pushed two tables together. We're chattering away when Sue arrives. We welcome her, she orders a drink and then, about five minutes in, I notice she hasn't said a word. Okay, this is shy Sue, I decide. Then I suddenly have this thought of her as that quiet kid in the junior high cafeteria who nobody thinks much about, nobody gets to know, everyone thinks of as kind of an out-group person and just ignores. She seems to be watching everyone with the same sort of social envy as that kid, too. I decide I'm going to chat her up because I'm sure there's an interesting person there, and I should rise above the junior high vibe that seems to be forming around us, and she happens to be sitting right across from me. I break away from the current lively round of What-Happened-to-Florida-Man-on-Your-Birthday game, based on a phone app, and I turn to Sue.

Turns out, Sue has a fantastic story, which we all do, really, if anyone just asks. She was an accountant in Chicago and one day, in her 30s she got the idea that what she really wanted was to be a yoga instructor living on the beach in Florida. A short time later, she sold everything, moved to Tampa, got a place on the beach, took yoga courses and soon was supporting herself teaching yoga. In the midst of all that, she met her husband. Then, at age 57, she decided she'd had enough of yoga-instructing, went back to school and got a master's degree in social work. She supports herself now as a contract therapist through an online service. I tell her it's an amazing story and she seems pleased that I said so. I get the attention of the rest of the table, tell them Sue has an amazing story, that she has gone and done what many people only dream of, and would she please share her story with everyone. She blushes and tells it, and everyone is thrilled, and, suddenly, so is she. Later that evening, I'm walking back from the Gregorian chant service in the little stone chapel up the road from our albergue, and suddenly there she is again. We talk about what a cool service it was.

Then there's a pause and she says, "You know I'd been feeling depressed, like the Camino was not everything I'd been hoping, but dinner tonight with all of you turned all that around." I was tempted to probe but felt it might be pushing things a bit so I just said I was happy for her. "Yeah," she said. "I think things are going to get better now."

There's a photo of the hospital at Fort Devens, the Massachusetts Army base, from World War I, taken during the flu pandemic. It shows an indoor space the size of a warehouse with rows of beds with white sheets and sick soldiers stretching the length and width of the building. The space is so big, the photographer couldn't get the whole scene into the shot. It was two days later on the Camino. What was mostly uphill on day one had turned mostly downhill on day two. I checked into the Albergue Ferramenteiro in Portomarin, 92 kilometers from Santiago. Check-in was normal: passport, pilgrim credential, and credit card. And the intro tour was also normal — wifi password posted on the wall, bar, shared kitchen, showers, and laundry area. Then we stepped into the dormitory. I felt instantly transported to Fort Devens, circa 1917, minus the nasty overtone of a deadly pandemic. Then, again, maybe not. The albergue lady, who was even dressed like a nurse, walked me down three columns of bunk beds with starched sheets, made a precision turn left past five rows of bunk beds, and pointed to mine, in the last row. I thanked her, she left, and then I took in the room. Looking down the length of the hangar-sized space, I counted 11 columns of bunkbeds. Looking the other way, I counted five rows. That's 110 beds. Turns out, though, I was wrong. I noticed, later, on the back of the door, it said "130 camas."

Shortly after I'd started out that morning, I found myself in the middle of a pack of what appeared to be high school students. Maybe fifty. I asked them, and, yup, high school field trip, walking from Samos to Santiago, a little over 100K. Pretty cool field trip. They reminded me of the group trips I used to take my high school students on — the energy, the excitement, the numbers!! Several other peregrinos I ran into during the day were trying to avoid the group, walking faster than usual to stay ahead, or waiting until they passed. I stayed with them. I wasn't trying to, but I wasn't trying to avoid them either. It was fun to be around all their chattiness and bravado and, well, noise.

I could feel the energy of the Camino rising as we closed in on Santiago. There were more people, and they were walking faster. Pilgrims who had started in the last town or two to meet the minimum requirement for the official pilgrim certificate were swelling the ranks. You could tell who they were with their clean sneakers, unsullied backpacks, and extra-lively step. Their fresh enthusiasm, like the energy of the teenagers, was contagious. When we got to the 100-kilometers-to-go point, a stone marker greeted us, like all the rest that appeared every few kilometers, only this one had, chiseled into its granite base, "100,000m." A clump of peregrinos were gathered by it as I approached. They were taking pictures of each other, swapping cameras, fist-pumping. Soon I was with them, doing the same.

Seems I couldn't get away from the high school group, even if I wanted to. When I checked into my 130-bed dorm, the whole gang had already arrived. The albergue manager had stuck them all the way at the far end, and all other peregrinos, including me, at the near end, but the mayhem was in full swing and they might as well have been sleeping right next to us. The traveling community of the Camino was morphing into a traveling party. Party-on companeros! Four days to Santiago.

"Yes, we have five. It's an adventure," This is Elizabeth. She means children. Five. She's walking with the two youngest, Sarah and AJ, and her husband, Phil. Sarah is 23 and about to start medical school. AJ, 21, is a junior in college studying biomedical engineering. They're from Minnesota, a suburb west of Minneapolis. I was halfway through a 15K uphill stretch from Portomarin to Ventas de Naron when I caught up with them.

Elizabeth says, "I always tag along and we do things to include them to keep them close." Tagging along in this case means walking 500 miles in a month across northern Spain. I met the four of them a couple weeks before, and we've been keeping roughly the same pace. We've become trail buddies. Phil gives me a fist bump whenever we run into each other.

But I'm interested in hearing more from Elizabeth, this woman who's raised five children as her principal occupation of the last 30 years while Phil has been lawyering with success, apparently. They stay in hotels that their travel agent booked and have their packs transported daily. The luxury version of the Camino. All the same, they're walking the distance, blisters, swollen ankles, strained Achilles, and all.

I say, "That's interesting, Elizabeth. I've done some reading about how women see adventure." She and her family know I'm working on a book. "In this one study, they interviewed a whole bunch of women who were accomplished outdoor enthusiasts—rock climbing, sea kayaking, mountain biking, you name it. One of the themes from the study was how some of these expert female adventurers said the biggest adventure of their life was raising children." Phil's walking just ahead of us. I think he's listening. I hope so. I continue, "They also found that, for many women, the essence of the adventure isn't risk or the uncertain outcome. It's building relationships."

After a thoughtful pause, Elizabeth says, "You know the fight and flight instinct?"

"Yup," I say.

"Well, I've read that women have a third option. It's a circle-the-wagons instinct."

"Okay," I say. "So, don't run away. Don't attack. Instead, turn to your people to figure it out together."

"Right."

"That's cool. I didn't know about that." I decide that Elizabeth is an expert adventurer. She knows the power of circling up with her adult children to keep them close. And she keeps up, with swollen ankles and all the rest because she is brave. Because she loves her family.

Every morning—minus two rest days—for the last month, I've followed this routine: get up with phone alarm, which means either the alarm wakes me up or I'm already awake and waiting for the alarm. I sit up, maybe remembering that I need to crouch to avoid whacking my head on the bottom of the upper bunk. Or I whack my head as my first move of the day. Then I pull on my pants and my "camp" shoes and tread to the bathroom in darkness, trying to remember the layout of the dorm and where on the floor people are likely to have left backpacks and gear I might trip over. The men's bathroom is usually a mess in the morning—trash can overflowing, water all over the floor, several toilets unflushed, a urinal blocked with paper towels, several sinks smeared with leftover toothpaste, hair, etc. I deal with it. I head back to my bunk, usually with limited eyesight due to the garish fluorescent lights that blast me when I enter the men's room, tripped by the motion sensor. I assess my situation in the dark, and how I need to vacate the dorm room with all my stuff without making any noise because it's early and everyone else is still sleeping (Even after I relaxed my pace, I was still up before most people). That's when the carabiner on my fanny pack that I'm adjusting drops and clanks annoyingly against the metal frame of my bed. So much for being quiet. I freeze for a few seconds thinking that if I keep the interruption to one, random, sharp noise, everyone will keep sleeping. It seems to work. One person stirs, then quiet returns. First step is roll up my bedroll, slightly complicated because it's a nylon quilt, safety pinned to a silk camp sheet. I have to turn it upside down, make sure all the complicated bits are squared up, fold it twice lengthwise then roll it into a little package that I secure with an adjustable strap. Then I have to find the adjustable strap which I put somewhere last night. All of this is in the dark. Next I have to locate the charger cord for my phone and my tablet and the outlet converter and then fish around in the mess that is the inside of my backpack to find the drawstring bag where they belong. So it goes, getting all my stuff into various drawstring bags, laying them all loosely in my backpack, which opens flat like a suitcase. It's a hybrid model. Then I lift it carefully, unzipped, on two outstretched arms so all the stuff doesn't fall out and carry it like a dining tray to the dorm door and out into the hall to whatever open floor space there is so I can put it down. I go back to my bunk to gather up the rest—water bottles, hat, guidebook—and use my phone-light to look around and make sure I haven't left anything behind. Then, out in the hallway, I pull everything out of my backpack, make sure each of the drawstring bags is all set, and then put them all in the backpack again, tightly organized in a manner I have figured out over many days is the most efficient configuration. I zip my backpack, feeling efficient. That's when I remember my laundry, which was drying overnight on the racks in the washroom. It's also when I remember that I'm still wearing my camp shoes, which at this point are supposed to be in my backpack because I should have gone to the closet where everyone puts their hiking shoes to swap them out. I get my laundry and my Hokas, redo the backpack and zip it up. Done! Time for breakfast. I will not miss this routine when I get home. I will not miss packing up all my possessions in the dark, in a painful crouch and attempting to do it all in silence. There are things I will miss about the Camino. This routine is not one of them.

Laia asked me, "What do you and your wife like to do together?" I had just said that the secret to a long-term marriage is doing some things together and some things apart. I think Laia was testing me. It was early afternoon. Fifteen minutes earlier, I'd stepped out of a café, boosted with a double espresso, and fallen in with a fast-moving crowd that happened to pass just then. Mostly women, speaking English. I gravitate to women for conversation. They're easier to talk with. Laia, maybe 50, with a short, no-nonsense haircut and a stocky build had commented on my colorful Hokas, and that started our conversation.

To her question, I said, "We like to go kayaking and hiking, and canoeing, and camping." All these examples rolled off my tongue pretty fast. Laia seemed okay with my answer. But then I thought, actually, those are things we do once in a while, like maybe three times a year we go kayaking, and maybe once a year we go camping, and maybe seven or eight times a year we go for a good day hike. I thought, what do we like to do together? That's when what's really true came to me. Not that the other stuff is untrue. It's just that's not the core of our days together. What is? It's a day when we're both working at home, mostly doing our own thing. We run into each other in the kitchen during early morning food prep, share a word or two, maybe have a nice hug, say, in a few words to each other, what our plans are for the day. Then we're off to our separate locations — office, yard, café downtown, Zoom meeting, doctor's appointment. Then, maybe later in the morning, one of us will pop into the other's office and say, "Want to go for a walk?" This will be fifteen minutes of "What are you working on? How's it going?" We may have one or two other brief encounters during the day with progress updates. Then somewhere around 5:30 p.m., I'll ask Laurie if she wants a drink. Three times out of four, it's yes to a gin and tonic which I make along with my martini. I bring it to her in her office, and I start organizing dinner. Usually, not always, we eat together. I'll make a salad for each of us, then we forage in the fridge for leftovers, or I'll make us one of our standards — spaghetti, veggie burger — and we'll settle in for dinner and a debrief of the day, then we'll watch the news together, mourn the state of the world. Eventually, we'll peel off for separate work sessions, Laurie usually works later into the evening than I do. I might watch a show. Laurie might join me, and we say goodnight, maybe with a hug or a touch, and I head upstairs. Laurie will be up for another couple hours, but I'll be two hours ahead of her getting up in the morning. That's what we do together mostly. The kayaking, hiking, etc. is fun, but it's not the core of who we are as a couple. The core of who we are is our daily interactions, mutual support, the occasional fight which gets resolved or blows over. It's our shared life. I didn't say all that to Laia because it came to me later, but it's what I'll say if I ever see her again on the Camino. Or if I see her in Santiago, which was, at that point, just another day away.

My final day on the Camino: I got up at 4:30 a.m. and started walking at 5:30. Nighttime dark! Light rain. After passing through the town center for O Pedrouzo, I entered a woodland trail. Pitch Black. Fortunately, there was a couple with headlamps just ahead of me. I quickly caught up and matched them step for step. They were moving fast and holding hands with matching yellow ponchos. It was raining on and off all morning—my first day of extended rain in the entire trip. Around 8:30 a.m., AJ and Sarah caught up with me. We walked together. Then Elizabeth and Phil caught up. Maggie, a tall 20-something American with a bright smile, who just finished a year teaching English in Madrid, joined us. The six of us walked into Santiago together, through the rain, in high spirits. The final approach was a long march through a modern city—not at all what I'd expected, with highways and overpasses, cars and buses, steel and glass buildings with lots of sharp angles. Until we entered the Old City. There we were greeted by narrow streets with cobblestone, balconies above, carved stonework, shops with goods spilling out onto the street in tiered display boxes, the crowd growing thicker the deeper we went, voices ricocheting off the building facades overhead, blending and falling back in a lively hub bub. None of us was sure what the final approach was supposed to look like. After 500 miles of very well marked trails, the familiar yellow arrows seemed suddenly hard to locate, painted in out-of-the-way spots. After walking longer than what seemed right, we started to wonder if we'd missed it. We kept going. Everyone was moving in the same direction so either we were all lost, or on the right path. Then we heard something that sounded like music, it was more than one instrument, an orchestra? Wait. Bagpipes? Yup. We turned a corner, walked down a staircase, into a darkened portico, where a man in a kilt and full get-up was shattering the air with his instrument's loud droning, the upper register piping some regal melody I did not recognize. The music startled me into the realization that something big was about to happen. And then we stepped out, into the light of day, onto the edge of a great plaza like a giant sports field, covered with stone instead of grass. The rain had stopped. A low hanging sky, streaked with gray, had given way to high, white clouds. It took me a moment to comprehend it. I scanned the scene. All across the plaza, clusters of people were milling around. Some were weeping. Some were hugging. Some were excitedly taking pictures. I stepped out onto the plaza and looked left, and, all of a sudden, there it was, looming over us with all its physical strength and its storied power, the great West Façade of the Cathedral of Santiago de Compostela.

It's several hours later, and I'm inside the Cathedral, standing just behind the last pew of the North Transept, waiting for the noon Pilgrim Mass to begin. I've had my extended moment in the plaza, greeting and hugging old friends, snapping pictures. I've obtained my certificate from the Pilgrim Office, where I got choked-up speaking with the man who stamped my Compostela. Seated behind glass in what looked like a row of bank tellers, he somehow managed to connect with my emotion, despite the fact that he likely stamps hundreds of these every day. I checked into my room, yes *my* room, in a slightly fancy hotel that I'd booked months before. I've also eaten a good breakfast in a real restaurant. I've also showered and put on clean clothes.

The Cathedral is packed. I arrived 30 minutes early and couldn't get a seat. The side aisles were starting to fill. It was standing room only. Seizing the moment, I'd quickly stepped just behind the last row of pews so I could get an unobstructed view of the altar, plus, I'd have the pew-back to hold onto for support. The excitement in the vast crowded space is electric, the mood expectant. No doubt, many of us are wondering if the mass will include the swinging Botafumeiro — the huge incense urn attached by rope to a pulley at the highest point in the ceiling of the great dome, seven stories above the altar. The service proceeds and, just as it appears to be winding down, there's a disturbance among the officiants. The botafumeiro appears, suspended at chest height over the platform in front of the altar. The crowd gives an audible gasp. Incense inside the botafumeiro has been lit and a team of attendants standing nearby manage the rope as a priest gives the urn a mighty shove. With rhythmic pulls on the rope, the attendants get the urn swinging, same as you would pump a playground swing with your legs. Gradually the large, silver-plated, brass canister, nearly the size of a refrigerator (it is five feet tall, weighing 140 pounds), expands its arc within the space described by the north and south transepts. The floor plan of the church is a gigantic cross laid flat. The main aisles of the church, with hundreds of pews, leading to the altar, would be the post, and the transepts, also filled with pews, would form the cross member. The urn widens its arc along the transepts. Shortly it is swinging almost all of those seven stories of open space above us. As it swoops from the far transept, falling with a powerful grace toward the altar, I can imagine the air rushing on the far side of the church, smoke billowing and trailing the speeding object. It passes the altar and swiftly starts its climb, up, up, over my head, slowing as it reaches its full height, stopping just before it reaches the ceiling, hanging motionless for a short beat, before beginning its return. A vocal soloist accompanied by a booming organ fills the great church with music, making the moment almost playful.

It is many, many years before. I am lying on the hard-packed dirt directly under the playground swing of the Edgewood Elementary School. My older brother is having a joyous ride, swooping and pumping with his legs, and rising nearly the height of the steel bar from which the swing is suspended. I squeal with a fear-filled delight as the swing falls back toward me, my brother's sneakers nearly, but not quite, touching my face. The swing-set is one apparatus in a playground fitted with monkey bars, see saws, a sandbox, plastic horses mounted on coil springs, ball fields beyond, then a little rise at the far corner of the school yard with a big rock, a glacial erratic that we climb during recess. We love hanging out on the far side of that rock where our teachers can't see us. This schoolyard was the setting of some of my earliest adventures, often during recess. We'd imagine a daring escape from bad guys as we pumped hard on the swings. Could we make the swing go all the way 'round? We'd plow roads into the sandbox and run our play-cars along them, imagining a cross-country trip. On the horses we were cowboys or Indians in pursuit or on the run. On that rock we were ascending Everest, and on the far side we were bank robbers hiding out in our lair. Our childhood adventures were safe, contained within a supervised schoolyard, bounded by a fence. The security we felt emboldened us to heighten our adventures. Climbing to the top of the monkey bars, we were on steel girders, constructing a skyscraper a hundred stories over the sidewalk. My adult adventures have been, really, one and the same: seeking out a path of uncertainty and risk and then surrounding it with safeguards, which provide security, while emboldening me to go farther. Adventures can go wrong. You accidentally eat poison berries and crawl into your sleeping bag to die. Plenty of adventures are foolhardy. It's almost part of the definition. That's where luck intervenes. It's the Chris McCandless paradox: if you succeed, you're a hero; if you fail, you're a fool. The narrative gets shaped by the outcome. Maybe that's the germ of the instinct to survive and strive. Steven Callahan and Tori Murden did not want to be remembered as "lost at sea" or the person who activated the emergency radio beacon.

I learned from my three great adventures that, for me, the heart of an adventure is striving for something difficult. You don't know, really, if you'll achieve it and there are stakes if you don't. That's what makes for the thrill. And that thrill elevates living. Maybe that's an alternative to the quest for deeper meaning-- living fully and well. Striving for something great, beyond yourself, experiencing the full range of emotions that go with that. It is the raw material from which you construct meaning and joy. Henry David Thoreau's famous lines from *Walden* come to mind as a much better version of what I'm trying to convey here.

> I went to the woods because I wished to live deliberately, to front only the essential facts of life, and see if I could not learn what it had to teach, and not, when I came to die, discover that I had not lived. I did not wish to live what was not life, living is so dear; nor did I wish to practise resignation, unless it was quite necessary. I wanted to live deep and suck out all the marrow of life, to live so sturdily and Spartan-like as to put to rout all that was not life, to cut a broad swath and shave close, to drive life into a corner, and reduce it to its lowest terms...[112]

What Thoreau sought in a cabin in the woods, I've undertaken on a bicycle, in a rowboat, on my own two feet. All of these are an attempt to strip life back to some kind of essence.

Back at the Pilgrim Mass, the botafumeiro is swinging madly. There is much I don't like about the Catholic Church, but I cannot deny the majesty, the thrill of this moment. I embrace it, I enter into it fully. We all crave something bigger to hold us, to assure us we are not alone. The difference between personal growth and spiritual growth is that one is about development of the self. Spiritual growth, on the other hand, is about the self in relation to something larger and difficult to comprehend: the universe, God, humanity, the natural world, the ultimate, whatever form Martin Buber's *thou* may take. Even if it is not sentient or beneficent, it makes us feel safe. And mystery is at its center, not because it is inherently mysterious, but because we need it to be so. Spiritual renewal, the kind you find in a splendid outdoor adventure, produces wonder, awe, gratitude, grace, and mystery, all of which are possible only in relationship to a universe that surrounds and holds us.

Epilogue
Bus Ride to the End of the World

Epilogue
Bus Ride to the End of the World

During my final days on the Camino, it occurred to me I could still get myself to Finisterre even if it wasn't part of my official walk. I'd booked a single room for three nights in Santiago, an unbelievable luxury at the end of my monthlong forced march. It would be easy to take one of those three days to visit the coast just 90 kilometers farther west. At first, the thought of taking a bus felt like cheating. It was, after all, my original destination, the revered, ancient path to the Celtic End-of-the-World, the further expression of my personal prowess, the big push past Santiago, that would prove I'm better than your average pilgrim (lesson there). But then I thought, wait a minute, I walked the whole damn Camino. I threaded my way along rocky paths, over mountainous terrain, across the great, flat boring Meseta, on foot, 500 miles to the official terminus. I'd done it. I'd accomplished the historic pilgrimage to its official destination. Nothing else was required. A bus ride to Finisterre would be a pleasant side trip.

I sat in the front row, opposite side from the driver, which afforded an unobstructed view through the enormous wraparound windshield. The comfortable tour bus threaded its way across the hilly landscape which gave way to an undulating coast of promontories and inlets. Towns blossomed at the edge of every harbor. The changing scenery passed before my eyes like an IMAX movie. I felt strange and giddy just sitting there as my body advanced effortlessly across the miles through the magical intervention of a mobile chair. Fisterra is the last town on Cape Finisterre and last stop for the bus. Fisterra hugs the harbor on the inside of the Cape. If you walk west, up and over hills above the town and keep going, you get a view of the other side. At first, you catch glimpses of the Atlantic coastline, and, as you descend toward the beach, the vista opens up. Before you is the great western ocean, arcing north to south as far as you can see. The highlands give way to dunes and then to a sandy beach. On the day I visited, it was sunny and warm and gentle waves pawed the sand. I walked barefoot onto the beach and then stepped into the rhythmic wash of the waves as they advanced and retreated up and down the sparkling shoreline. I decided to head toward a rock outcropping that ran into the water and marked the southern edge of this bit of beach. The cool salt water and the gentle abrasion of the wet sand against the soles of my feet felt like a day spa after all those miles of walking. A lone person was lying on a colorful towel higher up on the beach, but I saw no one else. Shortly, I came to the rocks. I clambered up several of them to get a slightly higher view and was just starting to take it all in when I heard something behind me and turned. A man, 50 feet away was walking briskly toward me. Not the beach towel person but someone else who'd come out of nowhere. He got closer, and I realized I knew this person. It was Arkady, from Ukraine, one of the first people I met on the Camino. He had a big smile. He marched right up to me, and we embraced. We hadn't seen each other in weeks, and here we were suddenly together on a lonely stretch of ocean beach at the so-called End of the World. We caught up. Arkady had arrived several days before, walked all the way. He said he'd been practicing deep meditation on the beach and was thinking of taking up residence in Fisterra. After a bit, we wished each other well and parted. It was a magical moment at the tail end of what was, and will always be, for me, an epic adventure.

In this book I've told tales of my adventuring over many years, and I've shared what I learned about adventuring from books and articles during a sabbatical year afterwards, which constituted the fourth journey of the book's title. It was an adventure, too. Those months of reading opened my eyes to some things I'd sensed only vaguely and some things I just never even considered. Here, as a reminder, is a summary of what all that reading had to say, rendered, in a few short paragraphs, from the essay chapters appearing in this book.

All adventures follow the same script, the hero-on-a-quest. Only, it's not so simple. Feminist writers in recent decades have demonstrated that female heroes tend to seek learning, growth, connection, and healing. Black people in the contemporary U.S. often do not participate in adventure, in the form of outdoor recreation, because of a history of racial terror. And people who live in poverty, including many people of color, do not crave the temporary hardship that adventures impose because they live hardship all the time. Also, there's a difference between heroes and adventurers. Heroes are selfless. Adventurers are all about fame and glory. When asked, modern male adventurers say they are out to test their limits, but for many women adventurers, it is also about building social connection. Adventure also has a dark side. Historically, it has been woven into popular literature to valorize war and justify colonization. Racism runs deep. Most White people are culturally imprinted with it and must work to manage it. Therefore, White people headed off on some adventure need to be cautious and do no harm, better still they should try to lend a hand.

Modern adventure education finds its roots in Outward Bound. It began as a school founded as an antidote to the perceived "decay" of society in the early 20th century. It was based on a romantic idea of the essential goodness of a child that must be drawn out and "muscular Christianity", a movement that emphasized character-building. The school included sea challenges of several weeks, which was the genesis of the Outward Bound program as we know it today. Research has shown Outward Bound has a lasting, positive impact. Modern efforts by BIPOC communities are evolving Outward Bound and similar adventure education approaches to match the interests and needs of communities of color.

Unfortunately, modern society, overall, is becoming more sedentary, with much less outdoor activity than at any time in history. The same goes for schools, which emphasize rote learning and tests. Children naturally want to run and play, but because school requires that they sit still, we diagnose them with a disorder and drug them into submission. Reformers have tried for nearly two centuries to make schools more progressive—drawing on curiosity, outdoor learning, physical exercise, cooperative problem solving, etc. Such reforms generally fade because our industrial society wants to batch-process everything, including children. We could learn something from Finland, which gives children 15 minutes of free play for every 45 minutes in class. Their ADHD rate is half what it is in the US. Outdoor adventuring is a powerful source of learning, but we are largely turning our back on it.

The Camino de Santiago has become a massive adventuring destination on a global scale. It has over a thousand-year history. At times, it has been heavily trafficked and other times, nearly forgotten. Its popularity has risen and fallen with politics and social trends. The Catholic Church promoted it during the Middle Ages. The Protestant Reformation discouraged it. The modern tourism industry is currently promoting it. Many people on the Camino seek a spiritual experience but are not specifically religious. They're also looking for a challenge to test their limits. It turns out, people have always had multiple reasons for pilgrimages beyond the narrow dictates of the Catholic Church. Nonetheless, spirituality is a prominent feature of the Camino and adventure in general. Walking, specifically, lends itself to spiritual, meditative practice. While the Camino is a very social form of adventuring, solo adventuring occupies a distinctive niche in our culture. We often read about famous solo adventurers, who defy the human instinct to be with others and who, like the heroes of the quest we learned about early in this book, return to society offering new learning and wisdom.

Where does all this talk leave us? Maybe here: adventure, historically has been the domain of the privileged-- mainly White men with money. However, things are changing, and, with change, our understanding of adventure, as feminists give voice to women who define adventure more expansively, and as diverse outdoor educators adapt traditional approaches to adventure learning and outdoor recreation for urban youth of color, and as society reckons with the ways adventure has been soaked in the culture of White privilege. Re-shaping adventure to be more race, gender, age, ability, and income inclusive is a great step forward. The bigger challenge, the societal challenge, is eliminating all those exclusionary forces in the first place. That's when all the positive aspects of adventuring— the learning, thrills, recreation, spiritual renewal, etc.—will be available, as it should be, to everyone. There's been personal learning, too, about access and ability. Over the course of three adventures, each with built-in stress tests, I learned there were limits to what I could take on physically, and there was evidence those limits were narrowing. Would I, at 65, be able to ride back-to-back centuries on my bike, like I did across the great flat midwest when I was 50? Maybe not, but I was also learning to take a page from my own journaling. It's not about the absolute scale of the feat. It's about a relationship between me and what I take on. If I'm still adventuring at 80, it will likely be a narrower scope from me at 65. But the same question will still apply. Is it challenging, risky, thrilling, *for me*, whatever my current abilities and limitations? That question opens up the possibility of adventure to everyone at any age.

There's also something beyond all this rational reflection, something beyond the reading and the learning, which I gained from the years of doing-- a kind of doing that is solitary, repetitive, physical, nearly free of intention. It's flow, and it's more. It's a place I know how to find when I need it. And the capacity I've developed for it is an enduring benefit of all these adventures. It is available to anyone. You just need to put in the time. Lots and lots of time.

Time, long stretches of it, spent cycling, rowing, walking, stroke upon stroke, step after step had taught me something about itself—time, that is. Namely, to live in its fullness—past, present, and future. Future is the realm of hope, anxiety, anticipation, dread, planning. The past offers up memory, nostalgia, regret, wisdom, knowledge, experience. And the present is the forge of living, where who we are gains its rough shape. In the present dwells sensuality, engagement with others (I-thou), action, unfolding experiences. To live fully and well is to embrace all three—past, present, and future. From that effort, we construct the deepest of meanings to inform our living. In the final analysis, meaning is not a quest. It's a construction project.

I used to own a framed needlepoint work that shows two children kneeling in prayer at their side-by-side beds. The caption underneath read, "Jesus loves me, this I know." A date, 1958, was stitched into the lower right corner. That's the year I was born, and I think my paternal grandmother made the needlepoint for me. I had noticed it in a box in our attic recently. Meanwhile, my brother, Tom, had a needlepoint hung in his front hall. It shows a stagecoach, and, underneath, a bit of verse that reads, "Travel East/ Travel West/ After All Home is Best." I asked my mother about it once when she was well into her 90s. I was aware it had come from her side of the family, and I believe it hung in her house when she was growing up.

She said, "Oh that? It was stitched by some ancient relative."

I really liked the caption and the stagecoach, and I liked that they were stitched into a bit of our family history. I wondered how Tom ended up with it and was a tad jealous. It wasn't until a few days after I came across the Jesus-Loves-Me needlepoint that I put two and two together. I sent Tom an email. Would he be open to a swap? He replied he would, and that Jesus would still love me. Upon my next visit to the farm a few months later, we made the exchange. Soon as Laurie and I got home, I enthusiastically hung my new needlepoint in our family room adjacent to the sofa.

Fast forward three years. I've beached my boat at Cape Hatteras at the conclusion of my rowing trip. I'm looking for a place to stash it for three days while Laurie and I will stay at a nearby motel for some celebrating and sight-seeing. A friendly guy who is walking his dog stops and chats me up. He says he lives a few doors up the road. I explain everything and ask him if I can store my boat in his driveway for a few days. He says yes. At the end of our three-day mini-vacation, Laurie and I stop by his house to retrieve the boat and heave it onto the roof of the Subaru. The couple across the street sees us.

"Mighty fine boat!" calls the man. Shortly we are in conversation. Turns out the woman is a craftsperson who makes quarterboards. She shows us her workshop set up in their garage. Instead of carving letters into the wood, the way quarterboard is generally done, she arranges, with glue, small seashells she finds on the beach into the shape of letters. One of the quarterboards on display, maybe a foot-and-a-half long, has the word EXPLORE laid out in a variety of pretty white and pink shells. I ask her how much. $60. I buy it. It now hangs underneath the travel-east-travel-west needlepoint in the family room. I love the pairing of these two small handicrafts because I love the idea of coming home and going out. For me, an essential part of adventuring is the movement between two poles: home and away, going out and coming back, excitement of a new adventure and the comfort of returning home.

I'm starting to think about my next adventure. The HI New York City Hostel on Amsterdam Avenue at 104th Street has beds for cheap — by New York standards. I have this idea. Book a dorm bed there for a week, and, each day, do a 10-mile walking loop of one of the City's five boroughs. End of the day, return and enjoy the company of fellow travelers in the kitchen. I'm calling it the Camino de New York City. I have another idea. Get myself and my bike to Yarmouth, Nova Scotia, the Canadian province's southernmost city. From there, ride north, as far I can go, and, where Nova Scotia runs out, take the ferry to Port aux Basques, Newfoundland. Ride north again, and, where the road ends at the Cape Norman Lighthouse, lift the bike over my head and shout into the wind, bellow across the sea, as blue, snowy icebergs drift slowly by, through the frigid North Atlantic. Here's another. Book an adventurous tour of India and trek with Laurie to some amazing places we've only ever seen in pictures. Okay, one more. For my 70th birthday, if the Universe allows, hop on my bike and ride it, in one big pull, coast to coast, from Washington DC to San Francisco.

How about you? Will you climb Mt. Kilimanjaro? Walk the park six blocks away that you've never explored? Step into a canoe for the first time ever? Take a boat and sail out of sight of land? Sleep in a tent under a giant Sequoia? Crawl through a storm drain to the next town? Cross a gorge on that rope bridge you've always been scared to navigate, despite the fact people use it every day? Join a multi-day group hike when you've only ever trekked alone? Conceive and raise a child? Remember, it is not about the scale of the adventure in absolute terms. It's about your relationship to the challenge. About *you* deciding whether it will be uncertain, scary, risky, thrilling, or rewarding. *—for you*?

What's *your* next adventure?

Endnotes

¹ In 2017, Alex Honnold became the first person to free solo the 3000-foot sheer rock face of El Capitan in Yosemite Valley. Free soloing means no ropes, no protective gear. His accomplishment is chronicled in H. A., & Roberts, D. (2018). *Alone on the wall*. W.W. Norton & Co.
² Strayed, C. (2013). *Wild: From lost to found on the Pacific Crest Trail*. Vintage.
³ Campbell, J. (1949). *The hero with a thousand faces*. Pantheon Books.
⁴ Campbell, J., & Moyers, B. (1988). *The power of myth*. Doubleday.
⁵ Interview with Neil Gaimon by Tim Ogline, Tree of Life Review, September (2007). http://treeoflifereview.com/neil-gaiman-interview-by-tim-ogline.phpp
⁶ Mythic Discovery Within the Inner Reaches of Outer Space: Joseph Campbell Meets George Lucas - Part I by Lucas Seastrom posted on Starwars.com, 2015.
⁷ Campbell, J. (1990). *The hero's journey: Joseph Campbell on his life and work*. Harper & Row Co.
⁸ Gill, B. (1989). The faces of Joseph Campbell. *New York Review of Books*.
⁹ Konner, J., Smith, H., Finch, R., Orr, C. W., Markman, R. H. (1989, November 9). *Joseph Campbell: An exchange*. New York Review of Books.
¹⁰ Murdock, M (1990). *The Heroine's Journey*. Shambhala Publications.
¹¹ Tatar, M. (2021). *The heroine with a 1,001 faces*. W.W. Norton & Co.
¹² Campbell, J., with S. Russi and D. Kudler (Eds.) (2018). *Goddesses: Mysteries of the Feminine Divine (The Collected Works of Joseph Campbell)*. Joseph Campbell Foundation.
¹³ Bond, S., & Christensen, J. (2021). The man behind the myth: Should we question the hero's journey? *Los Angeles Review of Books*. August 12.
¹⁴ Little, D., & Wilson, E. (2005). Adventure and the gender gap: Acknowledging diversity of experience, *Loisir et Société*, 28(1), 185-208.
¹⁵ *2021 Outdoor participation trends report*. Outdoor Foundation. (2021). www.outdoorindustry.org.
¹⁶ Hamilton, K. (2020, September 17). National parks are travel's next frontier in the movement for racial equality. *The Washington Post*.
¹⁷ Snowsports Industries America 2019-2020 Participation Study. Snowsports Industries America www.snowsports.org. Report available here: https://industry.traveloregon.com/wp-content/uploads/2021/04/SIA_Participation_Study_2019-2020_Nov.pdf
¹⁸ Raifman, M., & Choma, E. (2022). Disparities in activity and traffic fatalities by race/ethnicity. *Journal of Preventive Medicine*, 3(2), 160–167.

[19] Litwack, L. F. (2004). Hellhounds. In J. Allen, H. Als, J. Lewis, and L. Litwack. *Without sanctuary*. Twin Palms.

[20] Bad things happen in the woods: the anxiety of hiking while Black. (2018, July 13). *The Guardian*.

[21] Ibid.

[22] See, for example Harris, D. (1999). *Driving while Black: Racial profiling on our nation's highways*. An American Civil Liberties Union Special Report.

[23] Author. (2021). Cycling on the color line: Race, technology, and bicycle mobilities in the early Jim Crow South, 1887–1905. *Technology & Culture*, 62(4), 973-1002.

[24] Raifman &Choma. Ibid.

[25] Rose, J., & Paisley, K. (2012). White privilege in experiential education: A critical reflection. *Leisure Sciences*, 34, 136–154.

[26] Brune, M. (2020, July 22). Pulling down our monuments. *Sierra Club*. https://www.sierraclub.org/michael-brune/2020/07/john-muir-early-history-sierra-club

[27] Ramona Strategies. (2021). Sierra Club Restorative Accountability Processes Recommendations. (Report available here: https://www.documentcloud.org/documents/21046007-report).

[28] Lacayo, R. (1992, May 18). The two Americas. *Time Magazine*, 38-46. https://time.com/vault/issue/1992-05-18/spread/40/

[29] Climbing Mount Everest is work for supermen" *New York Times*.(1923, March 18).

[30] Walker, M. (2011, Sept. 8). 5 elements of adventure: Authenticity, purpose, inspiration. *Psychology Today*.

[31] Ewert, A., & Hollenhorst, S. (1989). Testing the adventure model: Empirical support for a model of risk recreation participation. *Journal of Leisure Research*, 21(2), 124–139.

[32] Ewert, A., Gilbertson, K., Luo, Y, & Voight, A. (2013). Beyond 'because it's there': Motivations for pursuing adventure recreational activities. *Journal of Leisure Research*, 44(1), 91-111.

[33] Green, M. (1991). Seven types of adventure tale: An etiology of a major genre. Penn State Univ Press.

[34] Livingstone, J. (2018). Travels in fiction: Baker, Stanley, Cameron and the adventure of African exploration. *Journal of Victorian Culture*, 23(1), 64–85. https://doi.org/10.1080/13555502.2017.1356586)

[35] *The Morning Post*, London, 4 December 1873, p. 3.

[36] My *Kalulu*, pp. vi–vii, as cited in Livingstone, ibid.

[37] Paris, M. (2013). Fiction and Britain's Middle East mandate. *History Today*, 63(5), 28-34.

[38] O'Brien, T. (1990). *The things they carried*. Houghton-Mifflin.

[39] Luna, J. M. (2021). De-Colonizing adventure: A cinematic road to El Dorado [Video].https://www.youtube.com/watch?v=uD4gWOpSvyQ
[40] Hahn, K. (1958). Address at the forty-eighth annual dinner of the old centralians. *The Central: The Journal of Old Centralians, 119*, 3-8. Passages in this paragraph quoted from page 4. kurthahn.org.
Baden-Powell, R. (1921). *Scouting for Boys.* www.gutenberg.org.
[41] Freeman, M. (2011). From 'character-training' to 'personal growth': the early history of Outward Bound 1941-1965. *History of Education, 40*(1), 21-43.
[42] Watson, N., Weir, S., & Friend, S. (2005). The development of muscular Christianity in Victorian Britain and beyond. *Journal of Religion and Society 7*, 1-25.
[43] Hahn, 1947, cited in Van Ooord, 2010; Hahn, K. (1947, February 20). *Training for and through the sea.* Address given to the Honourable Mariners' Company in Glasgow (privately printed).
[44] 'The Outward Bound Sea School, Aberdovey, Merionethshire: An Enterprise of the Outward Bound Trust': CUL, Add. 8270/26/39. Emphasis in the original. In Freeman.
[45] Outward Bound International. (n.d.). Outward Bound Global Impact Report, 2020. www.outwardbound.net.
[46] Hattie, J., Marsh, H. W., Neill, J. T., & Richards, G. E. (1997). Adventure education and outward bound: Out-of-class experiences that make a lasting difference. *Review of Educational Research, 67*(1), 43-87.
[47] Fang, B.-B., Frank, J. H., Lu, D. L., Gill, S. H. Liu , Chyi, T., & Chen, B. (2021). Systematic review and meta-analysis of the effects of outdoor education programs on adolescents' self-efficacy. *Perceptual and Motor Skills*, 1-27.
[48] Ewert, A. (1983). *Outdoor adventure and self-concept: A research analysis.* Center of Leisure Studies, University of Oregon.
[49] Mezirow, J. (2000). Learning to think like an adult. In J. Mezirow, (Ed.), *Learning as transformation: Critical perspectives on a theory in progress* (pp. 3-33). Jossey-Bass.
[50] Smock, J. C., &Clarkson, V. C. (1894). *Geological survey of New Jersey ron water-supply, water-power, the flow of streams and attendant phenomena* (Vol. 3, p. 290). John L. Murphy. ..
[51] Go to the website for the National Institute of Mental Health and follow the links to Mental Health Information, Statistics, and Mental Health. https://www.nimh.nih.gov/health/statistics/mental-illness. The source for information reported on the NIMH website is a national survey reported in the Journal of the American Academy of Child and Adolescent Psychiatry: Merikangas KR, He, JP, Burstein, M., Swanson, S.A., Avenevoli, S., Cui, L.,

Benjet, C., Georgiades, K., & Swendsen J. (2010). Lifetime prevalence of mental disorders in U.S. adolescents: Results from the National Comorbidity Survey Replication--Adolescent Supplement (NCS-A). *Journal of American Academics Child Adolescent Psychiatry, 49*(10), 980-989. doi: 10.1016/j.jaac.2010.05.017.
https://www.ncbi.nlm.nih.gov/pmc/articles/PMC2946114/

[52] Substance Abuse and Mental Health Services Administration. (2022). *Key substance use and mental health indicators in the United States: Results from the 2021 National Survey on Drug Use and Health* (HHS Publication No. PEP22-07-01-005, NSDUH Series H-57). Center for Behavioral Health Statistics and Quality, Substance Abuse & Mental Health Services Administration.
https://www.samhsa.gov/data/report/2021-nsduh-annual-national-report.

[53] U.S. Department of Health & Human Services. (2018). *Physical activity guidelines for Americans* (2nd ed., p. 51)
https://health.gov/sites/default/files/2019-09/Physical_Activity_Guidelines_2nd_edition.pdf
See also, Physical Activity Guidelines Advisory Committee. (2018). *2018 physical activity guidelines advisory committee scientific report* (pp. F7-F13). U.S. Department of Health and Human Services.
https://health.gov/sites/default/files/2019-09/PAG_Advisory_Committee_Report.pdf

[54] Physical Activity Alliance (2022). *U.S. report card on physical activity for children and youth.*https://paamovewithus.org/wp-content/uploads/2022/10/2022-US-Report-Card-on-Physical-Activity-for-Children-and-Youth.pdf

[55] Hofferth, S., & Sandberg, J. (2001). Changes in American children's time, 1981-1997, in T. Owens and S. Hofferth (Eds.), *Children at the millennium: Where have We come from, where are we going?* (Vol. 6), 193-229. Elsevier Science.

[56] Hofferth, S. (2009). Changes in American children's time – 1997 to 2003. *Electronic International Journal Time Use Research, 6*(1), 26–47. See Section 3.1, Table 1.

[57] The Aspen Institute. (2020). *State of play 2020.* .
https://www.aspenprojectplay.org/state-of-play-2020/introduction.

[58] Louv, R. (2008). *Last child in the woods: Saving our children from nature deficit disorder.* Alonquin Books.

[59] McMurrer, J. (2008). *Instructional time in elementary schools: A closer look at changes for specific subjects.* Center on Education Policy.

[60] Hodges, T. (2018). School engagement is more than just talk. Gallup.
https://www.gallup.com/education/244022/school-engagement-talk.aspx

61 Lange, K.W., Reichl, S., Lange, K.M., Tucha, L., & Tucha, O. (2010). The history of attention deficit hyperactivity disorder. *Atten Defic Hyperact Disord.* 2(4), 241–255. doi: 10.1007/s12402-010-0045-8..

62 See Epstein, J.N., & Loren, R.E. (2013). Changes in the definition of ADHD in DSM-5: Subtle but important. *Neuropsychiatry, 3*(5), 455-458. doi: 10.2217/npy.13.59. PMID: 24644516; PMCID: PMC3955126. For a scathing and deeply informed critique of the changes to DSM-5, see Frances, A. (2012). DSM-5 is a guide, not a bible: Simply ignore its 10 worst changes. *Psychiatric Times.* Frances chaired the task force that produced DSM-4.

63 Centers for Disease Contral &Prevention *ADHD Throughout the Years.* https://www.cdc.gov/ncbddd/adhd/timeline.html

64 Kazda, L., Bell, K., Thomas, R., McGeechan, K., Sims, R, Barratt, A. (2021). Overdiagnosis of attention-deficit/hyperactivity disorder in children and adolescents: A systematic scoping review. *JAMA Network Open, 4*(4), Article e215335. doi: 10.1001/jamanetworkopen.2021.5335..

65 Cousins, E. (Ed.) (2020). *Roots: From Outward Bound to EL education.* EL Education.

66 Bodilly, S. (2001). *New American schools' concept of break-the-mold design: How schools evolved and why.* Rand Corporation. See, pp. 50.

67 Berends, M., Kirby, S., Naftel, S., & McKelvey, C. (2001). *Implementation and performance in new American schools: Three years into scale-up.* Rand Corporation.

68 Bodilly, S. (2001). *New American schools' concept of break the mold designs: How designs evolved and why*
See, especially, Chapter 3, pp. 35-96.

69 Expeditionary Learning. (n.d.). *EL K-8 Language Arts Curriculum.* www.eleducation.org.

70 See endnote 67 (Berends et al.).

71 Berman, P., & McLaughlin, M. (1974). Federal programs supporting educational change (Vol. I). *A Model of Educational Change* . RAND Corporation. This is the first of five volumes, all of which are available at: www.rand.org/pubs/reports/R1589z1.html. See also McLaughlin, M. (1990). The RAND change agent study revisited: Macro perspectives and micro realities. *Educational Researcher* , 19(9), 11–16. This paper revisits the original study, largely affirming its main findings and suggesting modifications.

72 Schon, D. (1983). The reflective practitioner: How professionals think in action. Basic Books. See, especially, Chapter 2: From technical rationality to reflection in action(pp. 21-74).

[73] Dooley, K. (2004). Complexity science models of organizational change. In S. Poole, & A. Van De Ven (Eds.), *Handbook of organizational change and development* (pp. 354-373). Oxford University Press.

[74] For a fuller treatment of the three examples presented here, see Nehring, J. (2009). *The practice of school reform: Lessons from two centuries.* SUNY Press.

[75] Tim Walker is the author of Walker, T. (2017). *Teach like Finland: 33 simple strategies for joyful classrooms.* W.W. Norton. and Walker, T., & Sahlberg, P. (2021). *In teachers we trust: The Finnish way to world class schools.* W.W. Norton.. See related website for more about Walker's publications here: www.teachlikefinland.com.

[76] See, for example, Bloom, B.S. (1974).Time and learning. *American Psychologist, 29*(9),682–688. http://dx.doi.org/10.1037/h0037632. See also Stallings, J. (1980). Allocated academic learning time revisited, or beyond time on task. *Educational Researcher, 9*(11), 11–16. http://dx.doi.org/10.3102/0013189X009011011. Though research about time-on-task is nuanced, the popular conception in schools is that more time-on-task equals more learning.

[77] Organization for Economic Cooperation and Development. (2019). *Results from PISA 2018: Finland.* https://www.oecd.org/pisa/publications/PISA2018_CN_FIN.pdf Country Note: Programme for International Student Assessment (PISA)

[78] Pellegrini, A.D., & Bohn, C. M. (2005). The role of recess in children's cognitive performance and school adjustment. *Educational Research, 34*(1), 13-19.

[79] Danielson, M., Holbrook, J., Bitsko, R., Newsome, K., Charania, S., McCord, R., Kogan, M., & Blumberg, S. (2022). State-level estimates of the prevalence of parent-reported ADHD diagnosis and treatment among U.S. children and adolescents, 2016 to 2019. *Journal of Attention Disorders, 26*(13), 1685–1697. Also, Vuori, M. , Koski-Pirilä, A., Martikainen, J., & Saastamoinen, L.. (2020). Gender- and age-stratified analyses of ADHD medication use in children and adolescents in Finland using population-based longitudinal data, 2008-2018. *Scandinavian Journal of Public Health, 48*, 303–307.

[80] Robinson, K. (n.d.). *Divergent thinking* [Video]. https://www.youtube.com/watch?v=BHMUXFdBzik

[81] Nehring, J., Szczesiul, S., & Charner-Laird, M. (2019). *Bridging the progressive-traditional divide in education reform: A unifying vision for teaching, learning, and system-level supports.* Routledge Press. Nehring, J.. (2015) *Why teach?: Notes and questions from a life in education.* Rowman & Littlefield.

Nehring, J. (2009). *The practice of school reform: Lessons from two centuries.* SUNY Press.

Nehring, J. (2002). *Upstart startup: Creating and sustaining a public charter school.* Teachers College Press.

Nehring, J. (1998). *The school within us: The creation of an innovative public school.* SUNY Press.

Nehring, J. (1992). *The schools we have, the schools we want: An American teacher on the front line.* Jossey-Bass.

Nehring, J. (1989). *Why do we gotta do this stuff, Mr. Nehring: Notes from a teacher's day in school.* M. Evans & Company. Paperback reprint (1990) issued by Fawcett Columbine, a division of Random House.

[82] Talmud, Pirkei Avot, Mishna 2, Chapter 21.

[83] Buber, M. (1937). *I and thou.* T. and T. Clark, First English edition. Original German edition, 1923, *Ich und Du.* Im Insel-Verlag.

[84] Pilgrim Reception Office of Santiago de Compostela, www.oficinadelpergrino.com; www.caminolife.com.

[85] Franciscan Media, www.franciscanmedia.org

[86] Rahtz, P., & Watts, L. (1986). The archaeologist on the road to Lourdes and Santiago de Compostela in L. Butler, & Morris, R. (Eds.). *The Anglo-Saxon church papers on history, architecture, and archaeology in honour of Dr H. M. Taylor* (Report No. 60, p. 52). The Council for British Archaeology.

[87] The Codex Calixtinus, English version. https://codexcalixtinus.es/the-english-version-of-the-book-v-codex-calixtinus/

[88] Disputation of Doctor Martin Luther on the Power and Efficacy of Indulgences by Dr. Martin Luther (1517) Published in: Works of Martin Luther: Adolph Spaeth, L.D. Reed, Henry Eyster Jacobs, et Al., Trans. & Eds. (Philadelphia: A. J. Holman Company, 1915), Vol. 1, pp. 29-38. Available via Project Wittenberg here: https://www.projectwittenberg.org/pub/resources/text/wittenberg/luther/web/ninetyfive.html

[89] An Open Letter to the Christian Nobillity (1520): An Open Letter to the Christian Nobility of the German Nation Concerning the Reform of the Christian Estate, 1520, by Martin Luther. Introduction and Translation by C. M. Jacobs. Works of Martin Luther With Introduction and Notes, Vol. II. Philadelphia: A.J. Holman Co., 1915. Available here: https://christian.net/resources/selected-works-of-martin-luther-1483-1546/

[90] Lazure, G. (2007). Possessing the sacred: Monarchy and identity in Philip II's relic collection at the Escorial. *Renaissance Quarterly*, 60(1), 58-93.

[91] Ibid.

[92] Kissling, E. M. (2003). The Camino De Santiago in twentieth century Spain in *Tinta,* 60-68, Santa Barbara: University of California.

[93] UNESCO World Heritage Convention. Information available here: https://whc.unesco.org/en/list/669/

[94] See, for example, Kassam, A. & Mabel Banfield-Nwachi. Women walking Camino de Santiago speak of 'terrifying' sexual harassment. *The Guardian* (2024, Nov 18). https://www.theguardian.com/world/2024/nov/11/women-pilgrimage-camino-de-santiago-sexual-harassment

[95] See endnote 92 (Kissling).

[96] Oviedo, Ll., de Courcier, S. & Farias, M. (2014). Rise of pilgrims on the "Camino" to Santiago: Sign of change or religious revival? *Review of Religious Research,* 56(3), 433-442.

[97] Schmidt, C., & Little, D. (2007). Qualitative insights into Leisure as a spiritual experience. *Journal of Leisure Research,* 39(2), 222-247.

[98] Lion's Roar (2023, July 16). *How to meditate: Thich Nhat Hanh on walking meditation.* https://www.lionsroar.com/how-to-meditate-thich-nhat-hanh-on-walking-meditation/

[99] Nhat Hanh, T.. (2016). *How to walk.* Parallax Press.

[100] See Mihaly Csikszentmihalyi, M.(2004). *TED talk.* https://www.ted.com/talks/mihaly_csikszentmihalyi_flow_the_secret_to_happiness?language=en

[101] Csikszentmihalyi, M. (1990). *Flow: The psychology of optimal experience.* Harper.

[102] Grover, W. (2022, September 20). Inside the minds of the world's greatest solo adventurers. *Men's Journal.* https://www.mensjournal.com/adventure/inside-the-minds-of-the-worlds-greatest-solo-adventurers.

[103] Ibid.

[104] Guiness World Records (2013). First female to ski solo across Anarctica. *Guiness book of world records.* www.guinessworldrecords.com

[105] See several articles by Mike Libecki in www.Alpinist.com.

[106] See endnote 101 (Grover).

[107] Moitessier, B. (1974).*The long way* (W. Rodarmor, Trans.), Adlard Coles Nautical.

[108] Slocum, J. (1900). *Sailing alone around the world.* Century Books. https://gutenberg.org/ebooks/6317

[109] Turner, J. (2021). The solitary way. *Outside Magazine.* https://www.outsideonline.com/outdoor-adventure/exploration-survival/solitary-way/.

[110] Krakauer, J. (1996). *Into the wild.* Villard.

[111] Zwart, R. and R. Hines, (2022). Community wellness and social support as motivation for participation in outdoor adventure recreation, *Outdoor Recreation, Education, and Leadership* 14(1), 33-50. DOI: 10.18666/JOREL-2022-V14-I1-11139

[112] Thoreau, H.D. (1995) Walden: An annotated edition. Houghton Mifflin Company, p. 87

Acknowledgements

First, a big thank you to friends, colleagues, and family members who read and commented on early material, draft chapters, drafts of the entire manuscript, and, later, drafts of my query letter to publishers, and the book proposal. You are Jay Simmons, Laurie Sabol, Joanne Holdridge, Jack Schneider, John Kaag, Shanna Thompson, James Hibbard, dRae Sutherland, Laurie Nehring, Katherine Nehring, Maya Chhabra, Karen Fluet, and Joan DelPlato. Special thanks go to Brooke Warner for providing editorial guidance and Shanna Thompson for careful proofreading.

Numerous people provided practical support in a variety of ways. I could not have completed the three adventures without you! You are John Harris, designer of the expedition wherry and owner of Chesapeake Light Craft; Karen Fluet, Camino guide extraordinaire; Gene Kalajian and the team at Gear Works Cyclery; Pete Murray, Director of UMass Lowell Athletics; members of the Merrimack River Rowing Association; and Rob Nehring, Mary Jane Nehring, and Chuck Hendricks, who helped several summers with transportation logistics.

I am grateful to the owners, managers, and baristas who keep the several cafes I frequent, mostly in Central Massachusetts, running through the morning coffee rush, the lunch time bustle and the laptop crowd that lingers through the afternoon. You are Salt and Light Café in Groton, Wake and Bake and Union Coffee Roasters in Ayer, the Harvard General Store in the town of Harvard, The Java Room in Chelmsford, Boston Bean House in Maynard, and Cafes too numerous to mention along the Camino de Santiago, where this book started to take shape.

I am grateful also to the librarians, taxpayers and boosters who keep the idea of the public library alive and well. I am especially appreciative for Massachusetts libraries in Ayer,

Groton, Harvard, Pepperell, Chelmsford, Littleton, Chatham and Boston; also, the New York City Public Libraries, and, in Belfast, Northern Ireland, the Linen Hall Library, where the seed that became this book was planted.

My thanks go also to the Massachusetts Society of Professors and the Trustees of the University of Massachusetts for continuing to support the tradition of sabbatical leave, which provided me time and mental space to complete the first draft of the manuscript for this book. I am grateful also to the Provost's Office at the University of Massachusetts Lowell for establishing the Research and Scholars Investment Fund, which provided support for editorial services.

Thanks go also to Reagan Rothe and the Black Rose Writing team, superb collaborators in the birthing of a book! Thanks, also, go to dRae Sutherland for the route maps.

I am beyond thankful to my immediate family—Laurie, Reba, Abbie, and Anna-- for your support whenever I'm at work on a book, which is pretty much all the time. You patiently ride out my emotional ups and downs and encourage me to keep on. This burden falls most heavily on Laurie. Thank you, Laurie! I love you! What's our next adventure?

About the Author

James Nehring loves a good adventure, and he doesn't let his fear of heights, risk, and speed get in the way. Lacking trust fund, corporate sponsors and death-defying disposition, he pursues the kind of adventures available to most people reading this blurb, people who love thrills, uncertainty, physical and mental challenge, but on their own terms. Author of seven previous books, he's appeared on National Public Radio and CNN. His essays have appeared in the *Boston Globe*, *Washington Post* and *Chicago Tribune*. A life-long educator, and retired professor from the University of Massachusetts Lowell, he lives with his wife, Laurie, in central Massachusetts, and two cats who substitute for three kids who've flown the coop. When he's not teaching (part-time), you can find him outdoors on his bike or trekking through the woods just a few steps from his kitchen door.

Note from James Nehring

Word-of-mouth is crucial for any author to succeed. If you enjoyed *Everest and the Rest of Us*, please leave a review online — anywhere you are able. Even if it's just a sentence or two. It would make all the difference and would be very much appreciated.

For a fun ten minute read throughout the year, subscribe (for free!) to my substack, **"The Daily Adventure"** *Stuff happens all the time — funny, scary, unexpected. You just have to notice.* https://jamesnehring.substack.com

For photos, updates, and news, visit my website: www.jamesnehring.com.

Thanks!
James Nehring

We hope you enjoyed reading this title from:

www.blackrosewriting.com

Subscribe to our mailing list – *The Rosevine* – and receive **FREE** books, daily deals, and stay current with news about
upcoming releases and our hottest authors.
Scan the QR code below to sign up.

Already a subscriber? Please accept a sincere thank you for being a fan of Black Rose Writing authors.

View other Black Rose Writing titles at www.blackrosewriting.com/books and use promo code **PRINT** to receive a **20% discount** when purchasing.

www.ingramcontent.com/pod-product-compliance
Lightning Source LLC
Chambersburg PA
CBHW072146070526
44585CB00015B/1020